Feasts of a Militant Gastronome

Feasts of a Militant Gastronome

BY ROBERT COURTINE

Translated by June Guicharnaud

Recipes translated by Madeleine Kamman

WILLIAM MORROW & COMPANY, INC.
New York 1974

Calligraphy by Jeanyee Wong

Library of Congress Cataloging in Publication Data

Courtine, Robert J   comp.
    Feasts of a militant gastronome.
    1. Cookery, French. I. Title.
TX719.C61179   641.5'944   74–8826
ISBN 0–688–00296–X

À la mémoire de Curnonsky
Prince des Gastronomes

Contents

Preface

"You know, you're really lucky to eat such good food every day!"

I can't count the number of times I've heard that annoying remark. And I always want to answer, "All right. Come with me and see!"

For all isn't sweetness and caviar in the life of a militant gastronome. There are as many moments of glory and slavery in the profession of a gourmet as there were in the military career of Alfred de Vigny. And for one dinner that is a success there are countless others that are mediocre, deplorable, or just plain awful. Balzac, who had a talent for seeing and understanding everything, could have added another chapter to his *Comédie humaine*: "The Splendors and Miseries of a Courtesan . . . of the Table."

A few years ago a friend of mine and I wanted to set up a Hash House Prize. We wanted it to be the first prize of the year; in other words, it would have been awarded on December 31, one minute after midnight. We thought of inviting the press to meet us at a bench (we had chosen one on the Boulevard de Latour-Maubourg) where we would serve good thick sandwiches and a few well-chosen bottles of wine. After all, we'd been invited to so many meals that weren't worth a sandwich! But we gave up the idea. First, because in the winter we might have caught terrible colds, which would have unduly pleased the Hash House owners. Also, because we knew we'd be in an embarrassing situation: How could we single out one prizewinning Hash House? There are so many . . .

There are two kinds of disastrous meals: those that are naturally bad —because of total incompetence and the (bad) choice of products; and those that are pretentiously bad—because of a desire for farfetched originality, albeit it a desire to do (at least) *something* well.

We all have our memories, and Curnonsky did most especially. He loved to tell the story of the restaurateur from Lyons who—before the war —had invited him to taste his "marvelous bouillabaisse." They agreed on a date. And when Curnonsky arrived, with a friend, they found themselves to their great surprise in the midst of a huge crowd which had been attracted by a sign announcing: "Tonight Curnonsky, the Prince of Gastronomes, will taste our bouillabaisse."

9

In the middle of the room, on a stage roped off like a boxing ring, there were two chairs and a table set for two. The Prince and his friend climbed up and, surrounded by the cheering mob, were served the terrific bouillabaisse that everyone had come to watch them eat—like animals in a zoo. The mediocrity of the bouillabaisse made it even more difficult for Curnonsky to digest the joke.

Another time, in Montbard, Cur and I were guests of a good chef who, bowing and scraping like a dandy in a Molière play, announced that he'd created a dish for the Prince. We were served trout. The poor little things—stuffed with foie gras and surrounded by fried bananas—bore their burden of scalloped orange slices with more resignation than joy.

As we tasted—or, rather, as we swallowed—Cur, at the other end of the table, called out to me in his splendid, tangy voice, rolling his *r*'s the way they do in Anjou, "Crripes, old boy! This is verritable shit!" Through the half-open door I could see the chef in his *toque* and apron, peering at our faces for a sign of satisfaction. I was sorry for him, but the Prince was right. Or almost. If the dish had been what he said it was, the effect would scarcely have been more disconcerting.

I remember another adventure. A mutual friend had invited the boxer Georges Carpentier and me to a suburban inn near Paris. The huge innkeeper and his whole family were waiting for us, in front of a table covered with flowers.

"My chef," he said, "is king of the *sauce à l'américaine*. I hope you like anglerfish?"

We did. Or, rather, we like anglerfish when it's fresh and we like *sauce à l'américaine* when it's edible. Carpentier, who was brutal only in the ring, murmured gently that it was "very good" but that he would "appreciate something to drink"—if only to quench the fire that had been lit in our throats. Our host ordered a bottle of white wine (one bottle for seven of us!), which he poured fastidiously, pointing out that it was a vintage Burgundy. He even talked poetically about the old bottle, but alas, his poeticizing was loftier than the vintage, for the Burgundy turned out to be an acrid local wine. Then we had *choucroute*—in this case a mound of pale, washed-out sauerkraut, served, however, with a decent pork butt. We began to feel better. But again alas! There was just one pork butt and we weren't offered second helpings (for fear we would fight over the one slice that was left?). To make matters worse, we couldn't even catch up with the cheese, since there was only one tiny, very tiny, cheese that looked as if it had shrunk with terror before the lustful eyes of so many starving people!

After a dessert that was even more pathetic than the rest of the meal, the fat innkeeper dragged us off to see his "most beautiful" room, adorned with a round bed. Suddenly local photographers rushed in and began machine-gunning Carpentier and yours truly. Our photographs appeared in the regional newspapers to decorate ads publicizing that hash house of an inn, even though the food had already knocked us out in the first round.

Still, we very nearly awarded our Hash House Prize to the Lido, or, more precisely, to its food. When you think that people all over the world dream of Paris, and that Paris to them is the Lido, you feel somewhat ashamed of the food it serves. Although tourists don't go there mainly to eat, they should at least be given something respectable. For example, a few of us remember to this day the dinner to which we had been invited by Madame Bollinger (who had nothing to do with it, poor lady, for at least we had a lot of good things to drink!): fillets of sole rolled around frozen scallops and covered with two undefinable sauces; a piece of old mutton sweating grease, wrapped in the kind of pastry that sticks to your gullet; and a dish of synthetic sherbet. Most of us left everything there where it was, but those who ate weren't all there the next morning.

There is a well-known joke in France about Madame de Brinvilliers, the famous poisoner, to whom some gastronome or other compared a bad chef, saying, "The only difference between La Brinvilliers and him is that *he* had good intentions!" But it is a consolation to know that terrible meals are not the prerogative of this day and age. As Boileau stigmatized a ridiculous dinner:

> A conceited fool has just had me to dine
> In order, I believe, to poison me and mine.

Indeed, terrible meals are often caused by foolish conceit. Thus "big spreads" become synonymous with farfetched experiments and bad cooking. Often only courtesy has kept me in my seat when . . .

> . . . thinking, in rage, to hell with this feast,
> I almost left the table twenty times at least.

Therefore, out of courtesy I'll be discreet. I won't mention the name of the place in which I was brought a fowl to carve whose flesh I couldn't cut (I swear), not even with carving scissors and a hammer. We had to make do with bread soaked in the sauce.

So, readers, whoever you are, no matter how you marvel at the description of the following incredible meals, please do not envy me too much. Apart from the fact that, with these recipes, you now have the possibility of savoring the same sumptuous moments, never forget that they have been sifted out, that they are exceptions—a few rare experiences among a thousand culinary hardships which I shall spare you.

Wishing you a heartfelt *bon appétit!*

ROBERT COURTINE
de l'Académie Rabelais

Feasts of a Militant Gastronome

ABOUT THE RECIPES

Recipes for the dishes in FEASTS OF A MILITANT GASTRONOME have been faithfully translated from the original French recipes supplied by the author and by the chefs and restaurants mentioned in this book. Kitchen measurements are expressed in the customary American weights and measures.

However, because some recipes require further explanation to be used in American home kitchens, the recipe translator and editor has frequently supplied additional information which did not appear in the original French text. All such additions are set in *italics* to distinguish them from the work of the author and his contributors.

Basic recipes also supplied by the translator are to be found in the Appendix.

An Anniversary
at the Tour d'Argent

In 1970 he had surprised us.

He had died suddenly, without warning, and I was so taken aback that I didn't have the time to buy champagne for my friends.

But for November 9, 1971, the first anniversary of his death, we were able to organize a dinner in advance. In fact, it was exactly one year after the death of Charles de Gaulle that we met in a private suite of rooms at the Tour d'Argent.

I don't believe there is a place anywhere in the world that is more magical, more timeless. Not only does it boast "the most perfectly functioning mechanics of comfort," as André Gide put it, but those *salons,* new that very year, seem to have existed for centuries. It has an *apéritif salon* with light wood paneling, a disappearing wall, a dining room just dim enough for secret murmurings, and a window framing the world's most beautiful picture: Our Lady of the Night!

Notre-Dame de Paris. Our Lady of Eternity! One hears gentle music —perhaps sung by the angels? A mirrored partition, carefully dulled, reflects the flames of the candles. There are more movable panels, and the music swells on the threshold of a boudoir before discreetly subsiding.

One expects a magician to appear along with the anniversary cake. Will he be the ghost of the caterer Rourteau, who baked a heron torte here for his king, Henry IV? Or an impassive guardian of tradition? Or a smiling cicerone in the extravagant cast of a film about Paris high life and glamorous restaurants? For here, surely, there would be no lack of extras dressed in everything from armor to doublets, tunics to frock coats, tails to black tie. Perhaps, for instance, that crinoline is signed by Dior? No, no —*there's* the magician! Amazing, seductive, extravagant Claude Terrail appears—a man of olden days. The man of the Tower!

He is the Ruggieri of these daily fireworks which seem to have gone on since 1543. He is the page of all the great beauties who have stopped their coaches, victorias, or Rolls Royces on the quai de la Tournelle. He is the blushing violet that he wears in his boutonniere, as in an off-color drawing room drama of the Restoration. He is Claude Terrail.

15

La Tour d'Argent
Dîner
Le 9 Novembre 1971

———— • ————

(Bollinger R. D. 1961)

Le consommé Fabiola
Les homards Lagardère
Les noisettes de chevreuil Charles IX, sauce Diane
La terrine de foie gras des Trois Empereurs

(Château Filhot 1920)

Les poires en soufflé "Vie Parisienne"

It has been said, and rightly, that a Feydeau comedy was a mechanism. A meal at the Tour d'Argent is also a mechanism, and one which, like Feydeau's plays, would be nothing without wit, love, and . . . champagne as well, for champagne is its essence.

We had given complete freedom of choice to the amphitryon for our dinner of November ninth. We wanted to be nothing but dazzled spectators and, at the same time, actors directed by a genius. As we were finishing our glass of Bollinger R.D. 1961 (I do not need to explain that those letters, meaning "Recently Disgorged," are peculiar to Bollinger and bestow on the wine the double distinction of traditional wisdom and impassioned youth), the doors slid open and a resplendent acolyte announced: "Dinner is served, sir!"

He was young, had a pure and smiling face, and I thought of Proust, of whom this was also the anniversary. Proust—in a few exquisite and perceptive phrases—would have cleverly managed to set upon the page what was now on the stage, inviting a Guermantes to adorn, and a Swann to describe, this meal.

If I say nothing about the consommé Fabiola, it is not because there was nothing to say about it. But rather, in the words of the eighteenth-century epicurean Grimod de la Reynière, it was merely the peristyle of the building. And I ask you: Do you stop under a peristyle when everything inside invites you to enter?

We therefore entered . . . straight to the heart of the matter with a lobster Lagardère. What a lobster! It had first been poached in a court-bouillon, then diced and put back in its shell and dressed with a bracing sauce, full of joy and freshness, quite in keeping with the last bottles of Bollinger. The sauce had to have youth, as we shall see, to prepare our palates, for it was followed by another sauce—Diane (a *poivrade* with cream)—which was poured over *noisettes* of venison Charles IX. It's always somewhat difficult to offer game to connoisseurs—and connoisseurs whose tastes may vary as to how fresh it should be or how gamy. Moreover, venison, when freshly killed, is often a bit tough. Here it was precisely as it should be—rare, a tender pink, scented just like itself. And its sauce covered it like a poet's mantle! I should add that (contrary to a deplorable custom which has become a ridiculous mania with chefs) those tender fillets were not served on croutons. I should also add that two purées—celery and chestnut—completed the dish, reaching the sublime.

I can no longer remember which humorist remarked, "You'd even eat your mother with that sauce!" I would go him one better and conclude, "You'd even forgive Charles IX the Saint-Barthélemy Massacre for that dish."

Le Dîner des Trois Empereurs
Le 7 Juin 1867

——————— • ———————

Potage Impératrice
Potage Fontanges
Soufflés à la Reine
Filets de sole à la vénitienne
Escalopes de turbot au gratin
Selle de mouton, purée bretonne
Poulets à la portugaise
Pâté chaud de cailles
Homards à la parisienne
Sorbets au vin
Canetons à la rouennaise
Ortolans sur canapés
Aubergines à l'espagnole
Asperges en branches
Cassolette Princesse
Bombe glacée

Then came the terrine of foie gras *Trois Empereurs*.

It was on June 7, 1867, that the King of Prussia, the Emperor of Russia, and the Emperor of China dined together at the Café Anglais. I think I ought to give you the menu. So relax and listen carefully:

> Potage Impératrice; potage Fontanges; soufflés à la reine; fillets of sole à la vénitienne; collops of turbot au gratin; saddle of mutton with Breton purée; chicken à la portugaise; warm quail pâté; lobster à la parisienne; wine sherbets; duckling à la rouennaise; buntings on canapés; eggplant à l'espagnole; asparagus; cassolette Princesse; bombe glacée.

There was no foie gras, as you can see. Yet the tradition is nevertheless that this well-known dinner, which gourmets call the "Dinner of the Three Emperors," be remembered for one dish it never contained, a terrine of foie gras, which should be served with a great Sauternes. For our dinner this was a Château Filhot 1920.

For dessert, souffléed pears *"Vie Parisienne,"* a reference to another tradition. There is on the ground floor of the Tour d'Argent a small culinary museum lined with the paneling from a celebrated salon of the Café Anglais, the "Grand 16," where things—delicious things—went on which were immortalized by Offenbach in his *Vie Parisienne*.

> When morning comes, when dawn one sees,
> The high-living night-owls are ill at ease
> And in the "Grand 16" they ask for teas . . .

But for us the small suite at the Tour d'Argent gave shelter to the living rather than the high-living—shelter to epicureans whose wisdom begins with a wise rather than a copious bill of fare, an elegant rather than a knockout menu. We experienced a culinary fairy tale, thanks to Claude Terrail.

And, ah—one simple detail! We were brought finger bowls. I can imagine some nouveau riche wondering: *"What*? Nothing in it? No slice of lemon? No rose petals? How pathetic!" The nouveau riche would not have known that the plain clear water was scented with citron—and with a Guerlain perfume.

That's all!

Recipes of Claude Terrail
La Tour d'Argent

CONSOMMÉ FABIOLA

To make about 4 quarts

Prepare the following double consommé:

Step 1:
Put 6½ pounds plate beef, 6½ pounds shin beef, bone-in, 3 veal bones, 20 chicken wings, 4 carrots, the white part of 4 leeks and 2 small celery stalks with their leaves in a stock pot. Cover with water; bring to a boil, season well, skim and simmer for 4 to 5 hours.

As soon as the consommé is cooked, strain it into a clean pot.

Step 2:
Add to the strained consommé: 2 generous pounds of perfectly lean ground beef, 2 carrots, the white part of 1 leek and 1 small celery stalk with its leaves, all very finely minced. Season very well again and simmer gently for 1½ hours. Strain the consommé first through a sieve, then through a muslin. Correct the seasoning and serve piping hot.

LOBSTER LAGARDÈRE

To serve 6 persons

Immerse three 1¾-pound lobsters in a wildly boiling court-bouillon made of 3 quarts of water and aromatized and seasoned with 1 onion, ½ teaspoon thyme, 1 (Mediterranean) bay leaf, 10 peppercorns, a few parsley stems, ⅓ cup dry white wine, 3 tablespoons excellent wine vinegar and 3 tablespoons salt.

Bring the court-bouillon to a second boil over high heat. Turn the heat down a bit and continue boiling for 25 to 30 minutes.

Drain the lobsters and let them cool completely. Split them into halves.

Remove the meat from the tails and claws and slice it into fine *escalopes*. Arrange the *escalopes* in the reserved half-shells so they lightly overlap one another.

Chop very finely 1½ tablespoons each of fresh chervil and tarragon and 1 teaspoon fresh chives. Mash 2 hard-cooked egg yolks with a fork on a small plate. Transfer the mashed yolks to a small bowl; mix them with the chopped herbs. Add about ¼ teaspoon salt, a large pinch of finely ground pepper, 2¼ teaspoons strong Dijon mustard, 2 teaspoons vinegar, 1 teaspoon Madeira and a few drops of Worcestershire sauce; mix well. Gradually whisk 1 generous cup of oil into the mixture until the sauce thickens like a mayonnaise. Correct the seasoning to suit your taste but bear in mind that the sauce should be quite spicy.

Spoon some of the sauce between the slices of lobster, then coat the top of the lobster slices heavily with the remainder.

NOISETTES OF VENISON CHARLES IX

To serve 6 persons

To prepare the noisettes:

Purchase 6 venison rib chops. Have the butcher bone them to obtain 6 bone-, fat- and gristle-free *noisettes* and ask him also to chop the rib bones into small pieces; you will use the chopped bones in the marinade.

Prepare the following ingredients for the marinade:

Mix 2½ cups excellent dry white wine with 3 tablespoons Cognac, 2 tablespoons peanut oil and 2 tablespoons excellent wine vinegar.

Mince finely ½ small carrot, 1 shallot, 2 parsley stems. Mix those aromatics with 3 black peppercorns, a pinch of thyme and ½ bay leaf, crushed.

Place half of the aromatics in the bottom of a glass or china baking dish. Add the *noisettes* of venison and sprinkle them with the remainder of the aromatics. Surround the *noisettes* with the chopped rib bones and add the mixture of liquid ingredients to the baking dish. Marinate for 24 hours; turn the meat over several times while marinating.

To cook the noisettes:

Remove them from the marinade and pat them dry in a tea towel. Panfry them in 1½ tablespoons each of oil and butter heated almost to the smoking point. Keep them rare or medium rare and serve them with the sauce Diane.

Sauce Diane:

Strain the marinade through a fine strainer or sieve into a 1-quart saucepan and reduce it to 2 or 3 tablespoons. Brown half of the aromatics of the marinade and all the chopped bones in about 2 tablespoons oil. Add these browned ingredients to the reduced marinade and flambé with 1 ounce of Cognac. Add enough brown veal stock (p. 247) to barely cover the bones and vegetables. Bring to a boil and let simmer, uncovered, for 1 hour. Strain the sauce into a measuring cup; correct the seasoning (this sauce should be quite strong with pepper). Add 6 tablespoons heavy cream per cup of finished sauce. Reheat well before serving.

(Note: Flambéing the aromatics and bones in their frying pan before adding them to the marinade would bring additional flavor to the sauce, since the Cognac would dissolve the caramelized meat juices from the bones from the bottom of the frying pan. Also, M. Terrail's text instructs the reader to add a "little cream" to the finished sauce. The proportions indicated here are those of the classic sauce Diane which calls for ⅓ cup heavy cream for each 2 cups of finished sauce. As a matter of interest, the classic recipe calls for whipping the cream before adding it to the sauce. Ed.)

TERRINE OF FOIE GRAS "THREE EMPERORS"

(Note: This recipe must remain a description since, unfortunately, government regulations forbid the entrance of the raw goose livers into the United States. Ed.)

To make this terrine it is essential to have beautiful goose livers weighing about 1½ pounds each. The livers should be selected with great care, for the quality of the terrine depends on the quality of the livers used.

Taking great care not to puncture it, remove the gall bladder and all its surrounding tissues. Remove all the nerves and blood vessels. Season the livers with spices, which may vary with your personal taste, with salt and an infinitesimally small amount of saltpeter. Arrange the livers in a large mixing bowl, cover them with cold water, cover the bowl with a parchment paper, and store it in a cold place for 12 to 15 hours.

Stud each liver with peeled fresh truffles cut into quarters. Pack the livers in layers in a terrine, pressing down with the back of the hand. Cover the terrine with a large sheet of fresh unsalted fatback and a parchment paper.

Bake in a low 175°F. oven for 1 hour and 50 minutes. The baking is delicate and requires a bit of experience. Remove the terrine from the oven and pour off the cooking juices and all the fat. Replace them by new rendered and clarified goose fat. Let rest in a cold place for a whole day. Smooth the top of the terrine and pour over it a thin layer of melted lard, which will act as a sealer.

Prepared in this manner, the terrine keeps in the refrigerator for several weeks. Since its taste and flavor improve with time, it is advisable not to serve it immediately after baking.

SOUFFLÉED PEARS "VIE PARISIENNE"

(Note: M. Terrail's recipe consisted of an 8-line description. Since the recipe is pretty and could be made at home, it has been "rebuilt" completely here. Ed.).

To serve 6 persons

Step 1—Ladyfingers:
Prepare 24 ladyfingers: Mix 3 egg yolks with ⅓ cup sugar, a pinch of salt and the scraped seeds of a 2-inch-long piece of vanilla bean. Whip until the mixture is white and foamy and forms a heavy ribbon when falling from the beaters. Beat 3 egg whites until they can support the weight of an uncooked egg in its shell. Mix one quarter of the whites into the ribboned yolk mixture. Slide the remainder of the whites on top of the lightened egg yolks, sift ½ cup flour on top of the egg whites, and fold all these elements together at once and until homogeneous.

Pipe the batter through a pastry bag fitted with a plain ½-inch nozzle onto 4 bands of parchment paper 17 x 4 inches, forming sticks of batter 3½ inches long, separated by a 2-inch space. Place the bands of paper on 2 unbendable pastry sheets. Bake at 375°F. for 7 minutes. Reduce heat to 325°F. and continue baking for another 5 minutes. Remove the ladyfingers from the papers to a rack and cool them completely.

Step 2:
Purchase 9 beautiful and perfectly ripe Bartlett pears. Peel six of them and cut them into very fine slivers. Cook them uncovered with a squeeze of lemon juice and 6 tablespoons sugar until they fall into a fine purée. Uncover the pan and let the purée reduce until it becomes thickish and most of its liquid has evaporated. Add 1 tablespoon Kirsch. Set aside for later use.

In another deep saucepan, make a sugar syrup with 1¾ cups water and 1 generous cup of sugar. Add the scraped seeds of another 2-inch piece of vanilla bean. Bring the syrup to a boil and reduce to a simmer. Peel the remaining pears very carefully with a potato peeler. Core them, quarter them, and rub each quarter with some lemon. Poach the pieces of pear in the sugar syrup until a large sewing needle penetrates them easily. Drain the pears on a rack placed over a plate and keep them ready for later use.

Step 3:

Butter a large fireproof baking dish. Place on the bottom of the dish 6 groups of 4 ladyfingers placed side by side to make 6 cake bases. Leave a space of 2 inches between the groups. Sprinkle a reasonable amount of Kirsch on each ladyfinger base, then spread an equal amount of pear purée on each cake base. Spoon about 2 teaspoons melted currant jelly on the pear purée of each portion. Top each cake base with 2 pear quarters.

Step 4:

Now prepare a soufflé batter as follows:

Mix ½ cup sugar, ¼ cup flour and a pinch of salt. Dilute the mixture with 1 cup cold milk. Bring to a boil to thicken. Add the scraped seeds of yet another piece of vanilla bean. Add 8 egg yolks, one by one, beating well between additions. Beat 9 egg whites; mix one quarter of their volume into the base of the soufflé and fold in the remainder.

Spread the soufflé batter over the 6 portions of cake and pears, building 6 pyramid-shaped mounds. Sprinkle with confectioners' sugar and bake in a 375°F. oven for about 5 minutes. Serve with sabayon *sauce.*

Step 5—Sabayon Sauce:

Mix 1 cup sugar with 6 egg yolks and a small pinch of salt until they are foamy white and spin a heavy ribbon when falling from the whisk. Gradually whisk in 1 cup excellent dry white wine and continue whisking over direct but very slow heat until the mixture foams heavily and coats a spoon thickly. Whisk in ¼ cup Kirsch. Spoon over the souffléed pears. The sabayon *is best prepared in an enameled cast-iron saucepan.*

A Dinner with Perfume

When I was a boy, I used to dream of inventing names for perfumes. It seemed to me so poetic and easy. The other day I learned that it was neither, thanks to Monsieur Gosset.

I met Monsieur Gosset because of his champagne—which is good. While I was drinking his *brut* 1966 with him, I hoped to discuss those sparkling wines so dear to Dom Pérignon. But no, we didn't at all, for Monsieur Gosset is also connected with perfumes—he is one of the directors of Rochas.

You might tell me that perfumes, like champagne, are a mixture, a blend, and that to make a blended wine one must know not only how to taste but how to smell. The same sense of smell determines the harmony of a perfume. Agreed. Yet until my meeting with Monsieur Gosset it never occurred to me that either Madame Rochas and her "Femme" or Monsieur Rochas and his "Moustache" were that tongue-tingling and that worthy of accompanying a meal! Everything has changed!

But before getting down to my subject, let me tell you that I know now how difficult it is to find a new name for a perfume. Ah! If one could merely date them! We would then have "Madame Rochas 1971" and know that "Moustache 1970" has more body, a deeper hue, and a stronger scent than "Moustache 1957," whereas "Femme 1972" shows great promise . . .

Yes, it is difficult to find names like that, because so many of them are already copyrighted and untouchable. Also because they are short, easily pronounced by English-speaking people, have a pleasant sound to them, etc. In short, the choice must be audacious.

And, by the way, one of Rochas' new perfumes is called "Audace." For women, obviously!

Anyway, we were at Lasserre's, to have a chat, and were faced not only with a few magnums of Gosset's champagne but also a menu including . . . perfume!

I believe I have already paid homage elsewhere to Jules Maincave, a chef who died during World War I and was a true creator. He wrote the following, which is still relevant: "The culinary art drags along pathet-

25

ically with its twelve or thirteen recipes. The same dishes are served on every table, baptized and rebaptized, given hundreds of high-sounding names which conceal their mediocre uniformity. There has not been a truly new dish on this earth for three centuries. . . ."

He was a revolutionary who, even in his day, dreamed of chicken with lily of the valley, beef with kümmel, partridge à la rose. Actually he was not breaking new ground as much as he was going back to old sources, since over the centuries, to a true chef—or to a true creator of any kind (including Baudelaire)—colors, scents, and tastes correspond.

Jules Maincave would have been pleased by the meal we had at Lasserre's:

Red mullet with jasmine
Duck with lemon blossoms
Lettuce with Japanese chrysanthemums
Pink champagne sherbet
with rose petals

I believe that jasmine and roses contribute to the balanced combination of "Audace." The audacity in this case was to introduce them into the cuisine.

Jasmine, for example. It came to us from India and was first brought to Europe by Spanish sailors about 1560. The delicate sheen of its starlike blossoms was much admired, and one Duke of Tuscany, who had had some planted in his garden, forbade his gardener to give away so much as one blossom of it. But the man was in love and slipped a small branch of it into the bouquet he offered his girl to celebrate her saint's day. She in turn planted it in her garden; it remained green all year long and bloomed again the following spring.

We admired some potted jasmine on the table, naïve and happy as an alpine maid, while we tasted that unexpected red mullet.

Yet, as a creation, it was in a straight line of descent from cooking of the past. Indeed, in a *Portable Cooking Dictionary* (1770) I found thirteen recipes that use jasmine blossoms, including the following, which will be of no use to you until spring:

> Take whole jasmine blossoms and remove stems. Dip blossoms into beaten egg whites, then roll in fine granulated sugar. Dry over simmering water.

To produce his duck with lemon blossoms, Lasserre, the creator of chicken with lime blossoms, had only to delve into folklore—this time of

Chez Lasserre
"Un Dîner Parfumé"

❧

(Champagne Gosset Brut 1966)

Rougets - barbet au jasmin
Canard aux fleurs de citronnier
Laitue aux chrysanthèmes du Japon
Sorbet aux pétales de roses

China. And also into Édouard Nignon. This great nineteenth-century chef who is not known to modern chefs, although he was far superior to Escoffier and Montagné, frequently used that same lemon-blossom powder. He had the blossoms of the lemon tree, which is in its full glory throughout the summer, dried in the sun before rubbing them to powder. And he added that powder to tart or sweet pastry.

Finally, we had the sherbet that was made with Gosset's rosé champagne and decorated with crystallized rose petals. These are coated in the same way as the crystallized violets from Toulouse—which is how "the obscure violet, almond blossom of lawns," becomes useful indeed in cooking.

Recipes of René Lasserre
Chez Lasserre

RED MULLET WITH JASMINE

To serve 2 persons

Purchase 4 beautiful red mullets each weighing 6 to 7 ounces. Slit each of them open through the back, remove the backbone, and clean the fish without opening the stomach.

Stuff the fish with a mousseline made of 1 egg white, 3½ ounces each of whiting and salmon meat without skin or bones, and about ½ cup heavy cream. Flavor the mousseline with jasmine extract (see note). Place each fish on a piece of parchment paper. Fold the paper around the fish to make a papillote; before closing the papillotes, place them in a large baking dish and add to each of them 3 ounces dry white wine and 3 ounces fish *fumet* (p. 250).

Bake in a 350°F. oven for about 25 minutes. As soon as the fish are cooked, remove them to a long serving platter. Remove the papillotes and coat the fish with a classic white-wine sauce lightly colored with a bit of tomato paste. Serve very hot.

(Note: True Mediterranean red mullets of the size desired here can be purchased under the name of triglia *in fish stores located in Italian markets.*

The mousseline can be made very quickly by puréeing the whiting and salmon meats in an electric blender, using the egg white as liquid.

Strain the purée and chill it for 1 hour. Add salt and pepper, then beat in slowly and very gradually the chilled heavy cream mixed with the jasmine extract. If jasmine extract cannot be located, replace it by 1 dried jasmine flower completely powdered by rubbing it in the hollow of your hand.

To stuff the fish, use a pastry bag fitted with a small plain nozzle; it is recommended to sew the fish closed with a fine needle and thread before cooking it.

The easiest way to make the white-wine sauce in home cookery is to use the cooking juices of the fish; add to those juices 1 teaspoon tomato paste. Reduce juices to a scant cup over high heat; then reduce the heat. Thicken to a sauce by whisking into the simmering juices a beurre manié made of 3 tablespoons butter mixed with 1 tablespoon flour; correct the seasoning. Before coating the fish with the sauce, remove the threads and the top skin of each mullet. Ed.)

DUCK WITH LEMON BLOSSOMS

To serve 2 persons

Singe a 3½- to 4-pound duckling; remove its breastbone and truss it.

Use a pot just large enough to hold the duck and its giblets. Rub the bird with fresh lemon blossoms or, if blossoms are out of season, with a lemon half. Sprinkle it with thyme flowers, salt and pepper and put it in the pot. Surround the duck with its giblets sprinkled with 2 shallots, finely chopped, 1 large onion, minced, and 1 large carrot, minced. Add a generous amount of fresh butter and *poêle* the duck for about 50 minutes.

While the duck cooks, grate the rinds of 2 lemons very finely and squeeze and strain their juice. Peel another 2 lemons to the pulp and dice the pulp very finely. Set grated lemon rinds, lemon juice and diced lemon pulp aside for later use.

Melt 4 teaspoons sugar in a small pan and cook it to a light blond caramel. Dissolve the caramel with the lemon juice.

As soon as the duck is done, remove it to a platter and keep it warm. Defat its cooking juices and let them reduce completely over slow heat until they turn to a thick meat glaze. Add a good cup of rich cold chicken or brown veal stock (p. 247) mixed with 1¼ teaspoons potato starch and the grated lemon rind; simmer together for a few minutes.

Strain this sauce through a fine strainer into the small pan containing the caramel and lemon-juice mixture. Simmer the sauce and skim it for a few more minutes. Then, off the heat, whisk in 2 tablespoons fresh unsalted butter.

Present the duckling on a long platter. Sprinkle it with half of the diced lemon pulp and coat it with a few tablespoons of sauce. Mix the remainder of the sauce with the remainder of the diced lemon pulp and serve in a sauceboat.

(Note: The method of poêlage *given here by M. Lasserre is not applicable to American ducks, which are too fat and too large. To obtain about the same results with an American duck weighing 4 to 4½ pounds, place the duck and its giblets and vegetable garnish in a shallow roasting pan. Roast it slowly, uncovered, at 325°F. for 2½ hours. Prick the sides of the duck with a skewer or trussing needle to release the fat after the duck has been roasting for 30 minutes. When the duck is done, proceed exactly as indicated in paragraph 3 of M. Lasserre's recipe; there will be quite a lot of good gravy to prepare the sauce. Ed.)*

PINK CHAMPAGNE SHERBET
WITH ROSE PETALS

To serve 6 persons

Squeeze the juice from 4 large lemons and strain into a mixing bowl.

Mix 2 cups sugar with 3 tablespoons water, and let melt over medium heat; mix the obtained syrup with the lemon juice and let cool completely. Add 1 bottle of pink champagne. Strain the mixture through a muslin and pour it into the container of an ice-cream machine. Start the machine.

While the sherbet starts freezing, melt and cook ⅓ cup sugar mixed with 1 tablespoon water to 220°F. Beat 2 egg whites until they form soft peaks. Pour the hot syrup on the whites while you continue beating, and beat until the meringue is cold. Stop the ice-cream machine. Add the meringue to the semisolid sherbet and resume the churning until the sherbet has completely solidified.

Serve in champagne cups; sprinkle the top of each cup of sherbet with crystallized rose petals.

(Note: Crystallized rose petals can be purchased in fine food specialty stores. Ed.)

Persepolis at Maxim's

Dinner
offered by
THEIR IMPERIAL MAJESTIES
THE SHAHINSHAH
ARYAMEHR
and THE EMPRESS
of IRAN

in honor of their celebrated guests
participating in the
ceremonies of the 2,500 anniversary
of the founding of the Persian Empire
by CYRUS THE GREAT
PERSEPOLIS
Thursday, October 14, 1971

To quote a famous line from Féval's *Le bossu*: "If you don't go to Lagardère, Lagardère will come to you!" Since I did not go to Persepolis, it was Persepolis that came to me. And I had *my* Thursday, October 14, on Thursday, December 16, in Paris, at Maxim's.

Note, I could have gone to Persepolis. Louis Vaudable, the owner of Maxim's, had offered to take me on to poach quail eggs under his kitchen tents. But it seems that a pseudo-colleague of mine stooped to whatever was necessary to get the job. So I let him have it willingly: If travel broadens the mind, it can also broaden the waistline!

Anyway, I prefer *"mon petit Liré,"* as Du Bellay wrote of his village, to the hot dust of the desert and the promiscuity of the world's great men. To each his own place, and my place on that December evening was written in electric lights, piercing the fog on the rue Royale. The Madeleine, scraped and scrubbed down by Malraux—a wedding cake made of lard—seemed almost beautiful; the vista of the Concorde spread away from the Obelisk; and Maxim's doorman, perishing with cold, looked more like an

31

Maxim's
Dîner
Le Jeudi 16 Décembre 1971

— • —

Oeufs de cailles aux perles de Bandar Pahlavi

Mousse de queues d'écrevisses, sauce Nantua

Selle d'agneau des grands plateaux,
farcie et rôtie dans son jus

Sorbet au vieux champagne Moët 1911

Paon à l'impériale paré et entouré de sa cour
(Turban de figues garni de framboises au porto)

Poire Farah Diba

actor in a morose naturalist drama than anyone in Mirande's comedy, *La dame de chez Maxim's*. But it didn't matter, and I walked on briskly, as if in a dream starred with caviar. Indeed, what caviar? Iranian? The Shah's white caviar!

The meal, to honor the gastronomical press, took place in the bar-*salon* on the second floor. There were four tables set for twelve guests each. Which was three tables too many! For although a great spread had been laid out, it was spread too thin for so many. The lackeys (I suppose that's what they are called in Iran?) first served:

Quail Eggs with Bandar Pahlevi Caviar: A quail egg is extremely pretty in its shell, all spotted with blues, greens, and browns, which seems made of a precious and rare substance. It reminded me of a story. A few years ago, before quail eggs had become known, Raymond Oliver, of the Grand Véfour restaurant, served some—hard-boiled and in their shells—with apéritifs. A young woman exclaimed enthusiastically: "How very pretty! What are they?" "Quail eggs." "And how does one eat them?" "Like this," I replied, chewing one up conscientiously, but spitting out the shells when she happened to look the other way. My snobbish little friend did the same, and not wanting to confess her surprise, swallowed the entire egg. The expression on Raymond's face when he arrived and vainly looked about for the shells was a pleasure to see!

I can imagine how, in Iran, young boys are mobilized to go out in season and gather quail eggs from nests, and how luxurious they must be, soft-boiled, with their delicate yolks spilling out over a large, rich mound of caviar. At Maxim's we were served (and we might have expected as much) a very thin layer of the latter in pastry eggcups, with farm-bred quail eggs. It was excellent. Still, I couldn't help thinking of that well-known line:

> "Tell me, my dear, how did you find the caviar?"
> "Oh, quite by accident, when I lifted the quail egg."

Crawfish-tail Mousse with Nantua Sauce: We were back in France, with a classic dish from the region of Bresse, and Brillat-Savarin would not have had a word to say against it.

Saddle of Lamb des Grands Plateaux, *stuffed and roasted in its juice:* Lamb, I believe, is the one and only Iranian meat. The stuffing itself was unique, and the accompanying delicate green asparagus, just crisp enough, wreathed it admirably.

Champagne Sherbet, Moët 1911: A champagne *that* old is good for nothing but making sherbet, so I could hardly be enthusiastic about its being unique. But the old custom of serving sherbet between two courses always delights me.

Peacock à l'Impériale, adorned and surrounded by its Court: In France, during the Middle Ages, peacock was the meat of valiant knights. Actually, I believe that peacocks are still bred and eaten in Italy, in spite of the fact that their flesh is rather leathery. Do they eat peacocks in Iran? They did eat them (surely) in the times of Cyrus or Darius. At Maxim's, although we were treated to the sight of feathers adorning a fake peacock, we were served only its Court—that is to say, partridges (and farm-bred to boot!), stuffed and cold. The truffles were good. As for the salad invented by Alexandre Dumas (sic), I sought its origins in vain. In any case, I'm sure that even if that mixture of potatoes, lettuce, beets, etc., was signed by the author of *The Three Musketeers,* it was the work of one of his ghostwriters. It was just too mediocre!

"Turban" of Figs with Raspberries in Port: This was the surprise of the meal. There was no "turban"! The original dessert was replaced by pears Farah Diba. Others took the floor before I did (there are things one should never leave lying around—that damn floor, among others) to say that we'd just eaten *the* meal of the century. Still another meal of the century! What could I add?

That I would willingly have tasted the "turban" of figs with raspberries in port? That I admired the fact that an enthusiastic gastronome talked for five minutes about the quail we had just been served when it was partridge?

Or, quite simply, that the menu was truly fine?

I am obviously speaking of the very pretty menu itself, a small booklet of pink tissue paper printed in gold by the publisher Tolmer.

Recipes of Maxim's Restaurant

(Note: The style of the French writer was so concise that in these recipes three or four important operations were often described in only a few words. The very professional wording of the recipes made the text

difficult to follow for a nonprofessional cook. For the sake of clarity, the editor has rewritten the recipes, incorporating the chef's words into the text that follows. Ed.)

QUAIL EGGS WITH IRANIAN CAVIAR

To serve 6 persons

2 cups sifted flour
¾ cup unsalted butter
1½ teaspoons salt
6 tablespoons water
24 fresh quail eggs
1 cup heavy cream
salt and pepper
2 tablespoons chopped chives
6 ounces fresh Iranian caviar

Make a well in the flour. Add the butter, which should be very cold and cut into chunks the size of a tablespoon. Add the salt. With the fingertips, rub flour and butter together until a very coarse meal results, with pieces of butter about the size of a pea left in the mixture. Dribble in the water, tablespoon by tablespoon, mixing well with the fingertips and without kneading at all. When all the water has been used, gather the dough into a ball. Push nut-size portions of it 6 to 8 inches forward on the countertop; gather the dough into a ball again. Repeat this operation (which is called fraisage) *once more and refrigerate the dough for 2 hours.*

Butter six 3½-inch tartlet molds. Roll out the pastry and cut 6 circles of pastry 4½ to 5 inches in diameter. Fit the circles of pastry into the prepared molds. Prick the pastry with a fork. Line each tartlet mold with a parchment paper. Fill the paper with beans and bake in a preheated 425°F. oven for 7 to 8 minutes; remove the beans, then return the shells to the oven for another 4 to 5 minutes to dry their inside surfaces. Unmold and cool on a cake rack.

Poach the quail eggs for 2 minutes in simmering salted water acidulated with a bit of vinegar; cool them immediately in cold water to keep their yolks soft. Keep them cool between the folds of a clean napkin.

Whip the heavy cream with a bit of salt and pepper until quite firm. Chop the chives. Fill each tartlet shell with 1 ounce of caviar. At the center of each shell put 4 quail eggs. Spoon a large block of heavy cream over the eggs and sprinkle with chopped chives.

(Note: Unless the reader knows of a quail farm or where to go to collect quail eggs for poaching, he or she will have to make do with the canned hard-cooked quail eggs sold in fine food stores. Ed.)

CRAWFISH-TAIL MOUSSE WITH NANTUA SAUCE

(Note: This dish is much too fine to consider replacing the crawfish by shrimps. Only live Louisiana crawfish should be used here and the recipe should ideally be prepared only during the months of March to June when crawfish is in season. To order Louisiana crawfish, see page 272. Ed.)

To serve 4 persons

2¼ pounds large live freshwater crawfish
1 live 1-pound lobster
5 ounces pike meat without skin or bones
2 egg whites
2¼ cups heavy cream
salt and pepper
2 small carrots
1 large onion
10 tablespoons unsalted butter
1½ ounces Cognac
¾ pound fresh tomatoes, peeled, seeded, and finely diced
3 cups fish fumet *(p. 250)*
thyme
bay leaf
parsley
tarragon
2-inch piece of celery stalk with leaves
3½ tablespoons flour
¼ cup heavy cream
1 truffle, thinly sliced

Reserve 5 whole crawfish for decoration. For the rest of them, put all the heads with claws attached in a large pot. Shell all the tails by cutting the stomach membrane on both sides of the shell, then lifting the unblemished tail in one piece out of its shell. Add the shells of the tails to the pot containing the heads and put the meat on ice.

To shell the lobster meat, proceed as you would for an Américaine.

Sever the spinal cord, cut off the claws, and cut the tail into 3 pieces. Cut the head lengthwise into halves, remove the tomalley and any existing coral to a small container, and set it aside for later use. Discard the gravel bag. Extract all the meat from the pieces of tail, pushing out and discarding all traces of the vein or canal. Remove the meat from the claws after breaking them open with the back of the blade of a chef's knife. Keep the lobster meat on ice. Add the lobster shells to the crawfish shells.

To make the mousse, put the crawfish, lobster meat and pike in a mortar and pound, gradually adding the egg whites, until the mixture is homogeneous and rubbery. (Note: The same operation can be done in one third of the time with a professional mincer or in the home with an electric blender; if you use a blender, divide egg whites and meats into 4 portions and blend one after the other. Strain the purée through a fine sieve. Ed.)

Keep the obtained forcemeat on ice for about 2 hours. Then, using a spatula, gradually beat in the cream and about 1½ teaspoons salt and ½ teaspoon pepper (these amounts may vary with the shellfish). Add some of the lobster coral and tomalley. Before chilling the mousseline, gather a bit of it on a teaspoon and shape a small quenelle. *Poach it in salted simmering water to check the consistency of the mousse. If the forcemeat is too heavy add a bit more cream; if additional salt and pepper are needed add them now. Keep the mousseline deep-chilled until cooking time.*

To prepare the Nantua sauce:

Chop the carrots and onions into a fine mirepoix *(p. 267). Crush the crawfish and lobster heads and all the pieces of shells.*

Heat about 4 tablespoons butter in a large sauteuse. Sauté *the* mirepoix *until the onion turns translucent. Add the chopped heads and shells and raise the heat. Toss over high heat until the shells turn bright red. Add the Cognac, let it heat well, and flambé. Add the tomatoes, the fish fumet, thyme, bay leaf, parsley, tarragon and the small piece of celery stalk. Season with salt and pepper and simmer uncovered for about 1 hour.*

Strain the contents of the sauteuse *into a saucepan. You should obtain about 2 cups of concentrated shellfish essence. Add the 5 crawfish reserved for the decoration and poach them in the essence. Keep them warm.*

Mix the remainder of the lobster coral and tomalley with 3½ tablespoons flour and 4 tablespoons butter, mashing the mixture very well with a fork; whisk the obtained beurre manié *into the simmering shell-*

fish essence. Stir in ¼ cup heavy cream and whisk in 2 more tablespoons butter. Reheat well without boiling; strain the sauce again into a small clean saucepan.

To bake the mousseline:
    Butter a No. 24 (24 cm. or 9- to 10-inch) Savarin mold very generously and fill the mold with the mousseline of shellfish; tap the mold on the table or counter to pack it down. Butter a parchment paper, fit it on the mousseline, and trim its edges with the tip of a knife. Keep the mousseline cool until you are ready to bake it.
    Bake the mousseline in a hot water bath in a preheated 325°F. oven. The baking time will vary between 30 and 40 minutes. The mousseline is done when a fine needle pierces it easily and comes out dry and perfectly clean, and feels burning hot when quickly applied to the top of the hand.

To serve:
    Unmold the mousseline onto a round platter. Blot any clear liquid at the bottom of the platter with paper towels and coat the mousseline with about half of the sauce. Decorate its top with truffle slices and surround the mousseline with the 5 poached crawfish. Spoon some of the remainder of the sauce on each plate.

STUFFED SADDLE OF LAMB

    To serve 4 persons

    1 saddle of lamb, 4 to 5 pounds
    veal bones
    unsalted butter (about 10 tablespoons)
    1½ pounds fresh mushrooms
    salt and pepper
    lemon juice
    3 tablespoons chicken velouté, or 2 tablespoons chicken stock mixed with ½ teaspoon arrowroot
    2½ ounces goose-liver pâté (no replacement, please)
    24 spears of fresh large green asparagus

    Bone completely, or have the butcher bone, the saddle of lamb. Make sure that the tenderloins are left in place when the kidneys and the kidney fat are removed.
    With the chopped bones of the lamb and all the fat-free trimmings

plus a few meaty veal bones, prepare a good jus, *following the method given on page 247 for* jus de veau, *or brown veal stock.*

Wipe the mushrooms clean and chop them very finely. Sauté them in about ½ cup hot butter with salt, pepper and a few drops of lemon juice. As soon as the mushrooms have released their moisture into the pan, let about one third of it evaporate and add the velouté. Since velouté may not be available in a home kitchen, it may be replaced by ½ teaspoon arrowroot dissolved in 2 tablespoons cold chicken stock; add to the pan of mushrooms. Either velouté or arrowroot will thicken the mushroom juices. Let reduce gently until the mushroom hash is quite thick; let cool completely.

Dice the goose-liver pâté and delicately fold it into the cold mushroom hash. Stuff the boned saddle of lamb with the mixture. Roll and tie it, not too tightly (to prevent string scars on the cooked meat). Roast in a preheated 400°F. oven for 1 hour and 15 minutes. Let rest for 10 to 15 minutes before carving.

Cut the asparagus about 2½ inches below the terminal bud and peel off the skin with a potato peeler. Tie the asparagus spears in bundles and cook them in a large amount of wildly boiling salted water for about 8 minutes; they should remain bright green and crisp. Drain them and roll them while still hot in several tablespoons of fresh unsalted butter. Season them with salt and pepper.

To present the dish:

Set the saddle on a large serving platter. Defatten the cooking juices in the roasting pan completely and deglaze them with some of the prepared jus. *Brush some of that glaze all over the saddle. Surround the saddle with bundles of asparagus and serve the remainder of the* jus *in a sauceboat. Serve on hot dinner plates.*

PEARS FARAH DIBA

To serve 6 persons

The pears are poached, set on a piece of pain de gênes *well permeated with Kirsch, covered with a thin layer of Italian meringue, baked, and served topped with a Kirsch sabayon.*

To make the pain de gênes:
Cream 6½ tablespoons butter until white. Add ½ cup sugar and beat until well blended. Pulverize ¼ pound blanched almonds in the blender with 1½ tablespoons sugar. Blend the almonds into the sugar and butter

mixture. Beat in 3 small eggs, one by one, and 2 tablespoons rum. Continue beating the mixture until it is almost white and very foamy. Fold in 5 tablespoons sifted flour.

Butter an 8- or 9-inch cake pan and line its bottom with a parchment paper. Turn the cake batter into the cake mold and bake in a preheated 325°F. oven for 30 to 35 minutes.

To poach the pears:

Peel 3 large very ripe Bartlett pears. Cut them into halves and remove the cores with a melon-baller for the sake of neatness. Rub each pear with a piece of lemon as soon as peeled. Poach the half pears in a syrup made of 2 cups of water and 1 cup sugar and flavored with the seeds of a vanilla bean. Cool the pears on a cake rack placed over a plate to allow any excess syrup to drip.

To present the dessert:

Cut the cake into 6 pieces as large as each pear half (some recutting may be necessary). Moisten each piece of cake with at least 1½ tablespoons pure Kirsch. Top each piece of cake with one pear half. Set aside.

To make the meringue coating, beat together 3 egg whites and ¾ cup superfine sugar over low heat so that the meringue stiffens while being beaten. Add 1 tablespoon pure vanilla extract halfway through the beating. As soon as the meringue holds in peaks on the beaters, remove it from the heat and beat until cold.

Coat each pear and cake slice with an ⅛-inch layer of meringue and bake in a 350°F. oven for 10 minutes. Serve with the sabayon *sauce.*

To prepare the sabayon *sauce:*

Work in a double boiler. Place 6 egg yolks and ⅓ cup sugar in the upper container and beat until a heavy ribbon forms when the beaters are lifted from the batter.

Fit the upper container of the double boiler over the bottom part which should contain barely simmering water. Continue whisking, gradually adding about ½ cup warm water. When the mixture is thick, heavy and warm to the top of the finger, remove the sabayon *from the heat and whisk in 6 tablespoons Kirsch. Spoon the* sabayon *on the pears and serve promptly.*

Quest for the Big Aïoli

Some journalists and I had been invited to Arles for the Rice Festivals.

Since French journalists are the most ignorant in the world, I had astounded my colleagues on the train when I reminded them that rice was not nearly so exotic as they thought; that, rather, potatoes had been introduced into France more recently than rice. Actually they came to us from America; Christopher Columbus took them to Spain, and since the Pyrenees still existed as a barrier, they went from there to Italy, Savoy, and Germany before they ever reached France. Whereas rice had been grown in the Camargue for quite a long while.

The cultivation of rice was justified at the time because of famines and problems of transportation, but it seems somewhat ridiculous today. The Camargue should be merely a national zoo, where one only cultivates the art of living amicably with mosquitoes.

All the more so because long-grain American rice is the best. But enough of that . . .

We were speaking of the Rice Festivals. The Rhône was a joyous sight, with all the pretty Arlesian girls and the festive sun. We went to place after place and ate our fill, and ended up full. Full, but not gratified, for nothing is more debilitating than that type of official dinner at which the creamed fillet of sole precedes the beef Wellington, which is followed by the customary *bombe glacée,* and where the wine is undistinguished but plentiful and the speeches lend no flavor to the liqueurs.

On the last day there was to be a great official luncheon, presided over by the Minister of Agriculture (don't ask me his name; I've forgotten it if I ever knew it; and anyway, he was probably one of the unmentionables such as we have in this government's service). We could foresee the re-fillets of sole, the re-beef Wellingtons (a prestigious name to the British, but it makes gourmets mutter that well-known swearword immortalized at Waterloo), and the re-*bombes glacées.* Plus a suitably soporific speech, of course.

We were put up in a hotel the name of which still makes me smile, because of an untranslatable French joke. Le Nord-Pinus. It could be proud of its fine eighteenth-century building and its fine furniture, but not its

41

cuisine, which was as mediocre as it is in 99.99 percent of French hotels.

I asked the owner if he could make me an *aïoli*. The good man, thunderstruck, lifted his arms to heaven: "An *aïoli!* You want an *aïoli?* But, sir, today isn't Good Friday!"

Need I say that Arles is the capital of *aïoli?* And that that creamy garlic sauce is its glory? And that the Provençal poet Mistral guaranteed that "it saturates the body with warmth and bathes the soul in enthusiasm"?

So shouldn't one expect every hotel and restaurant in Arles to introduce *aïoli* to tourists? Not on your life! "They" are too stupid!

Then, since I persisted: "Oh, maybe you could get *aïoli* on Friday in some little bistro, but . . ."

But it was Monday and we were leaving on the next day after the official banquet. I was furious.

At cocktail time I walked around Arles, through some of those little streets that are known to be "shady" (even though the Fifth Republic of the landlords claims to be virtuous), in search of *the* bar. For in all French provincial towns there is at least one bar which—how shall I put it?—which is the hangout of the bad guys. And generally the bad guys are the best guys when it comes to good grub. Arles proved to be no exception. I went in. The owner was Corsican. After dropping the names of some of my Pigalle chums as passwords, I explained my predicament. The Corsican gave me the name of a sort of suburban dive, the owner of which—Dédé—was top-drawer when it came to *aïoli*. Then he phoned him, and with that first-class introduction I went out to find my man.

"Tomorrow, at noon, I can do it," he told me.

Tomorrow at noon was the official banquet. Rather annoying . . . But the *aïoli* I had been promised glowed like a sun on my epicurean horizon. Dédé added, "If there are five or six of you, I'll make you the big *aïoli*."

At this, any possible hesitation on my part disappeared. I ordered for six and was reassured.

Truth forces me to admit that I had no trouble corrupting four of my colleagues.

Aïoli is the cream of the South of France—a strong, unctuous mixture of garlic crushed with a pestle in a mortar and blended with egg yolks and olive oil. The marvelous exaltation of the triumphant garlic—*l'ail*—gave its name to this star dish, which should more precisely be called cod with *aïoli*. For it is cod—or stockfish—that best suits the sauce, although it is also served with any cold fish, cold meats, and boiled vegetables.

The "big *aïoli*," however, is something else again. A whole meal in itself, a monument. The Roman ruins of Arles are no more striking or

"Au Bar de Dédé"

Aïoli Arlésien

———— • ————

Morue

Escargots   Poulpes

Oeufs durs

Pommes de terre en robe des champs

Carottes   Topinambours

Raves   Haricots verts

Bettraves   Pois chiches

Chou-fleur   Artichauts

Gigot bouilli

perennial than the big *aïoli*. What am I saying? They are all on a par; they partake of the same Roman grandeur, the same classical authenticity.

Just think, fellow gluttons, the big *aïoli* includes . . .

Cod, with all the salt soaked out, poached in a court-bouillon, and flaked.

Snails, removed from their shells and cooked in a flavored court-bouillon.

Small blanched squid.

Hard-boiled eggs (at least two per guest).

Quantities of boiled vegetables (carrots, unpeeled potatoes, Jerusalem artichokes, string beans, beets, chick-peas).

One cauliflower.

One small artichoke per person.

A boiled leg or shoulder of lamb.

We arrived on time, with happy hearts, relaxed souls (in spite of our truancy, for the sin was that of those organizers who were too idiotic to have thought of offering us an *aïoli*), and fine appetites. There were five of us, as I said. We had ordered for six. The owner had prepared a big *aïoli* for twelve. We swore by Saint Trophime, patron of the Arlesian women, to stick it out.

We had good reason to be so resolved, because Dédé had called in some friends to make fun of us Parisian journalists. They were there, chanting anecdotes or playing cards as in Pagnol's *Marius,* drinking *pastis* after *pastis,* and peeking at us as they awaited our defeat.

"Impossible" is not . . . gastronomical. We attacked like General Kléber at Marengo, with drawn forks, slowly but surely. Undaunted. Midway to indigestion we had our *trou du milieu*—a shot of fortifying alcohol, in this case a good strong local *marc.* Then off we went, attacking again, besieging the last bastions of cod, assaulting the last hard-boiled eggs, goring the last snails, razing the final vegetables. We devoured everything. And, quite simply, the spectators who had come to sneer applauded.

We then understood Mistral's lyrical stanza: "When sitting down to a really fragrant *aïoli,* glowing like a golden thread, where—I ask you—are the men who would not consider themselves brothers?"

A few natives of the region must still remember the feeling. As for me, that lunch is unforgettable.

All the more so because, beforehand, I had sent my newspaper a brilliant report on the official luncheon, having quoted some witty, remarkable, definitive statements made by the Minister of Agriculture. It was perhaps the first time that gentleman had expounded, intelligently and relevantly, on a subject about which he knew nothing.

Except . . . Except for the fact that the Minister hadn't come!

Fortunately the editor of my paper never knew. Nor did its readers. Nor probably did the Minister . . . Indeed, those creatures never know much of anything at all!

That is why, a few years later, when the Minister (another one) awarded me a medal for my service to agriculture, I willingly accepted it. Of course, I had never raised any domestic animals except my cat, or farmed the land anywhere except in pots on my balcony. But I had once— the day I devoured a big *aïoli*—attributed immortal words to his predecessor!

Mistral's Grand Aïoli

(Note: Mistral, the great Provençal poet, was born in Maillane in 1834 and died in 1914. He wrote in Provençal and was the author of Mireille, *which Gounod made into an opera in 1904. The following is Mistral's description, rather than recipe, for* aïoli. *Ed.)*

Count 2 peeled garlic cloves per guest. Pound them to a paste in a mortar; add 3 egg yolks and a bit of salt. Drop by drop, add some olive oil (you want to use cold-pressed virgin olive oil) while you stir with the pestle, always in the same direction and at the same rhythm. As the *aïoli* thickens, add a few drops of lukewarm water and the juice of ½ lemon. Continue stirring constantly until the *aïoli* has "taken" (thickened) well.

You must be sure that the oil is at room temperature so that the *aïoli* does not turn. Should just this happen, empty the curdled *aïoli* into a small bowl. Clean the mortar and, with new ingredients, start a new thick *aïoli* into which you will gradually blend that first one.

In 2 separate pots, cook 1 potato in its jacket and 1 small artichoke per guest.

Poach a leg of lamb with a few carrots so it remains pink and juicy. Put some of the lamb cooking broth in 4 separate pots and in them cook separately some Jerusalem artichokes, white turnips, green beans and chick-peas.

Blanch, then boil a small cauliflower. Buy 2 cooked beets and bake them. Hard-cook 12 eggs and shell them.

Soak some stockfish in cold water overnight and poach it in a court-bouillon. Blanch some snails and baby squids, then finish cooking them in another court-bouillon.

(Note: Mistral's recipe stops here. The dish is usually presented on an enormous platter and is a symphony of colors and smells, especially of smells. The recipe can easily be prepared in the United States since all the vegetables, including the Jerusalem artichokes, are available.

For the sake of flavor and practicality, use a frenched leg of lamb without saddle. Make a larger than necessary amount of broth to poach it in, not only with carrots but also with all the vegetables usually entering a soup. The cooking time is 12 to 14 minutes per pound. While the lamb poaches, remove some of the broth and in it cook the 4 vegetables mentioned in the Mistral description.

Red beets in France are mostly sold already boiled in salted water; French people reheat them in a medium oven to concentrate their flavor.

Live snails and salted stockfish are easily located in Italian markets all over the country. To poach the snails and squids use the court-bouillon on page 251 and flavor it well with fennel seeds, or dried fennel stalks, if you can locate them. Ed.)

A Bourbonnais Luncheon

I was writing my book *Les vacances dans votre assiette,** a work devoted to what I call folklore cooking because it springs from the soil itself and is now, alas, becoming a thing of the past. I was at Vichy, in one of the oldest and least-known French provinces, Bourbonnais, the door to Auvergne, the cradle of our Bourbon kings. Yes, even more than Touraine, Bourbonnais was the very essence of the French monarchy until the Orléanais, accomplices of the Republicans, assassinated it.

Curnonsky liked to tell me that the cuisine of the *"bourbonnichons"* (I'm afraid that *is* what they're called!) is robust and derives from both the peasantry and the bourgeoisie.

Jacques Aletti, a friend whose hobby is cooking, suggested taking me to lunch in an authentic Bourbonnais home—the Lamoureux. Lucien Lamoureux, a former minister of the Third Republic, was one of those literate men who could be described as serious without being austere, forthright, and unaffected—in other words, the type that, because of Gaullism, we rarely have now as statesmen. His wife, Madeleine, a reflection of his simplicity and charm, was, and still is, a peasant housewife in the noblest sense of the word, a mistress of the house at a time when there were no houses (in the patriarchal sense of the word), who reminded me of the wife of the poet Théodore de Banville:

> You, you do everything, the washing and baking,
> All with a light hand, never quaking,
> You know, too, how to preserve citrons . . .

I found that first lunch marvelous. I have had others there since, and it now has become a tradition: every year I have a Bourbonnais lunch at Madame Lamoureux's. Her husband is unfortunately no longer alive, but we always imagine that he is there with us, rejoicing at our appetites, at our appreciation of his wine (he had his own vineyards), and at our jokes. For I might add that the *chansonniers* and humorists Jean Rigaux, Jacques

* Published by Fayard.

47

Meyran, and Pierre-Jean Vaillard were also invited and contributed, as Balzac said, "samples of French talk" in the gay and healthy tradition of the kind of wit that, since Rabelais, had made one hungry.

Yes, that first meal will always be engraved in my mind and on my taste buds. We had just enough time to walk around on the terrace of the lovely Bourbonnais house in Creuzier-le-Vieux, which overlooks the non-chalant river Allier and its sand dunes, when Madame Lamoureux came out of the kitchen, *her* kitchen and her kingdom! For, as in all good families, the cook and her little platoon were merely soldiers in the service of the mistress of the house. One could feel that, even the day before the meal, everyone had been given his share of direction, a specific job, and the materials to work with according to custom and tradition.

The house smelled of floor wax, orange blossoms, and serenity. The kitchen itself smelled of warm bread, milk curdling into fresh cheese, rich stews, and unctuous sauces. The dining room glowed in the shade of blinds lowered to veil the summer sun and the buzzing bees. It was alive—the main and most serious room in the house. The sturdy wooden table was covered with those mouth-watering appetizers which, in every corner of France, seem to inscribe, indirectly, the epicurean richness of the soil, its inspirations and its aspirations! On platters large enough to satisfy Gargantua, there was the *pompe aux grattons,* the meat pie, and the potato cake, not to mention the *sanciaux.*

When hog fat is rendered for lard—which, in spite of butter and oil, is still the best cooking grease for rustic and honest dishes—it forms *grattons,* or cracklings, which can be obtained at any pork store in this region. *La pompe* is actually a kind of brioche, which, with cracklings, is a local delicacy usually found at every regional festival. The meat pie is yet another and one for which there are as many recipes as there are local housewives. It may be served at either the beginning or the end of a meal. It originated in the region of Montluçon, where, for Saint George's Day, the inhabitants carry a painted cloth dragon through the streets, praying to their saint not to freeze the vineyards, after which they all, in a body, eat a meat pâté *(pâté à la courniaule)* made of highly spiced horsemeat.

The potato cake, soaked in cream, is fortifying and delicate. *Sanciaux* are crêpes. Native-born Bourbonnais exiled in Paris have a society called *Les Sanciaux,* which shows how traditional these buckwheat-flour and buttermilk pancakes are. Today, *sanciaux* are sometimes made of ordinary flour, of grated potatoes, or, in keeping with another old tradition, of oat flour.

These tempting appetizers on the Lamoureux table, washed down with white wine from the family vineyards, had the true aroma of good

Déjeuner bourbonnais
offert par
Monsieur et Madame Lucien Lamoureux
à Creuzier-le-Vieux

.

Pompe aux grattons
Tourte à la viande
Gâteau de pommes de terre
Sanciaux

.

Poulet aux carottes
Canard à la Duchambais

.

Galette au fromage
Fruits du verger
Piquenchâgne

.

home cooking—the kind of cooking that draws men and inspires their respect for the "mistress," the guardian, of the house, and also the person who "controls" all the work and the daily life and the conversation about them: Autumn will be fine this year—there won't be much game—the vineyard could use a few days of rain—didn't we harvest the wheat too early?—*La Fanchette's* newborn calves are thriving . . .

We were then served two dishes of fowl. Madame Lamoureux apologized, insisting that this was not a classical meal but rather a sampling of regional recipes. The chicken with carrots was a happy surprise, even if it didn't have a story. But the duck *à la Duchambais* was one of those dishes that my late colleague Francis Amunatégui called "history-making." Such dishes might even be called "historical," or at least this one could, given its authenticated origins: in 1815 hare *à la Du Chambet* was created; then, by extrapolation, there came duck *à la Du Chambet;* and now both dishes are known as *à la Duchambais.*

The Du Chambet château, near Lapalisse-en-Bourbonnais, was then occupied by allied troops that had come to free France from Napoleon I. It was an Austrian contingent that was billeted there, and the officers naturally asked their cook for something that reminded them of home—in other words, sour-cream sauces which turn the entire dish somewhat sour. Monsieur Du Chambet's own cook watched them at work. When the troops left, she tried to please her master by imitating their hare concoction, which she found strange but realized was interesting. Soon, during the hunting season, all the receptions at the château included that hare dish from Central Europe, and it became known as hare *à la Du Chambet.* Then, after the game season, she got the idea of preparing farmyard ducks in a similar way, and her preparation became known as duck *à la Du Chambet.* I have never been able to find out why we say *Duchambais* today. Nor had the Lamoureux. In any case, their purpose was to provide us with a real feast.

Fresh cheese from the farm, fruit from the orchard, and *piquenchâgne* (pear cake), which got its name from an old French game mentioned by Rabelais, the children's game "oak fork" or *châgnedret*—the lunch was admirable, rare, even astonishing. Later we talked it over in Lucien Lamoureux's library, its shelves dappled with sunlight that filtered onto the faded bindings, as we sipped a liqueur that was as local as the food.

"Good heavens!" exclaimed Madame Lamoureux in dismay. "I forgot to have the cheese tart served!"

Recipes of Madame Lamoureux

CRACKLING BREAD (Pompe aux Grattons)

Dice finely a generous pound of pork cracklings. Mix them with 3½ cups sifted flour. Make a well in the flour. Add 7 tablespoons very soft butter, 3 whole eggs beaten, a scant ½ cup milk and 1¼ teaspoons salt. Work the flour slowly into the liquid ingredients to make a dough. Grease a pastry sheet and shape the dough into a crown. Bake in a preheated 350°F. oven for 1 hour.

(Note: In Bourbonnais, this bread is often made with an ordinary brioche dough. The preceding dough can be lightened considerably if one adds 2½ teaspoons dried yeast to the milk and allows the mixture to start bubbling before making the dough. One should then allow the finished dough to rise to twice its original size. Then punch it down and shape it into a crown. Let the shaped bread rise again until one and one half times its original size. Bake it in a preheated 375°F. oven for 40 minutes. Ed.)

MEAT PIE (Tourte à la Viande)

To serve 6 persons

Prepare one recipe for puff pastry (see p. 268). Roll out half of the pastry into a ¼-inch-thick sheet. Transfer this sheet to a buttered baking sheet rinsed under cold water. Cut a 10-inch circle out of it.

Prepare a highly seasoned forcemeat (see veal and pork forcemeat on p. 266). Shape it into a dome on the circle of paste so that its thickness is about 2½ inches at the center. Leave 1 inch of dough free at the edges and brush it with *dorure* (p. 270).

Roll out the other half of the pastry into a second sheet ½ inch thick. Cut a circle of pastry 12 inches in diameter. With a pastry cutter cut a 1-inch hole at the center of the circle to make a "chimney." Transfer the second circle of pastry over the first one; this is best done by wrapping the dough over your rolling pin. Seal the circles of pastry by pressing the edges well together and cutting small indentations into both layers of pastry with the tip of a paring knife.

Bake in a 375°F. oven for 1½ hours. As soon as baked, pour a few tablespoons of melted lard through the chimney of the pie. Let cool completely before serving.

POTATO PIE (Gâteau de Pommes de Terre)

To serve 6 persons

With 1 pound flour, 1 cup butter, 1 egg, lightly beaten, 2 teaspoons salt and about 2 tablespoons cold water, make a short pastry (see p. 268). Let the dough rest for 20 minutes. Then roll out two thirds of the dough and fit it into a buttered 10-inch porcelain pie plate.

Slice 6 baking potatoes into paper-thin slices. Chop enough fresh parsley, chervil, tarragon and chives to obtain 2 tablespoons of each herb. Mix the herbs well. Alternate layers of potato slices with layers of chopped herbs. Salt and pepper each layer of potatoes.

Roll out the remainder of the dough. Cut an 11-inch circle of dough out of it; at its center cut a 1-inch hole to make a "chimney" and transfer the circle of dough on top of the potatoes to make the top crust of the pie. Seal the edges well.

Brush the pie with *dorure* (see p. 270) and bake at 400°F. for 45 minutes.

When the pie is done, pour 1 cup heavy cream into the chimney. Serve piping hot.

(Note: Heat the heavy cream before pouring it into the pie or the potato starch will cool off too fast and acquire a cardboard taste; use a funnel to pour the cream into the pie. Ed.)

BUCKWHEAT PANCAKES (Sanciaux)

To serve 4 to 6 persons

Put 1 cup buckwheat flour in a bowl. Make a well. Add 2 eggs, 1⅓ cups buttermilk, salt and pepper. Stir until smooth. Add ¼ cup sunflower oil.

Heat a crêpe pan very well. Pour about 3½ tablespoons of the batter into the hot pan to make crêpes about ⅛ inch thick.

(Note: These crêpes are thick. In Bourbonnais, they are enjoyed with fresh cheese, honey or jam. Use any crêpe pan from No. 18 to No. 22 to obtain 18 to 12 crêpes. Ed.)

CHICKEN WITH CARROTS IN MILK COURT-BOUILLON

To serve 6 persons

Sauté 2 large onions, sliced, 1 large garlic clove, mashed, 1 large carrot and 1 large turnip, both sliced, in 2 tablespoons butter.

Add 3½ cups chicken broth and 1½ cups milk. Bring to a boil; add a *bouquet garni* and the giblets of the chicken. Let simmer uncovered for 1 hour and strain.

Cut a 3½-pound chicken into 8 pieces (2 drumsticks, 2 thighs, 4 pieces of breast). Heat 2 tablespoons butter in a large *sauteuse*. Add the pieces of chicken and let them stiffen in the hot butter, as nearly as possible without letting them color. Salt and pepper the chicken and pour the court-bouillon over it. Barely simmer, covered, for 15 minutes. Add ¾ pound of baby spring carrots and continue simmering for another 20 minutes, still covered. Remove the chicken pieces to a platter and keep them warm.

Uncover the pot, raise the heat, and finish cooking the carrots over high heat to reduce the cooking broth to a semi-glaze. Blend in 1½ tablespoons each of heavy cream and sour cream. Reheat without boiling. Correct the seasoning of the sauce and pour it over the chicken pieces.

DUCK À LA DUCHAMBAIS

Cut a 4-pound duck into 6 pieces. Cut a 4-ounce piece of fresh unsalted pork brisket (fresh unsalted unsmoked bacon) into lardoons 1¼ inches by ⅓ inch. In a large enameled cast-iron braising pot, gently render the lardoons until they turn golden; remove them to a platter. In the melted pork fat, sauté 3 coarsely chopped shallots very gently until they start browning. Remove the shallots to the same plate as the lardoons.

Still in the same fat, brown the pieces of duck well on both sides. Salt and pepper them well. Add ¼ cup excellent wine vinegar and toss well together. Sprinkle the pieces of meat with 2 tablespoons flour and let the flour brown while you toss the meat again with a wooden spoon. Add just enough brown veal stock (see p. 247) to cover the duck (*about 2 cups, Ed.*) and return the lardoons and shallots to the pan. Cover the pot and bake in a 325°F. oven for 1 hour or more.

The duck is done when a skewer inserted into one of the thighs comes out without resistance. Remove the pieces of duck to a warm platter. Defatten the cooking juices completely and add ⅓ cup heavy cream mixed with 2 tablespoons sour cream. Correct the seasoning of the sauce and strain it over the duck. Decorate with chopped parsley and butter-fried croutons.

(Note: For proper reducing of the duck juices during the oven braising, cover the meat first with a piece of aluminum foil placed flush on its surface and forming an inverted lid to catch the steam; then cover with the pot lid. Ed.)

FRESH-CHEESE TART (Galette au Fromage)

(Note: The quality of fresh cheese varies from one end of France to the other. In a country home like Madame Lamoureux's, this cheese (called fromage frais) *is most probably homemade with naturally soured and curdled full-cream milk. The curdled milk is put to drain through a cheesecloth and used while fresh and fragrant. As no store-bought cream, cottage or ricotta cheese would be able to take the place of such a "personal" product, the recipe below is a description only.*

If unpasteurized raw milk can be located, let it sour at room temperature and make fresh cheese as indicated above; use 2 cups of that cheese to make the pie described here. Ed.)

Make a short pastry (see p. 268). Line a pie plate with it.

Lighten the consistency of some fresh cheese with a bit of milk; add 1 egg beaten with 3 tablespoons flour, salt and pepper. Pour into the pastry shell and bake in a hot oven for 45 minutes.

PIQUENCHÂGNE (Pear Cake)

To serve 6 persons

Make a short pastry with 2 cups sifted flour, ¾ cup cold butter, 1½ tablespoons sugar, a pinch of salt and 5 to 6 tablespoons ice water. Peel and slice very thinly 6 ripe Bartlett pears. Macerate the pears for 3 hours in a mixture of 3 tablespoons sugar, a vanilla bean, a pinch of white pepper, 1 ounce dark rum and ½ cup heavy cream.

Roll out the pastry into a thin oval sheet. Put the pears at its center and fold the pastry over to make a turnover. Seal the edges. Brush with a mixture of egg yolk and milk (see *dorure,* p. 270). Bake in a 375°F. oven for 45 minutes.

(Note: By the time the pears have macerated for 3 hours, there will be quite a bit of liquid in the bowl. Do not discard it! Put it in a little pan and slowly reduce it to a syrup which you can brush on the baked piquenchâgne *to glaze it. Ed.)*

Table for Seven

In 1972 the one-hundredth anniversary of Curnonsky's birth was celebrated. The Prince of Gastronomes, Maurice Sailland, was born in Angers on October 12, 1872.

Having come to Paris to study literature at the Sorbonne, he decided in favor of journalism and, on the advice of the writer Alphonse Allais (who always had a penchant for mystification), chose an appropriate pseudonym, given the then friendly relations between France and Russia: *Cur non sky*—Why-not-sky?

He soon became one of those boulevardiers whose wit constitutes Parisian life. Léon Daudet, in his *Souvenirs,* describes him as regularly frequenting the Café Wéber in the company of the painter Forain or the journalist-politician Adrien Hebrard, while the ethereal shadow of Marcel Proust, his elder by one year, hovered above them. He could also be seen at Maxim's, sitting at Feydeau's table, and some evenings he would join the poet Paul Fort in Montparnasse. Or else he would invent rhymes with the poet from Béarn, Paul-Jean Toulet, in their "pavanatorium," or accompany the good Bacchic poet Raoul Ponchon on his nocturnal wanderings.

But mostly he wrote! He was devoted to his native tongue, the clear language of the Loire—that of Du Bellay; even then he said that he preferred his Gallic Loire to the Latin Tiber, and declared:

> Anjou's mild and gentle sheen
> Was mirrored in its fine cuisine.

For he was a gourmet from the very start, having been initiated into the simple pleasures of the table by a first-rate cook, an old peasant woman in his family's service whose name his friends will always recall with deep feeling: Marie Chevallier.

Provincial cuisine, more than in Paris, was then the work of women, and in its empiric simplicity was to introduce a new element to gastronomy. Still, it needed an epicurean writer to become its bard.

Curnonsky (for that is how he has been known ever since) made no distinction between literature and food. "If you want to say it's raining, say it's raining," he was advised by one of his teachers. Addressing himself to cooks, he added: "And, above all, keep it simple!" Somewhat later, in Brittany on a visit to Riec-sur-Belon with some painter friends, he met the cook Mélanie Rouat and her daughter and for them wrote a quatrain, the last two lines of which have become a golden rule for good eating:

> *La cuisine, c'est quand les choses*
> *Ont le goût de ce qu'elles sont!*

> "Cuisine" means that
> Things taste just like what they are!

He traveled all through the French provinces—often with his friend Marcel Rouff, author of *La vie et la passion de Dodin-Bouffant* and the most Parisian of Swiss writers—seeking out inns where the folklore of food and the nature of things were still respected. Curnonsky published in collaboration with his friend twenty-eight small volumes of epicurean escape, *La France gastronomique*.

A writer of quality and clarity, Curnonsky was the author of varied works—novels, ana, columns, and memoirs—in that classical style "which was the man himself." According to Colette, he "raised culinary art to the fine, high level of French art," and, as the author of *Les vrilles de la vigne* wrote, he was "the most provincial, crisp, and golden brown" of men. In fact, this is a marvelous image of the man whose perspicacity and epicureanism were strikingly "lucid and strongly fragrant," and who sang of them "in words that smacked both of modesty and perfect self-confidence."

The evolution of the French cuisine, its "renaissance" after World War II, owes much, if not everything, to Maurice Sailland-Curnonsky. Because he categorized all types of cuisine, he probably did not underestimate "Great Cuisine"—the rather showy kind that has a leaning toward "those forcemeats that, alas! often lead to force-feeding." But he extolled simple cooking and regional cooking, which are often—but should always be—the same thing.

When traveling, he loved to eat "at the local houses" (which, after all, could well be those of innkeepers) because they had a sense of the soil and of its friendship. His little masterpieces of kindness, cheerful good sense, and hearty appetite, which enlivened the review *Cuisine et vins de France* from 1947 to his death, indirectly reflected France herself, with her vineyards, her pastures, her orchards, the honey of her hives, the fowl of her farmyards, and the mushrooms of her forests—that France which, as Georges Duhamel wrote, is a happy country "which produces both olive oil and sweet butter, wine and beer; which reaps chestnuts and oranges, rye and lemons; which breeds cattle, looks after her game, grinds her wheat, cultivates vegetables galore, even those whose yield is small or inferior; invents cheeses, distills spirits, differentiates between mushrooms, gathers honey, catches fish, manufactures sugar, honors her eggs and disdains nothing that is eatable, not even frogs, not even truffles."

Cuisine et vins de France is still published. On the seventh of each month the review invites its close associates to dinner in some Parisian restaurant. I am sometimes asked to those "Dinners on the 7th." I'd be lying if I said that all of them were completely successful, more especially because I, along with one of Balzac's characters, claim that there should never be more than seven at the table . . . And those "Dinners on the 7th" are not dinners for seven.

Yet I should like to speak of one that, to my taste, was absolutely remarkable. I planned it, but don't sneer. The editor of the review, Odette Kahn, upon the publication of my *Vacances dans votre assiette,* had asked me to make the menu myself, based on recipes I'd given in the book. One is never so well served as by oneself, as the saying goes!

I dedicated the dinner to our friend Curnonsky, for the very good reason that it consisted of simple cuisine and regional dishes, and also because it took place in the kind of admirable 1900 setting he so loved.

It was at the Train Bleu, the "restaurant-buffet" at the Gare de Lyon in Paris.

That huge nave, built in 1900, was inaugurated in April, 1901, by the President of the Republic, Émile Loubet. But naturally, since this was in France, all work on the structure had not yet been completed. Indeed, it took a few years more, and the last frescoes are dated 1905. All around the inside and on the ceiling are enormous smoothed-out chromo paintings, touchingly naïve and characteristic of the "artiste" style of the period, with all the most sordid and wondrous aspects of academicism. When you think that Van Gogh had just died, that Claude Monet was painting his Nympheas, that Toulouse-Lautrec still had one year to live, to mention only a few, and that the State commissioned paintings like those! So what! Let us rejoice, since today they are what constitutes the attraction, if not the value, of that stupefying décor . . . Émile Loubet was the President of the Republic who was caned on his top hat as well as at the Longchamps racetrack. Those were happy days!

So the dinner took place in that rare and incomparable setting of the Train Bleu

> "Where everythin's blue . . .
> And like a train that's takin' off . . .
> There's no reason for not takin' you,"

sang Léo Ferré. I had asked our friend Georges Neu, owner of the excellent Train Bleu, to have his chef prepare the following menu:

Le Train Bleu
Restaurant - Buffet de la Gare de Lyon

"Dîner du 7"

———— • ————

Tartelettes bourguignonnes au fromage blanc
Soupe froide aux tomates
Morue à la lyonnaise
Gigot d' Yvetot
Fromages: cantal Saint - Nectaire fourme d'Ambert
Baba au rhum

Burgundian cream-cheese tartlets
Cold tomato soup
Codfish à la Lyonnaise
Leg of mutton Yvetot
Assorted cheeses
Baba au rhum

I was sure it would have delighted Curnonsky as representative of the provinces he loved, which are not only the soul of France but also the source of her true cuisine. The cold tomato soup had all the fragrance of Provence—not the alluvial scent of the Mediterranean seacoast, but the authentic fragrance of the interior. Cod *à la lyonnaise* is abundantly garnished with onions. Lyons is still the epicurean capital of France, and Curnonsky often extolled those he had baptized his "Holy Mothers," the first-rate cooks of the city watered by three rivers: Rhône, Saône, and Beaujolais. Cod with onions is one of those common dishes that delights me.

The leg of mutton Yvetot was greeted with a variety of reactions. It is boiled. The birds of prey who feed only on grilled meat, very rare, do not understand that meat can be boiled. And yet . . . ! Perhaps this old recipe that dates from the Middle Ages crossed the Channel with the companions of William the Conqueror and became enhanced by mint sauce? It would not have been the first time that the French and the English exchanged recipes across the strait, as one returns a tennis ball. That leg of mutton, surrounded by the vegetables that had been boiled along with it, was bracing (since, of course, it was mutton, not lamb) and fortifying.

I had ordered a trilogy of cheeses from Auvergne—cantal, Saint-Nectaire, and fourme d'Ambert. And, to end the meal, the dessert was a blend of Lorraine and Paris, since it was King Stanislas Leczinski, at his court in Lunéville, who had had the idea of transforming a Polish pastry into a French cake, which was then commercialized by a Parisian pastry cook, Sthorer, under the name of ali-baba (soon shortened to baba).

It was (in all modesty and, most especially, because of the chef) an admirable meal. Its only sins were the wines, for which I was not responsible. I hope you won't mind if I take this opportunity to suggest those that I would have preferred:

A champagne (Moët et Chandon's "Saran nature") as an apéritif to accompany the cream-cheese tartlets.

A Beaujolais Villages for the cod *à la lyonnaise*. But a Beaujolais that is rarely found in France and never in the United States, a Beaujolais of the year—light, tongue-tingling, even a bit tart, with its fruity flavor and mauve color indicating that no dealer had ever got near it!

A red Graves (Domaine de Chevalier) for the leg of mutton. A Saint-enay (Domaine des Hautes Cornières) for the cheeses. And water, almost iced, for the *baba au rhum.*

Recipes from My Vacances dans Votre Assiette

BURGUNDIAN CREAM-CHEESE TARTLETS

(Note: Before starting to prepare this recipe, read the note on French cream cheese or "fresh" cheese on page 54. Ed.)

To serve 6 to 8 persons

Strain a generous ½ pound creamed cottage cheese through a fine strainer. Cream ¼ pound unsalted butter; beat in the strained cottage cheese; add 2 tablespoons flour, some salt and a lot of pepper; continue beating until the mixture is smooth. Add 2 eggs, one at a time, beating well after each addition.

Line 6 to 8 tartlet molds (3½ inches in diameter) with short pastry (see p. 268). Fill them with the cheese mixture and bake in a 350°F. oven for 35 to 40 minutes.

COLD TOMATO SOUP

To serve 4 persons

Mince very finely the white part of 2 large leeks. Heat 2 to 3 table-spoons olive oil in a thick-bottomed saucepan. Add the leeks and let them cook gently over slow heat, stirring occasionally, until the vegetables are translucent. Add 5 large or 6 smallish sun-ripened tomatoes, peeled, seeded and quartered. Add a *bouquet garni,* 1 large garlic clove, mashed, salt and pepper. Toss with the leeks.

Add enough water to barely cover the tomatoes; bring back to a boil

and simmer, uncovered, for about 30 minutes. Remove the *bouquet garni*
and strain the soup through a fine sieve; let cool. Serve chilled.

CODFISH À LA LYONNAISE

To serve 4 persons

In a large frying pan, sauté 3 minced onions in plenty of butter.

Add 5 medium-size potatoes, boiled in their skins, peeled and sliced,
and finally some cooked codfish already poached, drained and flaked. Add
salt if needed and pepper to your taste.

Let fry in the butter over high heat; add a trickle of vinegar just before
serving; sprinkle with chopped parsley.

*(Note: Use 1 pound of salted codfish. Soak it in cold water for 24
hours, taking care to keep the fish on a cake rack immersed in the water.
Renew the soaking water at least twice. Poach the fish in unsalted water
for 10 to 15 minutes. The potatoes should be in ¼-inch-thick slices. Ed.)*

LEG OF MUTTON YVETOT

To serve about 8 persons

Boil together for 2 hours 6½ quarts water, 5 carrots, 5 leeks, 2 white
turnips, 3 large onions, each stuck with 2 cloves, and a large *bouquet garni*.
Add 2 crushed garlic cloves and 2 tablespoons Calvados.

Add a "frenched" leg of mutton and bring back to a boil. Turn the
heat down so the water barely simmers and let the leg of mutton poach
for 15 minutes per pound.

While the meat poaches peel, cut, and trim neatly 1 carrot, 1 white
turnip and 1 leek per person. Cook these vegetables in some of the mutton
cooking broth in a separate pot.

Serve the leg of mutton surrounded by the vegetables and accompanied
by a white caper sauce.

*(Note: Yvetot is a Normandy town near Rouen and Dieppe. A
"frenched" leg of mutton is shortened and does not include any part of
the saddle. To make the sauce: make a white roux with 3 tablespoons
butter and 3 tablespoons flour and moisten with 2 cups of the mutton cooking stock. Bring to a boil to thicken and simmer and skim for about 20
minutes. Add capers and fresh butter to suit your taste. It is a good idea
to flour the meat and wrap it in cheesecloth before cooking it. Ed.)*

BABA AU RHUM

To make 12 *babas*

Make a well in 1 pound of flour. Add 2 cakes of fresh yeast, crumbled, *(or 2 envelopes of dried yeast)*. Dissolve the yeast in ⅓ cup lukewarm milk. Let the yeast start to bubble; add ¾ teaspoon salt and 7 whole eggs. Gather the flour, yeast and eggs into a soft dough. Cream 1¼ cups butter and work it into the dough bit by bit.

Put the dough into a large bowl. Cover it with a towel or muslin and let it rise until double in bulk. Meanwhile macerate ¼ cup each of light and dark raisins in 3 tablespoons dark rum.

Sprinkle 2 tablespoons sugar over the dough and as you punch it down work the sugar and raisins into the dough.

Butter generously 12 *baba* molds. Put in enough *baba* dough to fill one third of the mold. Let the dough rise again to one and one half times its original volume. Bake in a 425°F. oven. Let the *babas* cool in their molds and saturate them with rum syrup. Make the syrup with 1 cup sugar and 2¼ cups water; heat it just enough to allow the sugar to melt. Let it cool and mix it with ¼ cup dark rum.

(Note: The best way to saturate a baba *is to immerse it completely in the syrup. Push on the immersed* baba *with a soup ladle, then slowly release the pressure to allow the cake to absorb the rum syrup. Ed.)*

Le Dodin-Bouffant

I never knew Curnonsky's great friend Marcel Rouff. I regret it not only because Curnonsky talked so much about him, but because Rouff dedicated one of his books to his potluck companion, and the dedication delights me as it reveals the intelligence Rouff put into the art of living: "To the friend with whom I have tasted of life, loved Balzac, adored Food, celebrated Wine, loathed ill-bred cads, sung the praises of Women, and taken this ridiculous planet as a joke. To thirty years of friendship, obesity, and thirst. Marcel Rouff, the Genevan."

Obesity? Or rather, let's say, with Brillat-Savarin, that both their bellies "tended to be majestic." Besides, that is why one day, glancing at the menu of a restaurant in Normandy and reading: "Lobster . . . according to weight," Rouff said to Curnonsky (or vice versa), "Well, old boy, this one's going to cost us a fortune!"

Yes, Marcel Rouff was a literate epicurean of great quality, a gentleman (in the sense of *"honnête homme,"* a type that is fast disappearing), and, yes, indeed, a great writer.

One has only to read his culinary novel—unique in its genre— *La vie et la passion de Dodin-Bouffant, gourmet,* to be convinced. I have often claimed that certain pages of it ought to be printed in anthologies and that schoolchildren would learn far more from them than from reading all those wretched fashionable writers from Sartre to Malraux, not to mention Camus.

But forget it. Since there is little that is not forgotten in the end, those knights of blah-blah-blah will be forgotten, too; whereas both Balzac and, for initiates, Dodin-Bouffant will be with us forever!

Although Dodin-Bouffant is a fictional character, he is very much alive. In the tiny provincial town where his amphitryon qualities are unanimously acknowledged, he was called the Beethoven of cuisine, the Shakespeare of food: "Princes had tried in vain to make their way into that modest dining room in which no more than three tested and worthy guests were allowed to sit at the table."

Among the great men who wanted to share his table and his food, prepared by Adèle Pidou (the cook whom Dodin finally marries), was the Prince of Eurasia. So he invited Dodin-Bouffant to his princely table for a meal that turned out to be as ridiculous as Boileau's. In the hopes of knocking out his man, the Prince ordered a typical nouveau-riche menu, in which "the shocking solecisms of the composition of each piece and of the orchestration of flavors" might worry a true gourmet. Still Dodin-Bouffant said not a word, but after the meal he asked the Prince to be a guest at his own house. Delighted, the Prince accepted. Thus one fine day the Prince of Eurasia and Dodin's usual guests sat down to a meal prepared by Adèle Pidou. The menu was as follows:

Delicacies before the soup

Soup Adèle Pidou

Tiny fried fish Brillat-Savarin

Boiled beef Dodin-Bouffant, dressed
with its own vegetables

Onions Soubise

Desserts

You can imagine how shocked the snobbish Prince was when he read the menu. What's this? Does one dare make fun of a Royal Highness? Dodin's friends themselves were worried: Was their idol going to fall into a ridiculous trap? I won't give details, but I must say that Dodin's *pot-au-feu* —his simple, vulgar boiled dinner—proves that no dish is vulgar when culinary genius is involved.

To me the description of this *pot-au-feu* Dodin-Bouffant is the high point of Marcel Rouff's novel. Like the dish itself, it reaches poetic heights; it is the dreamlike utterings of a culinary bard, a creation of spirit when the spirit applies itself to the most unbridled epicurean fantasies.

In short, it is a dish one dreams of being able to taste once in a lifetime.

I wrote those words one day in an article for the weekly paper *Carrefour* and, in addition, called for a patron. That was over twenty years ago. The patron didn't take over twenty hours to make himself known. I received a special-delivery note, signed Jean Barnagaud-Prunier, the gist of which was: "Gather a few friends of your choice around Prince Curnonsky, choose a date and a time, and let me know. The Dodin-Bouffant will be awaiting you."

And that is precisely what happened.

We were at the famous seafood restaurant Prunier's, on the old rue

Le Dîner de Dodin - Bouffant

Les friandises avant le potage

Le potage Adèle Pidou

Les fritures de Brillat - Savarin

Le pot - au - feu Dodin-Bouffant paré de ses légumes

Le purée Soubise

Les desserts

Duphot, which still delights me because one of Balzac's heroines, Madame Rabourdin, lived on it. It was an admirable opportunity to replace the courses preceding the *pot-au-feu* (delicacies, soup, fried fish) with abundant and varied seafood, on a platter as long as a torpedo boat.

Here, then, is the menu of the first Dodin-Bouffant:

Seafood platter

Pot-au-feu Dodin-Bouffant

Brie

Pears Belle Angevine

I say the "first," for there have been others here and there, and the last to date was made by Jacques Manière (in his restaurant, Le Pactole). One day Raymond Oliver even got the idea of a mini-Dodin-Bouffant served in a casing. But that falls into the category of diversions for chefs. For example, I am perfectly willing to admit that goose liver is better when cooked in its own juice and served cold than when it's hot and cooked in Chambertin, even if Chambertin *was* Napoleon's favorite wine. But no matter. There is not a gourmet alive who could be insensitive to the *pot-au-feu* which was created in a gourmandizing poet's imagination.

Francis Amunatégui, in his amusing and witty book, *L'Art des mets*, classified his favorite dishes under these headings: dishes that don't make history, dishes that have a history, dishes that make history, and dishes that will go down in history. Dodin-Bouffant (which, like every classic, is called *the* Dodin-Bouffant, just as one says "the Ninth" or "the Chartreuse") seems to me not only a dish that has a history but one that is history-making and will go down in history.

And I shall always remember the exchange of savory anecdotes at that dinner at Prunier's, with all of us gathered around the wonderful talker Curnonsky. As someone has said, conversation is the spice of food.

Yet the most wonderful story of all will forever be the description of the dish by its author: read and salivate.

"The boiled beef itself, rubbed lightly with saltpeter and sprinkled with salt, was cut in slices, and its flesh was so delicate that one's mouth felt it in advance, and guessed it to be deliciously fragmentable and tender. The aroma that emanated from it came not only from beef juices, steaming like incense, but from several—not many—cubes of lard, transparent and immaculate, with which it was pierced. The slices, which were fairly thick and whose texture one could anticipate, rested gently against a cushion of a large circle of sausage in which the meat, coarsely chopped, was pork

Prunier - 9, rue Duphot

Déjeuner

Plateau de fruits de mer
Pot-au-feu Dodin-Bouffant
Fromage de Brie
Poires Belle Angevine

accompanied by the most delicate veal, and seasoned with herbs, chopped chervil, and thyme. But these delicacies, cooked in the same bouillon as the beef, were themselves supported by generous cuts of the white meat— a breast and wing—of a fat capon simmered in its own juice with a veal knuckle and rubbed with mint and wild thyme. And to prop this magnificent, triple super-imposition, the rich and robust buttress of a comfortable layer of fresh goose liver, cooked simply in Chambertin, had been audaciously slipped behind the white meat of the fowl, which had been fed only on bread soaked in milk. The disposition of the platter repeated the same alternation, creating sections each neatly encircled by an envelope of assorted vegetables cooked in the bouillon and rolled in butter. In one motion, with a fork and spoon, each guest was expected to ladle up the quadruple delight which was vested to him and then carry it to his plate."

Recipe from the
Restaurant Prunier

PEARS BELLE ANGEVINE

To serve 4 persons

Peel 4 ripe Bartlett or Bosc pears. Remove their cores, wash them, and put them in a *sauteuse*. Barely cover them with a good red wine (Champigny, perhaps, or Saint-Émilion). Add 3 to 4 tablespoons sugar and a piece of cinnamon bark. Cook slowly, covered. Drain the pears and arrange them in a compote dish.

Reduce the cooking juices to obtain a light syrup. Let it cool and flavor it with a few drops of pear brandy. Pour it over the fruit. Serve the dessert chilled.

A Farm in Bresse

Every year in December, Bourg-en-Bresse has a poultry fair. As everyone knows, the blue-footed chickens, *poulardes,* and capons from Bresse, fed on corn, are one of the wonders of the farmyard. These days, when the French are fed mass-produced chickens under the pretext of agricultural "planning," a fowl from Bresse seems somewhat archaic and brings to mind these lines by the poet Gabriel Vicaire:

> Suddenly we saw—gay, fresh, and hale
> As a smiling new wife—
> A capon from the banks of the Veyle
> That had bloomed with new life. . . .
> It was so unctuous to behold
> The cook gave the impression
> Of someone who marches
> In a religious procession.

The Veyle is a tributary of the Saône which rises in the Dombes and flows near Bourg-en-Bresse.

Also, every year at the same time as the blue-ribbon poultry fair, the "Académie Granet," named after a local clog-maker and philosopher, holds a meeting. This takes place at table, before a feast of *daubes* and capons. The Granet *daube* is one of those Pantagruelic dishes which seem to come straight out of the Middle Ages, but which one is pleased to eat again each year in memory of the local clog-maker.

Now, once—and I mean once a long time ago—a few of us got together at Bourg-en-Bresse for that dual and happy occasion of the poultry show and a sampling of the fowl, as fattened as you could wish, and the annual meeting of the "Académie Granet" (which is also a sampling).

My crony Henri Clos-Jouve, author of *Promeneur lettré en Bourgogne et en Beaujolais,* suggested that we culminate these frolics of the fork with a few jaunts on foot into the surrounding countryside. He set up a whole itinerary and gamboled about at the head of the troop of our gastronomadic colleagues. But after a little while I, who prefer driving, began to trail behind. To begin with, it was snowing as hard as it does in Victor Hugo's poems. The harsh winter was swooping down like an avalanche, and my city shoes were acting like sponges. I'd reached the point of chewing over bitter thoughts (which, for a gourmet, is certainly not ideal) when, at a turn in the road, my savior appeared, in the person of a local colleague I had met the night before. He had two passengers in a jalopy whom he introduced to me: one was a director of the Union of Cheese Cooperatives in the province, and the second seemed to prefer *one* of his titles to fame to all the others—that of farmer.

After he had asked me to climb in, our driver said, "We're all going to have a bite to eat at La Bérezière. Come on with us . . . if a simple peasant meal doesn't scare you!"

It was still snowing, just as it had during the retreat in Russia. The Veyle must have been frozen to the bottom. A frigid wind blew over what to me was unknown territory, and though I was not barefoot like the heroes of Napoleon's army, my feet were as cold as ice. I climbed into the car.

Bresse is a region of long, low farmhouses. The roofs are so near the ground that they themselves seem to spring from the soil, and on the beams of the porches outside the kitchens ears of corn (called "golden *panouillons*" in that part of the country) hang in clusters, like symbols of friendship.

The Bérezière farm was a classic quadrilateral, with sloping roofs covered with Roman tiles and a large fountain in the middle of the courtyard. The snow was by now almost a foot deep, and we rushed straight into the huge kitchen.

"Natives of Bresse love to live alone and proud on their domains," the president of the "Académie Granet" had told me the night before. Like all good natives, the farmer's wife loved her life on her domain, in front of her hearth, with her stoves and all her pots. She greeted us with a big, somewhat frightened smile, then shoved us into the next room, where the table was set for us.

But before that I was made to swap my drenched shoes for a pair of slippers that were quite suitable to good digestion, for as a poet once said: "At the table, warm feet are an indispensable complement to one's belly."

I must admit that I really felt for Clos-Jouve. Was he still wandering about the snowy countryside or was he gulping some snack or other at an inn? But the farmer's wife slipped a menu between my plate and glass—a menu handwritten in a very old-fashioned style, with touching and obsolete flourishes:

Velouté soup

Ham cornets jardinière

Chicken-liver cake Bressan

Poached chicken in cream sauce

Sautéed string beans

Pickerel Dombes style

Roast wild rabbit

Salad

Fresh cheese

Aunt Amélie's tart

Fruit

Dauntless, we lit into the velvety *potage*, which warmed us up body and soul. The farmer informed us that everything we were eating came from the farm except the salt, pepper, and coffee. Yes, everything was born and bred on his territory: the pig, the chicken, the wild rabbit, the pickerel from his pond. Everything had grown on his land: the wheat in the bread, the vegetables, the fruit. The cheese came from his cows' milk, as had the cream, which is absolutely essential to this regional cooking, and the wine came from his vineyards, and the oil from his walnut trees . . .

I thought I could catch him in error. "But what about the sugar in that wonderful tart?" I asked. I was wrong. The tart was sweetened with honey—honey from his own hives!

We ate—for a long time. The women, who had stayed in the kitchen, were still bustling about; they had put on a big spread. Could I say that I didn't much appreciate the vegetable salad with the ham? That I should have liked the pickerel at the beginning of the meal? That, to my taste, there was too much vinegar in the salad dressing? That cream in every dish, even in the region of Bresse, was too much? I couldn't.

Besides, I was too comfortable in that warm room, with the skies outside falling down, while I, transported to another century, was having one of the most extraordinary meals of my life.

Déjeuner Bressan
à La Bérezière

—— • ——

Potage velouté

Cornets jardinière

Gâteau de foies de volailles bressan

Poulet à la crème

Haricots verts sautés

Brochetons dombistes

Rôti de garenne

Salade

Fromage frais

Tarte de la Tante Amélie

Fruits

Recipes from a Farm in Bresse

VELOUTÉ SOUP

To serve 4 persons

Prepare a golden *roux* with ½ cup each of flour and butter. Moisten it gradually with 5 cups of chicken stock. Let simmer for 15 minutes; strain through a muslin.

Cut 5 to 6 ounces of mushroom caps into a fine julienne. Toss them in a frying pan with a bit of hot butter to evaporate their moisture and to brown them lightly. Salt and pepper them.

Add to the soup a *liaison* made of 2 egg yolks and a scant ½ cup of heavy cream. Correct the seasoning. Add a few nuggets of butter and beat with a wooden spoon.

Put the mushrooms in a soup tureen and pour the soup over them.

HAM CORNETS JARDINIÈRE

Prepare a rémoulade sauce by diluting 2 tablespoons strong Dijon mustard with 2 generous tablespoons of wine vinegar and gradually adding some walnut oil. Salt and pepper the mixture.

Grate a celery root. Put the pulp into a cloth and squeeze well to discard the excess moisture. Chop 5 or 6 walnuts. Mix them with the grated celery root and toss with the rémoulade sauce. Roll as many slices of country ham as you have guests into cornucopias. Fill the cornucopias with the rémoulade and arrange the cornucopias on a platter. Chill in the refrigerator for 1 hour.

CHICKEN-LIVER CAKE BRESSAN

To serve 6 to 8 persons

Rub the inside of a mortar lightly with garlic. Put 6 large chicken livers and ¼ cup diced poached marrow in the mortar and pound them to a paste. Add ⅓ cup meat juices and about ½ cup milk to obtain a very liquid purée. Add 3 whole eggs and 3 egg yolks lightly beaten together. Salt and pepper the mixture and strain it through a fine sieve.

Oil a 4-cup charlotte mold; turn it upside down on a towel to allow the excess oil to drip down. Line the bottom of the mold with a circle of oiled parchment paper just large enough to cover it. Pour the liver mixture into the mold to fill it to within ½ inch of the rim.

Set the mold in a cold-water bath, making sure that the bottom of the mold does not touch the bottom of the water container. Heat the water bath progressively without ever letting the water come to a boil. Cook the loaf for 1½ hours.

Remove the mold from the water, pat it dry, and unmold the loaf on a shallow serving dish. Coat the loaf with a thick and spicy tomato sauce (see p. 258).

(Note: Instead of meat juices, meat glaze, strong veal stock or leftover gravy from roasted or pot-roasted chicken or veal may be used. The gravy should be natural and unfloured. To keep the mold from touching the bottom of the water bath, set a cake rack in the water bath and rest the mold on it. Ed.)

POACHED CHICKEN IN CREAM SAUCE

To serve 8 persons

Clean and wash ½ pound leeks, 1 small leafy celery rib, ¼ pound carrots and as much of white turnips. Put these vegetables into a soup pot together with an onion stuck with a clove, 1 garlic clove, 1 bay leaf and the giblets of a chicken. Add 3 quarts water. Bring to a boil and simmer for 1 hour. Skim two or three times.

After 1 hour, add a 3½-pound chicken and poach it for 45 to 50 minutes. Halfway through the cooking time of the chicken, add a small handful of coarse salt.

While the chicken poaches, heat well ¼ cup butter in a saucepan. Add the same amount of flour; stir well with a spatula. Add a bit of cold water, stirring with a whisk to prevent the formation of lumps, then add about 3½ cups of the chicken stock; you will obtain a rather liquid sauce. Bring it to a boil, stirring constantly, and let simmer for 10 minutes. Correct the seasoning.

Drain the cooked chicken in a colander. Carve it into 8 serving pieces. Add ⅓ cup heavy cream and the pieces of chicken to the sauce. Simmer together for just a few minutes and serve.

PICKEREL DOMBES STYLE

To serve 4 persons

Prepare a court-bouillon with 1 quart each of dry white wine and water, parsley, thyme, bay leaf, salt and pepper (see p. 251). Let it boil for 20 minutes and strain it.

Put 4 cleaned pickerels each weighing about ½ pound in a fish poacher. Pour the hot court-bouillon into the poacher so it covers the pickerels and let the fish poach, barely at a simmer, for about 20 minutes. Let cool to lukewarm.

Drain the pickerels. Remove their skins and put the fish in a shallow serving dish. Strain 2 cups court-bouillon into a saucepan and reduce it to ½ cup. Whisk 4 tablespoons unsalted butter divided into small pieces into the reduced court-bouillon. Pour over the pickerels.

(Note: The Dombes is part of the French province of Bresse. It is a marshy area rich in freshwater fish and aquatic game birds. Ed.)

ROAST WILD RABBIT

Salt and pepper the saddle of a wild rabbit. Put the saddle and some butter in a *sauteuse* and roast it in a medium oven. Baste the saddle often with the cooking butter to keep it moist and tender.

Ten minutes before the cooking time of the saddle is finished, brush it with some strong Dijon mustard and finish cooking it.

Remove the saddle to a platter and keep it warm. Defatten the cooking juices, deglaze them with 1½ to 2 ounces of *marc,* and flambé. Add 1 generous cup of heavy cream and let reduce to coating consistency. Correct the seasoning. Return the rabbit to the cooking pan and serve it.

(Note: The total cooking time of a young wild rabbit is about 45 minutes. The cooking time may vary, however, from one animal to the other. Ed.)

AUNT AMÉLIE'S TART

To serve 6 persons

Crumble well enough day-old bread to obtain ½ cup of crumbs. Moisten the crumbs with 1¼ cups milk. Add ¼ cup liquid honey, 3 to 4 tablespoons *marc* or Cognac, ½ cup ground almonds or walnuts. Fold

4 beaten egg yolks and 2 beaten egg whites into the mixture.

Line a 9-inch pie plate with ordinary short pastry (see p. 268). Pour the nut filling into the pastry shell and bake for 30 to 35 minutes.

(Note: Use a 375°F. oven. Bake the tart on the bottom rack of the oven for 15 minutes and on the top rack of the oven for the remainder of the baking time. Ed.).

What Is It in English?

Of all modern languages, argot is the most alive. Just as one says that an old man is still green, so "green language" (to go back to François Villon and his thieves)—in other words, slang—is still the liveliest source for our best modern neologisms and racy expressions.

I feel a somewhat astonished friendship for argot—the kind you have for a language you were not born to, but love. Those who studied the humanities in the dives of the Parisian working-class suburbs probably don't feel all that tender or even amused about the words they use every day, however skillfully they handle them. When a hoodlum *se met à table* (sits down at the table), it means, in slang, that he is making a full confession. At dinner, the table, in argot, is the *carante,* and when the *nourriture* (food) or cuisine appears, it may be called *la fripe, la croûte, la briffe, la cuistance, la bèquetance, la jaffe, la graine, la daronge, le frichti,* or *la tortore.*

To talk this language, you've got to have an *estome* (or breadbasket), and to live, you've got to *manger* (or eat)—that is, *claper, croquer, cacher, grainer, claboter, clapoter, claquer, gousser, morfiler, morfier,* or *tortorer,* and if the chow is good, you eat like a pig; that is, you *se morfale, fricote,* or *se bégale.*

On the *carante* you first have *pain*—in other words, bread, or *la gringue, l'artifaille, la brèque, le brigeton,* or *le brignollet.*

Then comes the wine—that is to say, *le sirop, le pivois, le jaja, le pive, le tutu, le busard, le picrate, le pichtegom,* or *le picton!* If it happens to be a cheap red wine that "stains," it is called *coaltar.* If it's a good light wine, it is called *coulange.* It may be *rouquin* (red) or *blanco* (white) and sometimes a *beaujolpif,* but then you'd buy it by the *bouteille,* or bottle (*betterave, boutanche,* or *rouille*) rather than by the liter (*kil* or *kilo*). But if it's a bottle of *champ'* (champagne), the bottle becomes a *roteuse* (a burper), and you drink it not in a *verre,* or glass, but in a *guindal,* a *bennard,* or a *glasse.*

You start off with an *apéro* (apéritif), go on to *la bouillante* (the soup), and end with *calendo* (camembert, the king of ratfoods), having already eaten the *barbaque* or *bidoche* (the meat) or the *saussiflard* (salami), along with *navarins* (turnips) or *loubiats* (beans). You finally get to coffee (*caoua*) and to the last bottle of wine, which you drink before leaving the table and which is called the *consolante,* or consoler.

There are no professors of slang, but if there were, the best one would probably be Albert Simonin. *Mon pote!* My buddy!

A kid from Belleville, that "dagger" province of Paris, he was nursed on freedom like Victor Hugo's Gavroche. Later on, at the wheel of his *rongeur,* or taxi, he meditated on real life, the kind one doesn't learn about in books, and he decided to write his own. His first was *Touchez pas au Grisbi,* an epic of the underworld, voyage to the end of the riffraff, and initiation into the life of mobsters—a little masterpiece which found its scenario writer in Michel Audiard and its knockout of an actor in Jean Gabin.

It was, then, for the première of the film *Touchez pas au Grisbi* that the producers got in touch with me. Simonin had given them the word: "For *la tortore,* see Courtine!" A dinner was to be given for the press to celebrate the opening.

It had to take place at Lasserre's. And the menu had to be written in argot.

I remember that the author and the screenwriter, as well as Gabin and the other actors, were surrounded by the cream of the movie critics. Those ladies and gentlemen had been asked to wear costumes of "local color." The real beauty (in any case, she thought she was), France Roche, who had come dressed as a moll, reigned over a variety of chippies and a handful of pimps. Gabin looked the critics over with an unnecessarily paternal eye, but Simonin must really have laughed inside at this bunch of freaks. And so did I. We didn't have to go back to Noah to understand each other, damn it!

The menu, however, consoled us. This is how I drew it up:

Par ici la bonne soupe

Les petits frangins de Pigalle
et leurs dames en soufflé

Les G'men à la chaise électrique

La salade du panier

Les demi-sel

Et une bonne gâterie, une!

(pour les dames)

Chez Lasserre
Dîner "La Bonne Croque"

Par ici la bonne soupe
Les petits frangins de Pigalle
et leurs dames en soufflé
Les G'men à la chaise électrique
La salade du panier
Les demi-sel
Et une bonne gâterie, Une!
(pour les dames)

All of it washed down with pitchers of wine and the house *roteuse*.

One day I showed the menu to a friend from the provinces and realized that I should have attached a glossary to it. For what I had thought so clear to a person with any imagination turned out to be far from that to a middle-class man. And yet . . . ! I had best comment, all the same, on the utter simplicity of my text:

Par ici la bonne soupe ("the good soup's over here") is an expression that is very familiar to the Frenchman who, for example, has a stroke of luck and collects all the bets during a poker game. Actually, though, it was not soup but a *potage*.

Les petits frangins de Pigalle ("the little brothers from Pigalle") were none other than small mackerel, which, in French argot, also means pimps. The fish was so baptized because it has the reputation of always following another fish in the sea, the *pucelle* (a tiny water flea, but also a virgin), although clearly *leurs dames* hadn't been *pucelles* for ages, but were rather —in the lingo of the underworld—*des morues* (cod, but also whores). And, in fact, what they served us were codfish soufflés.

Apropos, and parenthetically, René Lasserre had first told me: "They sound amusing, but, in fact, I'm going to have turbot soufflé made for you. Turbot is a far more delicate fish." I protested and explained my belief in sincerity. So the chef tried cod, and the soufflé proved to be a great success. It had an incomparable flavor, and its scent was somewhat gamy and delectable.

Les G'men à la chaise électrique ("G-men on the electric chair") could only have been broiled chicken (*poulets* is the slang word for "pigs" or, if you prefer, "cops") American style.

La salade du panier means salad that has been shaken dry in a wire basket (*panier*). But it also implies a *panier à salade,* which is slang for the paddy wagon with metal bars which the pigs offer as transportation to delinquents.

Les demi-sel, a lightly salted cream cheese (more popular early in the century than it is today), is also, in argot, the term for young men who do not yet belong to the underworld but have high hopes. As for *une gâterie pour les dames* ("a treat for the ladies"), it was one of Lasserre's great desserts, *timbale Elysée*.

In any case, everything considered, behind the jokes there was the substance of a great epicurean meal. Simonin, who likes solid and healthful food (in his book *Du mourron pour les p'tits oiseaux* the hero feasts on a *blanquette* which is slowly simmered by his concierge and which is one of the proud moments of his culinary life), will not contradict me.

We had—what is it in English?—a good feed? Or, if you prefer, we really had a bellyful.

Recipes of René Lasserre
Chez Lasserre

MARINATED MACKEREL

To serve 8 persons

Choose 8 small firm-fleshed mackerels; clean each of them and remove the heads. Put the mackerels side by side in a braising pot or a *sauteuse*.

Sprinkle 1 onion and 1 lemon, both sliced thinly, a large pinch of thyme, 1 crumbled bay leaf, 6 fennel seeds, some peppercorns and 1 clove on the fish.

Add a mixture of 2¼ cups water, ½ cup white-wine vinegar and ½ cup dry white wine. Bring to a boil, reduce the heat, and let the fish poach for 18 to 20 minutes. Let the mackerels cool in the marinade and refrigerate for a few hours.

CODFISH SOUFFLÉS

To serve 4 persons

The small soufflés are served on prebaked 6-inch round puff-paste croutons.

Use 4 round puff-paste croutons, 6 inches around and ¼ inch thick, or 4 plain toasts of the same size; 2¼ pounds salt cod, 2 egg yolks, 4 egg whites, ⅓ cup thick Béchamel sauce (p. 256), ⅓ cup olive oil, ½ to ⅓ cup peanut oil, ¾ cup grated Parmesan cheese, a bit of heavy cream (¼ cup at least, more if necessary).

Soak the salt cod in several successive baths of cold water for 24 hours. Put the cod in a large saucepan, cover it with cold water, and slowly bring to a simmer. As soon as the water simmers, turn the heat down and let the cod poach for 10 minutes, taking care never to let it boil.

Remove the cooked cod to a warm plate; skin it with the help of 2 forks; flake the meat into small bits. Put the flaked cod in a pan rubbed with garlic; mash it well; add salt if needed, pepper, a pinch of nutmeg and, if you desire, a little bit of chopped truffle. Add the heavy cream and mix well until you obtain a soft well-homogenized purée of not too thin consistency. It is most important that while you prepare the mixture, the saucepan be kept warm. When the mixture is ready, keep it over warm water to keep it from cooling.

In another saucepan, whisk 2 egg yolks into the Béchamel sauce to obtain a smooth cream sauce; beat the 4 whites in a copper bowl, starting slowly and accelerating as the foam thickens. Fold the egg whites into the Béchamel base to obtain a soufflé mixture.

In a small heavy saucepan, mix the remaining 2 egg yolks with 2 tablespoons water and a bit of salt and pepper. Whisk over low heat until the mixture foams and thickens as the egg yolks poach. Gradually dribble in the olive and peanut oils, which should be barely more than lukewarm, still whisking, as if you were making a mayonnaise. You will obtain a sauce Mireille, which is nothing more than a hollandaise made with oil.

On each puff-paste crouton, heap about ¼ cup of the cod purée. Then, smooth about one quarter of the soufflé mixture on top of the cod and sprinkle each portion with 3 tablespoons of Parmesan. Bake in a very hot oven for 6 to 10 minutes. Serve immediately on warm plates accompanied by the sauce Mireille.

BROILED CHICKEN AMERICAN STYLE

To serve 2 persons

Clean and singe a 3-pound chicken. Remove the backbone and cut the bird into halves. Flatten each half with a meat bat. Using a small paring knife, remove the small rib-cage bones and cut through the leg joints. Season with salt and pepper and brush liberally with oil; use at least ⅓ cup oil.

Place the chicken halves on a rack. Sear the "meat side" for 5 minutes under the direct flame of the broiler, then reduce heat to 350° F. and let cook for another 7 to 8 minutes. Brush with 1 tablespoon Dijon mustard, sprinkle generously with 3 or 4 tablespoons of fresh bread crumbs, and baste with melted butter. Let color under the direct flame of the broiler for 3 or 4 minutes.

Turn the chicken halves over and repeat exactly the same procedure on the skin side of each chicken half.

Serve the chicken on a large platter. Put 2 rashers of bacon on each chicken half. Surround the chicken halves with broiled tomatoes, mushroom caps and small bunches of watercress. Decorate the edge of the platter with scalloped slices of lemon.

TIMBALE ELYSÉE

Place a 1-inch-thick slice of *génoise* at the bottom of as many dessert dishes as you have guests. Spoon enough liqueur of your choice onto each portion of cake to lightly permeate it. Set a scoop of vanilla ice cream on each portion of cake; flatten the top of the ice cream and cover it with fresh strawberries. Dot the strawberries with rosettes of cream.

At Lasserre's, each timbale is made in a tart shell and is closed with a cage of spun sugar, the making of which requires a bit of patience.

Butter very lightly a soup ladle. Cook ½ cup sugar with ⅓ teaspoon of light corn syrup and 2 tablespoons water to the hard-crack stage. When the syrup turns a light amber color, put the pot on a thermostat burner set at 300°F. to keep the syrup from hardening.

Dip the tip of a spoon into the syrup and let the syrup drop into a fine stream, forming parallel lines which you should try to space as regularly as possible. Trace another series of fine lines in the opposite direction so as to form a net and finally trace a slightly thicker line passing all around the edge of the ladle. Let the cage harden and delicately remove the cage from the ladle. Decorate the side of each cage with a natural flower.

(Note: To remove the cage from the ladle, twist the cage gently to the right and the ladle to the left. Ed.)

Paris–Dumaine:
260 Kilometers

I am more than a little proud to be the author of that phrase.

Admit that it is far more attractive than the banal "Paris–Saulieu: 260 kilometers." Not that there is anything wrong with Saulieu, the capital of the region of Morvan. Its churches, Saint-Andoche and Saint-Saturnin, are interesting to visit, and its Bourguignon museum has its charm. But for a gourmet, Saulieu for a long time meant the famous chef, the late, beloved Alexandre Dumaine—nicknamed "Alexander the Great"—at the Hôtel de la Côte d'Or.

This mild, plump little man, who was almost stutteringly modest, knew how to speak incomparably about the incomparable dishes he prepared. His prelate's hands seemed to envelop the food's aroma, leading it straight to your nose, and when he explained one of his recipes, your mouth watered, or, rather, "wined" with Burgundy.

I remember an expedition we made to Dumaine—René Lasserre, Raymond Oliver, and I. We had driven the hundred and sixty miles without having a drop to drink, knowing that upon our arrival, at a sign from Jeanne Dumaine—a charming and serene hostess—champagne would flow straightaway. Then we would dine.

The menu included, among others, the following words: "Morvan trout." We were served sweetbreads with leaf spinach.

"My friends," said Dumaine, "when I am unable to get brook trout, these sweetbreads are what I baptize trout. For I refuse to serve those absorbent-cotton trout that are bred in the hatcheries!"

An admirably clear conscience! A final judgment!

And René Lasserre, who sat next to me at the table, leaned toward me and confessed that he had never in his life tasted such perfect leaf spinach—not only with respect to its cooking (cooking spinach is a very delicate process, for it must remain intact, almost *al dente*), but also to its subtle flavor. At the end of the meal I repeated Lasserre's comment to Dumaine. He smiled. His nice round face lit up with inner satisfaction and a blush of modesty.

"The fact is, my good friends," he said, "I remember the lessons I got

84

from my great teacher Burtin, who adored and respected vegetables. I make my spinach as you all do. Except, just before serving it, I take a wooden fork, stick it into a clove of garlic, and turn it about in the spinach three times—no more. That's all!"

But that "all" makes all the difference. It is the touch of genius. No, his spinach did not smell of garlic, absolutely not. But it had been, as it were, exalted by it.

Another time Dumaine had made one of those pâtés of bygone days— a culinary monument that Brillat-Savarin called "the pillow of the Beautiful Aurore," because the crust was as puffy as a pillow, and because his mother, Aurore Brillat-Savarin, made it to perfection. The pâté contains not only foie gras but five or six different types of game, including the sublime woodcock. As well as Chambertin, Napoleon's favorite wine. But it was not for a general, not even had he been an emperor, that Alexandre had prepared this historic dish. It was for a field marshal, the only one left to us, the only one spared by de Gaulle—the Maréchal Juin.

I arrived the next day, about nine o'clock in the morning. There was still some pillow left—cold. So I had a marvelous, strange, and unexpected snack—the leftovers of the victor at Carigliano—washed down with a Juliénas 1958, Clos des Mouilles, which had come straight from Abbé Gonard's wine cellar. A worthy abbot! If all his wines are of the same quality, there is no doubt whatever that, when taking communion, he does not have to wince before Almighty God!

But I'd like to describe another meal I had at Dumaine's. It was a lunch in May, 1959, at which there were seven of us (the golden number), including Dumaine himself. The menu was simple. I mean that, given Dumaine, and given Dumaine's skill, and given the meals one could eat at Dumaine's, the three dishes on the menu might appear ordinary. But a great cook's skill consists precisely in linking simplicity and grandeur. One of dear Alexandre's dishes that I liked the most was his steamed *poularde*. He had meditated on it for months and months, and he made a masterpiece of it. And yet "nothing is simpler than a boiled fowl," remarked someone who was envious, smirking.

But listen, let me explain Dumaine's steamed *poularde*. To begin with, the fowl comes from Bresse—a great well-bred lady with unctuously firm and fat flesh, who is marbled with large strips of truffles. She is first set on a copper tripod, then placed in the copper pot, with, beneath her—and almost reaching her—a concentrated bouillon made from another fowl. Then the cover is put on and sealed hermetically—that is, soldered with pastry. The bird is then steamed until the cover is removed. The cooking time must be calculated by three simple rules (but requiring patient preliminary study): according to how much the fowl weighs, how hot the burner is, and how hard the water boils. Too little would be fatal, but too

Hôtel de la Côte d'Or à Saulieu

Déjeuner

Mousseline de saumon aux queues
d'écrevisses Antonin Carême

Jambon du Morvan rôti aux primeurs

Aiguillettes de caneton Montmorency

Salpicon royal Paillard

Fromage sélectionnés

Fraises Romanoff

much would be too much. Ah! Picture Dumaine's admirable serenity while the dish was being prepared—and while we dreamed about it!

Now, to get back to our dinner for seven. But before I do, I must add that Dumaine, when he retired, was replaced at Saulieu's Côte d'Or by the chef Minot, whose cooking is also worthy of a detour.

Here is the menu of that memorable lunch:

Salmon mousseline with crawfish tails
Antonin Carême

Baked Morvan ham with spring vegetables

Sliced duckling Montmorency

Salpicon royal Paillard

Cheeses

Strawberries Romanoff

I must admit that I am not terribly fond of those *mousselines* (which are merely glorified *quenelles*), since, in all things, I prefer what is natural. But a *mousseline* à la Dumaine is something else again. I remember as if it were yesterday how enthusiastic I was about the ham, and I might have said, like Jean-Jacques Rousseau in his *Confessions:* "Glancing out the corner of my eye at that roast which looked so good and smelled so good, I could not help but bow to it. . . ."

The ham was merely a step leading to ecstasy, and with the *salpicon* Paillard I could feel it coming over me. Fortunately, as Cur used to say, champagne quells all passions. Thank you, Dom Pérignon, I thank you!

Recipes of Alexandre Dumaine
Hôtel de la Côte d'Or in Saulieu

(Note: M. Dumaine's style was so very concise that the text has been amplified. The editor's additions are in italics and parentheses. No measurements were indicated by the author. Those indicated here have been taken from M. Dumaine's book Ma Cuisine, *published in Paris in 1972 by Les Éditions de la Pensée Moderne in French only. Ed.)*

SALMON MOUSSELINE WITH CRAWFISH TAILS ANTONIN CARÊME

(Note: Please use only Louisiana crawfish. Ed.)

Bone a piece of fresh salmon to obtain 1 pound of salmon meat without skin or bones. Season the salmon meat with 1½ teaspoons salt and pepper it lightly.

Pound in a mortar *(until the meat acquires a slightly rubbery consistency; the natural fat should appear at its surface as a shiny layer which keeps it from sticking to either mortar or pestle)*. Strain the meat through a fine sieve and gradually whisk in 2 lightly beaten egg whites.

(Chill the salmon purée for 1 hour or so. Place it in a bowl embedded in a large bowl containing crushed ice and) gradually add about 1¾ cups of heavy cream. Turn the mousseline into a buttered mold and poach it in a hot-water bath *(in a 325°F. oven)* for about 35 minutes. Prepare a *mirepoix (p. 267);* cook it gently, covered, with a pinch of salt and pepper. Sauté 32 crawfish in butter, let them turn bright red, season them with salt and pepper. Add the *mirepoix,* the Cognac *(1 ounce)* and dry white wine *(⅓ cup)*. Do not flambé, but cover the *sauteuse* and let the liquids reduce completely *(this will be achieved only if you leave the lids slightly ajar)*. When the pan juices have completely evaporated, add some tomato essence *(3 to 4 tablespoons; see p. 258)* and a *bouquet garni*. Add some fish fumet *(1 cup; see p. 250)* and heavy cream *(1 cup)*. Bring briskly to a boil, reduce the heat to a minimum, and let poach for 8 to 10 minutes.

Shell the tails and claws of the crawfish. Dry the crawfish shells in a slow oven and crush them well, weigh them and add to them the same weight of butter; let the butter melt and keep it warm in a hot-water bath to allow it to absorb the crawfish taste. Strain the butter.

(Reduce the sauce until it thickens lightly.) To finish it add the crawfish butter *(the sauce may not reboil after that last addition)*. Strain the sauce over the crawfish tails and mix well.

Unmold the salmon mousseline onto a plate and spoon the crawfish sauce over it.

BAKED MORVAN HAM WITH SPRING VEGETABLES

Prepare the following marinade 2 days before starting the marination of the ham:

(Sauté 2 sliced onions, 1 sliced carrot and 2 sliced shallots in 1 generous tablespoon of olive oil. Add ¾ cup each of dry Madeira and Cognac,

4½ cups dry white wine and 2½ cups red wine. Simmer together for 30 minutes and let cool. Keep in a cool place for 2 days.)

Two days before cooking the ham, *piquer (its meat side with fatback strips, ¾ x ¼ inch, using a larding needle)* and immerse the ham in the marinade. Turn the ham several times while it is marinating.

Brown the ham lightly in butter on all sides; add some *mirepoix (1½ cups; see p. 267);* let steam covered for a little while. Discard the browning fat. Add the strained marinade, let it reduce; add *(about 1 cup)* white stock and let it reduce completely. Add *(another cup)* white stock, let it reduce again completely. Finally add enough white stock to half-cover the ham and bake covered *(in a 325°F. oven)* for 2½ to 3 hours.

When the ham is done, remove the rind *(and all but ¼ inch of its fat covering)* and sprinkle it with confectioners' sugar. Glaze the ham in a hot oven.

Defatten the gravy completely, reduce it well *(by one half at least)* and blend it with *(½ cup)* very strong veal stock *(see p. 247).*

Slowly sauté ¼ cup very finely chopped shallots in butter. Add ½ cup dry white wine, reduce the wine completely, and add the shallots to the prepared ham gravy.

Serve the ham with a vegetable garnish in season.

SLICED DUCKLING MONTMORENCY

(Note: This is a description of the dish rather than a recipe. Ed.)

Roast a duckling, keeping it rare. Remove the skin from the breast meat. Cut the breast meat (off the bone lengthwise) in strips called *aiguillettes.*

1. The cherries

Use about 10 sour cherries per person. Poach the cherries in a mixture of half port and half Bordeaux wine. Reduce the cherry poaching liquid by half. Add 2 tablespoons currant jelly.

2. The chaud-froid *sauce*

Prepare a brown sauce with the duck's carcass and its leg and thigh bones (p. 250). Mix the sauce with the reduction of the cherry cooking juices.

3. The forcemeat

Prepare a forcemeat with the duck's liver and the meat from the legs and thighs; bind the forcemeat with a bit of the *chaud-froid* sauce.

Build the forcemeat into a dome; wrap the *aiguillettes* over the dome of forcemeat so they slightly overlap one another. Coat them first with the *chaud-froid* sauce, then with a layer of aspic (made with duck *fumet*).

Surround the *aiguillettes* with cherries glazed with aspic.

(Note: In classic cuisine, this preparation is more often than not prepared with 2 ducks; the legs and thighs of one are used for the forcemeat and the breast filets of both ducks are cut in aiguillettes. The forcemeat is piled into the breastbone of the second duck and it is topped with the overlapping aiguillettes. The decorated duck is then coated with chaud-froid sauce and aspic. Ed.)

SALPICON ROYAL PAILLARD

Prepare a *salpicon* of ham, mushrooms, fat goose liver, cocks' combs and kidneys; season it and mold it in Dariole molds; bind the *salpicon* with aspic prepared with duck *fumet* (see p. 250).

STRAWBERRIES ROMANOFF

Macerate some beautiful strawberries in a mixture of orange juice and Curaçao. Pile them into a timbale and cover them with Chantilly cream (sweetened whipped cream flavored with vanilla).

A Royal Meal

By repeating that their cooking is the best in the world (which is not true, for good cooking exists everywhere; theirs is merely, though undeniably, the most varied), the French have given natural gourmets from other countries rather unnatural complexes.

The Belgians or the Swiss, for example, scorn their own best dishes, and it would not take much to make them ashamed of a *papet de poireaux* or a *waterzoï*. What they do is replace them with imitations of great French cooking, ersatz copies of our famous dishes, "Palace-Hotel" slops which they ingurgitate, murmuring with confidence, "French cuisine! Not bad, huh?"

Worst of all, they make their French visitors ingurgitate it and then wonder at our lack of enthusiasm.

And *still* worse, they call in French chefs for all great gastronomical occasions. For two weeks the master chef Something-or-Other is taking over the culinary duties of the famous What's-His-Name. When one thinks, first, that there are as few culinary geniuses running kitchens as there are artistic geniuses running the streets; secondly, that only a few of them are born every hundred years; thirdly, that truly good chefs are not all that anxious to leave their own pots and pans in order to "stand on their hind legs" on tour, one gets a good idea of the mediocre types who generally agree to cook for those gala occasions.

And the foreign gourmet (who is the customer at such affairs) perpetuates the error that it is not as serious to mistake Piraeus for a man as it is to mistake lobster Thermidor and beef Wellington for great cuisine!

Yet when the president of the Club des 33 invited me to a Brussels dinner, I did not hesitate for a moment. Because the meal was to be prepared by Jean and Pierre Troisgros, two brothers from Roanne, who not only have a good sense of cooking (in fact, a genius for it) but also the good sense to have organized that dinner during the season when their restaurant was closed, so that they took the time (and what a time!) during their holidays and did not deprive their customers of one second of it.

The Club des 33 is *the* aristocratic gourmet club of Belgium. A bit like the Club des 100 in France, but with a touch of something more . . . Or perhaps it's the French Club des 100 which has a touch of something less and is in the process of devaluating and popularizing itself, a reflection of the tendency of the entire French elite. No matter. The Club des 33 was so named for two reasons: it was founded in 1933 and it has thirty-three members. That gave me the idea for a heading in *Le Monde:* "2 Troisgros at the 33."

There are really three Troisgros, Jean and Pierre, plus their father, Jean-Baptiste, the patriarch. It was he who, half a century ago, left his native Burgundy to settle in Roanne and run a simple little hotel across from the railroad station. But he had lots of enthusiasm. Even today, the culinary art of the Troisgros brothers, who supplement each other, taking turns at the stoves in their illustrious restaurant (worthy of a crowned red cock in the *Guide Kléber*), indirectly reflects Jean-Baptiste Troisgros' *joie de vivre*.

Many people know the anecdote that has been attributed in turn to Talleyrand, to the mentor of the Prince of Wales who became Edward VII, and to a few others. It happened that a great vintage wine, already poured, was about to be drunk too quickly.

"No, sir! You must look at such a wine and watch it glitter like rubies in the glass. You sniff it, you breathe it in, you admire it. And then . . ."

"You drink it," exclaimed the other man, thinking he had understood.

"No, sir! Not yet. You talk about it!"

There are many ways of talking about wine. Affected people, who are not necessarily connoisseurs, smugly comment that it "has real guts" or that it slides down "like a hat over your ears." Papa Troisgros is not one of these. But if you are lucky enough to chat with him about one of his wines (which he always serves cool, ah! the saintly man), you will have a splendid time.

In his Burgundian voice, rolling his *r*'s like carriages rolling over stony vineyard paths, Jean-Baptiste discusses wine like a seer, a peasant poet, and a gentleman. He has a sense for images that speaks to the heart as well as the palate, plus a touch of pertinent irony that whets your appetite. He knows what he is talking about. His theory about uncooked salt and pepper, for instance, can be verified on each and every occasion. He claims that salt and pepper cooked with food lose their strength and change the nature of the product. Therefore one should put in only a bare minimum. But once the food is cooked, a touch of salt and pepper actually brings out its flavor. As we all know, a grind of the pepper mill over oysters gives them a marvelous taste. The same may be said for melon. Still, most people would not think of doing it to strawberries, and never to meat. But once the wonderful ribs of beef Charollais at the Troisgros' restaurant are served on the plate, they are even better heightened by a bit of salt which divinizes their aroma.

In fact, Papa Troisgros' enthusiasm in his explication of culinary theories (all based on good sense and experience) and in his comments on wines is not only infectious but exalting. He sets an example!

But only Jean and Pierre Troisgros had come to cook the dinner for "33" in Brussels, bringing with them not only all the foodstuff—the hibernating snails, the salmon newly caught at the mouth of the Loire, the turkey hens, and the truffles—but also the wines (chosen by Jean-Baptiste) and . . . their own dinner plates, which were so large that the most sumptuous portions seemed comfortable on them.

The meal took place at Comme Chez Soi—one of the best restaurants in Brussels, run by the Wynants, father and son—on a day when it would normally be closed. I have often feasted there, and often on their kidneys *liégeoises,* which are made according to an admirable recipe (in spite of the fact that the elder Wynant had insisted that I taste his kidneys with mustard *bourguignonne:* that old French complex again!).

No women are allowed at the table of the Club des 33, which delights me, as does Joseph Despaze's poem "Dinners without Women," which I came across in Grimod de La Reynière's *Almanach des gourmands:*

> . . . If you'd like us not to be witty,
> And to kill our spirits and transports,
> Just put ten women who are pretty
> At our table, even at mid-course.

> . . . Friends, let's stay alone, now as then.
> Can our senses lead us astray?
> For dinners we'll keep just the men,
> And for suppers, the women so gay.

On the other hand, that particular evening the smile of Eve illuminated the "33" dinner, because King Leopold and Her Royal Highness Princess Lillian of Belgium, the Princesse de Réthy, were invited.

I had the honor of sitting near the fairy-tale princess, a woman of grace, intelligence, and a hearty appetite—a combination of qualities so rarely applicable to women in general and to princesses in particular. It prompted me, during cigar time (Davidoffs, of course), to tell Jean Troisgros that Her Highness's enthusiasm for his cooking was not per-

Dîner des Messieurs Jean et Pierre Troisgros
pour Le Club des 33
au Restaurant Comme Chez Soi
à Bruxelles

—

Escargots poëlés
Cassolette de queues d'écrevisses
Foie de canard aux navets
Escalope de saumon à l'oseille
Granité champenois
Dindonne pochée comme dans le Bourbonnais
avec son gâteau de foie
Fromage frais
Tartes aux pommes chaudes
Pralines

functory or a way of thanking him; it was, on the contrary, "structured" according to the dishes that were served.

Here is the list:

Sautéed snails

Crawfish-tail cassolette

Foie gras of duck with glazed turnips

Salmon cutlets with sorrel sauce Troisgros

Champagne granité

Poached turkey hen Bourbonnaise
garnished with a forcemeat of its liver

Fresh truffle salad with walnut oil

Fresh cheeses

Warm apple tart

Pralines

The lowly, plebeian snails were so high-flying that they surprised those who don't know as well as I that, in Roanne, they may make a charming breakfast, washed down with some Beaujolais *nouveau*. You need a strong stomach and true affection for them, of course, but they are a splendid rebuff to the everlasting café au lait!

The crawfish tails, wrapped in the rich shroud of their sauce, opened the dance (not at all *macabre*) of gustatory contrasts. As for the foie gras . . .

"It's perfection!" exclaimed Her Highness.

And the Swiss ambassador to Brussels approved: "On every point we submit to your judgment, Madame!"

Actually, I should like, in all humility, to take issue with one of them. The turnips (an admirable, unappreciated, and neglected vegetable), merely braised, would have been enough as an escort for the duck liver, with its gamy overtones. The Périgueux sauce that covered them was no more than a stylistic performance, perhaps (and I say perhaps) distracting from the Racinian purity that should characterize a dish of that type.

Sometimes the same thing happens in literature. One starts out trying to be a Racine and ends up a Corneille, and it's not all that serious. However, if this meal had not been prepared by the Troisgros, one would have started out with George Sand and ended up with nothingness—that is to say, Françoise Sagan!

Apropos of the salmon cutlets, a short novel could be written called *The Birth of a Dish*. Alex Humbert was the first to think of cutting salmon into cutlets instead of steaks (slices). The cutlets were just as thick but sliced with the grain, which is natural, rather than against it. The Troisgros followed his example. Then, since their gardener—who had planted sorrel so they might flavor their soups with it—had planted so many seeds and had such an overwhelming crop, they got the idea of using the extra sorrel in the vermouth sauce. Finally, a customer (an American, which proves yet again that the pleasures of the table are not limited to one country), Joe Hyde, suggested they flatten the salmon cutlets as one does veal cutlets—that is, pound them between two pieces of oiled, sulphurized paper. A great dish was born, which provoked me to confess a sin: their fresh salmon, cut in that way, was no longer the vulgar blotting paper smelling of cod-liver oil that I had always accused it of being!

The turkey hen surprised and revived the spirits of all those for whom cuisine is merely cuisine, as codified by the chefs Saint Carême, Saint Escoffier, and Saint Philéas Gilbert. To tell the truth, the malicious Troisgros somewhat mystified their flock on this occasion by serving them a common, peasant, folkloric dish from Bourbonnais: poached fowl (with its accompanying vegetables) and salad. Here it was a truffle salad—noblesse oblige. But on the farms it is just as good with greens, dressed also with walnut oil. Moreover, the cake made with the fowl's liver (in fact, a modified forcemeat more than a cake) was covered with puréed tomatoes that heightened the flavor of the vegetables. In the past, at wedding dinners, that was the way to serve chicken boiled in bouillon—the chicken with a walnut-oil and vinegar dressing, the oxtail with french-fried potatoes and tomato sauce. Everything has already been invented! But one characteristic of very great men is that they know how to rediscover and how to take a chance—which is what my Troisgros friends did that evening.

It was truly a royal meal!

I dared to say that to the Princesse de Réthy, as I lifted my glass of Chambolle-Musigny les Amoureuses 1966, from the Comte de Voguë's vineyards.

"One *talks* about a wine like this, gentlemen!"

Which is what we did, until late into the night, finishing off the last Davidoffs wedded to a great Cognac, after Their Highnesses had left.

But perhaps they did, too, after they were gone. . . .

Recipes of Messieurs Troisgros

SAUTÉED SNAILS

(Note: This recipe is described in the chefs' own words. Ed.)

Remove the membranes of "sleeping" winter snails. Use 18 snails per person. Wash the snails in several waters. Sprinkle them with coarse salt and let them stand for a couple of hours.

Blanch the snails in boiling water, drain them, and extract each snail from its shell. Discard the curly end. Put the snails in a saucepan, add 2 glasses of dry white wine and just enough water to cover them, 2 sliced carrots, 2 onions, 2 garlic cloves, a *bouquet garni*, 2 cloves and some cracked black pepper. Salt with 1½ teaspoons of fine salt per quart of liquid.

Cook, skimming at regular intervals, for 1½ to 2 hours. At 5 minutes before serving, drain the snails. Sauté them in a copper *sauteuse*. Deglaze the *sauteuse* with a bit of the cooling broth and bind the snails with a classic snail butter containing a lot of parsley. Serve in very hot soup plates.

(Note: When snails hibernate, they build a membrane of chalk to seal their shells. A lesser version of this recipe can be executed in America with canned small snails of the type called les petits-gris *in France, not the large Burgundy-type snails; use the canning juices of the snails to deglaze the pan and finish the dish with the snail butter on page 262. Use 3 tablespoons of snail butter for each dozen snails prepared and add an additional tablespoon of chopped parsley.*

If one prefers to use live snails, they can be purchased very easily in fish stores located in Italian neighborhoods; although the snails are of the same type as the petits-gris, *their flavor will be different from their French cousins since the flavor of snails depends on the vegetables they feed on. Ed.)*

CRAWFISH-TAIL CASSOLETTE

(Note: Please use only Louisiana crawfish. Ed.)

To serve 6 persons

Shell 4½ pounds crawfish cooked in unsalted water. Set the tails aside.

Prepare an excellent court-bouillon with 4½ cups water, 2 sliced carrots, 2 onions sliced thick, 2 celery sprigs chopped, 2 garlic cloves,

1 large *bouquet garni,* rosemary, sage, cloves and peppercorns. Cook it for 10 minutes.

Drain completely the water from the court-bouillon and replace it by 1 cup of white Sancerre wine. Bring to a violent boil, do not let the wine reduce, but without breaking the vegetables, add immediately ¼ pound of butter. Add the crawfish tails and remove from the heat. Season with a pinch of tarragon and a squeeze of lemon juice.

(Note: By adding the butter at the center of the boil, tablespoon by tablespoon, it will form an emulsion with the wine and vegetable mixture and will remain emulsified. To prevent the vegetables breaking, do not use a whisk, but shake the pan back and forth over the heat as you add the butter so that the contents of the pan move across the whole surface of its bottom. Ed.)

FOIE GRAS OF DUCK WITH GLAZED TURNIPS

A description:

Poach a fat duck liver weighing 1 to 1¼ pounds in salted simmering water for 5 minutes. This poaching should be done 24 hours ahead of time. The next day, slice the liver and remove all its nerves and vessels.

Prepare a sauce with ½ cup old port, ½ cup truffle juice and 2 cups brown veal stock (p. 247). Reduce to a heavy glaze and fluff in 4 tablespoons unsalted butter.

Cut some white turnips and trim into small olive-shaped pieces. Use 8 pieces of turnip per person. Cover the turnips with brown veal stock and cook them until they are glazed. Blend the turnips with the sauce.

Panfry the slices of liver quickly so they turn a beautiful golden color. Coat them with the sauce and turnips.

(Note: This beautiful recipe will have to remain a description unless one fattens one's own ducks. The canned foie gras de canard au naturel is damaged beyond repair by the canning process and should not be used here. The white turnips should be blanched before being cooked in that beautiful sauce. Ed.)

SALMON CUTLETS WITH SORREL SAUCE TROISGROS

To serve 6 persons

Bone and skin a salmon to obtain 2 fillets each weighing a generous pound. Cut each of the fillets with the grain—that is to say, parallel to the skin—into 3 scallops; flatten the cutlet between 2 layers of lightly oiled parchment paper.

Prepare a fish *fumet* (p. 250) from the heads and bones of such excellent fish as soles, turbots, whitings and conger eel, 1 carrot, 1 onion and water to cover. Cook it for about 10 minutes. Strain it.

Put ½ cup of that *fumet*, ¼ cup dry white wine and 1 tablespoon dry white vermouth in a saucepan. Add 1 finely chopped shallot. Let reduce until almost dry. Add then 2 tablespoons heavy cream per person and whisk over medium heat until the cream thickens.

Prepare 1 generous ounce of fresh sorrel leaves per person; clean and wash the sorrel very well. Blot it dry in a towel and add it to the prepared cream. Mix well with a wooden spoon; as soon as the sorrel has wilted into the cream sauce, remove from the heat.

Off the heat, whisk in ¼ cup unsalted butter. Add salt, pepper and lemon juice. Pour some of the sorrel sauce into each plate. Top each portion of sauce with 1 salmon cutlet panfried in hot oil and seasoned on its prettiest-looking side only.

(Note: Upon query from the editor, MM. Troisgros gave the precision that each cutlet usually looks better on the side which was originally closest to the bone; they called this side of the scallop its "interior face" [face intérieure]. Ed.)

CHAMPAGNE GRANITÉ

To serve 6 persons

Squeeze the juices of 2 lemons and 2 oranges. Add those juices to a cold sugar syrup made of 2 cups of sugar dissolved in 3¼ cups of water.

Pour the mixture into the container of an ice-cream freezer. Embed the container in crushed ice but do not turn the machine on. As the ice crystals form around the sides of the container, remove them with a spoon. The granité should have a granular texture and therefore should not be churned.

Pour about 2 ounces of champagne *blanc de blancs* into balloon-shaped glasses and add 2 heaping tablespoons of granité to each glass.

POACHED TURKEY HEN BOURBONNAISE

To serve at least 8 persons

Choose a small turkey hen weighing about 6 pounds. Clean and truss it; poach it in white stock reinforced with the turkey giblets and a few chicken carcasses; add the classic vegetable and aromatic garnis The poaching time is about 1½ hours.

Pour some of the poaching stock into another pot and use it to cook 12 carrots, 12 white turnips and 8 celeriacs all cut and trimmed into cork-shaped chunks, plus the white part of 8 leeks.

In yet another pot, cook in boiling salted water ½ pound of broccoli flowerets, which should be kept green and very firm. Just before serving, reheat the broccoli in some of the stock.

Prepare a truffle salad with 5 ounces uncooked truffles shaved into fine slivers and seasoned with salt, pepper, wine vinegar and walnut oil.

Slice both turkey breasts into fine slices; garnish the dish with the vegetables and coat the slices of meat with the truffle salad.

WARM APPLE TART

To serve 8 persons

Set a 9-inch flan ring on an unbendable pastry sheet; line it with classic puff paste (p. 268). Prick the bottom and sides of the uncooked shell heavily; line the shell with a parchment paper and fill the paper with dried beans. When the shell is three quarters baked, remove the beans and paper and return the shell to the oven for another 6 minutes.

Peel 8 excellent apples and cut them into halves. Core them and slice each apple half into ½-inch-thick slices. Do not separate the apple slices but keep them lightly packed together.

Put the cut apple halves in a buttered baking dish. Dot them with more butter and sugar them well. Bake them until they are golden. Garnish the tart shell with the baked apples.

Melt 3 tablespoons sugar with a bit of water in a copper *sauteuse*. When the sugar turns to light caramel, add the cooking juices of the apples remaining in the baking dish and another ⅓ cup of sugar.

Let the sugar melt. Pour the mixture over the tart, and serve it.

(Note: Use one quarter of the puff paste recipe given on p. 268. Preferably, use Cortland apples and bake in a 350°F. oven. Ed.)

The Dinner of the Century

In the eighteenth century it would have been one of the Regent's "little suppers," and the *Chronique de l'œil de bœuf*, which reported all the court news, would have made a thing of it. Or else Louis XV, the "Well-Beloved," would have asked Madame du Barry to receive both her king and his attendants. Mauconseil, the chef, would have prepared *animelles*, ram's testicles to which the aging king attributed hidden and wondrous qualities.

Yes, a "dinner of the century" in the eighteenth century—with every courtier rushing to the kitchen to get in the good graces of the monarch, leaving to posterity a recipe named after him—would have been truly dazzling. A dinner with a favorite! Imagine one, for example, at the home of the Duc de Richelieu—that adventurous and sybaritic marshal, lascivious gourmet, and gallant ladies' man—Richelieu, a man who, according to the President of the Chamber of Deputies, Hénault, once ordered a meal composed uniquely of beef and vegetables, from a *garbure gratiné* (a cabbage soup which is a specialty of the region of the Pyrenees), to beef consommé, to jellied beef with wine from Alicante, to plums from Verdun—no less than twenty-two courses in all.

Those were the days when a Villeroi, the only French field marshal never to have won a battle, added a sauce thickened with the yolks of hard-boiled eggs to the science of eating; when the Cardinal de Bernis invented *crêpes dentelles* for Madame de Pompadour; when the Marshal of Luxembourg discovered *chaud-froid de volaille,* or cold jellied fowl—thanks to the fact that he was late for dinner. In sum, it was a great century for food.

In the nineteenth century it would have been a dinner at the home of Cambacérès, apparently named Arch-chancellor of the Empire merely to shame his master, Napoleon, for eating so badly. Or at the home of Charles-Maurice de Talleyrand-Périgord, the "Lame Devil" who discovered the great chef Carême. At the end of the meal there would have been a Brie comparable to the one that Talleyrand had had crowned King of the Cheeses at the Congress of Vienna—a Brie from Meaux, straight from the farm, the kind one hardly ever finds nowadays. And that Dinner of the Century would have been both a "restauration" and a "restoration."

Le Café de Paris
Biarritz

Dîner du Siécle, 1971

———————

Consommé moscovite
Louvine braisée au Graves rouge
Timbale de queues d'écrevisses
Canard sauvage au Haut-Brion blanc
Ragoût de truffes
Purée de mais au foie gras
Fromage
Corbeilles des Dix

In 1900, guests at the Dinner of the Century would have included dauntless gourmets such as the Marquis de Rougé (who knew how to take communion alone at Larue's by way of pressed duck and a great Burgundy) and the courtesans of Maxim's, for that was a happy period. Perhaps a few years before it would have been given in the "Grand Seize," the sumptuous *salon* of the Café Anglais, whose wood paneling is still with us, having been transferred to the Tour d'Argent at the same time that Cora Pearl's vermeil dinner service was. An Offenbach tune would have started off the saraband of courses, and we would have had shelled crawfish until dawn, as in the Café des Ambassadeurs.

Those were my dreams in a plane that was flying me to Biarritz, where I had been invited to the Dinner of the Century—the last half of the twentieth century. I was dazzled in advance. I had quite forgotten that every century has the dinner it deserves. . . .

Great French Cuisine . . . No, no, it's not what you think . . . It has nothing to do with art, with epicureanism, with gastronomic subtlety—in short, with pleasure in food—but rather, with some association or other, with a commercial deal, with, as it were, business. The ten chefs who were there had enough ambition for a hundred, and although I have friends among them, that does not keep me from saying what I think. As a business, Great French Cuisine is no more than a great French racket. To begin with, why were those particular chefs asked, and they alone? Why this one and not that one? Why does the man who serves awful rubbery loaves of daily bread in his restaurant claim to represent quality? Why does another, who serves farm-bread quail, claim to honor true gourmets?

No matter. Here is the menu . . . of the century!

Consommé Moscovite
Louvine braised in red Graves
Crawfish-tail timbale
Wild duck in a white Haut-Brion
Ragout of truffles
Purée of corn with foie gras
Cheese
Fruit basket "des Dix"

The consommé Moscovite was no more than a cold consommé mixed with caviar. And one might question whether there was any rhyme or reason for it. It reminded me of the story of the millionaire whose car broke down and who was put up by some peasants. Since they would not accept money for their hospitality, the millionaire, once he was back in Paris, had a magnum of champagne and a jar of caviar sent to them. He received a thank-you note: Your bubbly wasn't bad, but your jam tasted too much like fish!

In the old days—I mean for a dinner of the last century—a "cubed" bouillon was prepared. The strained bouillon from one piece of boiled beef served to boil a second piece of beef. The result was a "squared" consommé, in which yet another piece of meat was boiled, producing a "cubed" consommé. And the meat? It was kept for family stews. The Laportes' consommé at Biarritz's Café de Paris was excellent, full-bodied, perhaps squared . . . In other words, it was sumptuous enough to be spoiled by the caviar!

Louvine is the Côte Basque's name for bass (called *loup* when it comes from the Mediterranean). The dish was perfection. Why? Because the fish not only was at home in Biarritz and could stand a red-wine sauce, but its flavor was actually heightened by it. Another disappointment awaited us, however: the duck. That wild bird was served along with stewed truffles. Didn't those gentlemen, those great chefs, know that in that particular season one could get only canned truffles? Yes, probably they did; but they believed in all their naïveté that truffles are indispensable to great cuisine, even when they are not first-rate. Whereas great cuisine must be just that—first-rate. So the stew was plain ordinary. But in this case it did not make the purée of corn with foie gras any worse than it was. "Tournedos Rossini" is an insult to foie gras, which is heated and thrown onto some piece of tasteless flesh. Here the insult was even more outrageous because it was intentional. The "Rossini" dish is generally imitated out of sheer intellectual laziness, because it is a sacred monster, the Mary Marquet of food.

But in 1971, to create a purée of corn mixed with foie gras was more than a crime or a sin. It was depravity!

Coming back on the plane, I kept repeating the phrase to myself: the Dinner of the Century? So be it. Every century has the dinner it deserves . . . It took ten chefs to produce that one! And a hundred people to sample it. Ah, those guests of the Regent, of Richelieu, of Talleyrand, of the "Grand Seize" . . . As I considered the caricature called *le Tout Paris*—with everybody who "is" anybody now in Paris—with all its bogus glory, its wailing stars, its hustling painters, its simpering dancers, and its dashing swells—as I considered them all, I told myself that that dinner was *their* dinner!

Recipes of Pierre Laporte
Café de Paris, Biarritz

CONSOMMÉ MOSCOVITE

To serve 4 persons

You need meaty beef bones, two 4-pound roasting chickens, 3½ pounds lean beef meat, onions, carrots, celery stalks, leeks, egg whites, fresh tomatoes, pepper, coarse salt, 6½ ounces caviar.

Preparation:

Prepare a white stock with about 6 quarts of water, the unbrowned beef bones and the vegetables. Let it cook for 8 hours. Strain the stock. Bring the stock back to a boil. Add new soup vegetables and the 2 roasters. Poach the roasters in the stock. When they are done, strain the stock again.

Mix the diced lean beef; the green tops of the leeks; some celery and carrots, both finely minced; fresh tomatoes, peeled, seeded and crushed; coarsely cracked peppercorns; 2 cups lightly beaten egg whites (about 10 egg whites); and the lukewarm stock. Bring to a boil, stirring constantly. Let simmer over very low heat for 40 minutes. Turn the heat off and let stand for 5 to 10 minutes; strain through a muslin. Let the consommé cool completely before refrigerating it.

Presentation:

When the consommé is firm, ladle it into small soup tureens or bowls. Spoon about 1¼ ounces of caviar on top of each cup of consommé. Since no additional gelatin was used, the caviar will slowly sink into the jellied consommé.

SEA BASS (LOUVINE) BRAISED IN RED WINE

To serve 4 persons

You need one sea bass, 3½ to 4 pounds, ½ pound unsalted butter, ¼ pound mushrooms, ¼ pound silverskin onions, fish *fumet*, 2 cups red Burgundy wine, shallots, 1 cup heavy cream, fish glaze, hollandaise sauce, white bread.

Preparation:

Fillet the fish. Season the fillets with salt and pepper. Crisp both sides of ecah fillet in butter. Remove the fillets to a plate. In the same butter, sauté the sliced mushrooms and the silverskin onions. Return the fish fillets to the pan; place them on top of the vegetable garnish, then add red wine and fish *fumet*. Cover with a buttered paper and let the fish cook through for another 6 to 8 minutes.

Drain the cooking juices into a *sauteuse*. Add a bit of fish *fumet* (p. 253) and let reduce slowly; fluff in some butter, cream and hollandaise. Season and strain through a muslin.

Presentation:

Drain the fillets of the bass on a tea towel. Remove the skin and arrange fillets on a serving platter surrounded by the vegetable garnish. Coat with the sauce; glaze with a salamander and serve with butter-fried white bread croutons.

(Note: The author gave no exact proportions for the balance of the ingredients in the making of the sauce; here are a few suggestions. Rather than using 2 cups of red wine to poach the fillets of 1 bass, it may be a better idea for the home cook to start by making a red-wine fish fumet *with good red Burgundy wine (p. 252). Reserve 1 cup* fumet *to poach the fillets and reduce 2 more cups to ½ cup of glaze.*

The fillet can then be poached with 1 cup of red Burgundy wine mixed with 1 cup of red-wine fish fumet. *The following proportions would be used to build the sauce:*

Reduce the cooking juices of the fish by half; you should obtain a very generous cup of flavorful liquid to which you add the fish glaze. Reduce again over high heat to 1 cup; add ½ cup unsalted butter bit by bit at the center of the boil, then remove this mixture from the heat and blend in a mousseline sauce made with 1 egg yolk, 6 tablespoons unsalted butter and ¼ cup of heavy whipped cream. See Hollandaise Sauce, p. 258. Ed.)

CRAWFISH-TAIL TIMBALE

(Note: Please use only Louisiana crawfish. Ed.)

To serve 4 persons

You need ¾ pound shelled crawfish tails, onions, carrots, celery, tarragon, chervil, dry white wine, butter, lemon, salt and cayenne.

Preparation:

Prepare a classic *nage* or court-bouillon for crawfish (p. 251) with sliced carrots, sliced onions, celery, water and seasonings. Bring to a boil; add the crawfish to that court-bouillon and let cook 8 minutes. Remove the crawfish from the court-bouillon and shell them. Reduce some dry white wine; add the vegetables from the court-bouillon, the crawfish tails and butter. Season highly and serve in a timbale, sprinkled with chervil and chopped tarragon.

(Note: No proportions. May I suggest that you reduce 1 cup of dry white wine mixed with the vegetables of the nage *to ½ cup over high heat; then fluff ¼ pound butter into the violently boiling mixture while shaking the pan back and forth over the heat. Remove from the heat; blend the crawfish into the vegetable sauce and reheat without boiling. Ed.)*

WILD DUCK WITH RAGOUT OF FRESH TRUFFLES

To serve 4 persons

You need 1 wild duck, 1 bottle white Haut-Brion wine, 1 pound truffles, butter, port, 2¼ cups demi-glace sauce *(in this dish use a brown sauce made with duck carcasses as on p. 250, or a real demi-glace made with pure brown veal stock as on p. 255),* shallots, pepper.

Preparation:

Truss the duck. Roast to a pink juiciness. Remove the duck to a platter; keep it warm. Discard all traces of fat in the roasting pan, add a nugget of butter and a bit of chopped shallots, and let cook gently for just a few minutes. Add the Haut-Brion *blanc* and let it reduce. Bind the sauce lightly by blending it with a ladle of demi-glace sauce. Strain through a fine conical strainer.

Ragout of Truffles:

Cut the truffles into quarters; let them steam, covered, in a bit of butter. Add port and demi-glace sauce. Let simmer together for 40 minutes. Correct the seasoning.

Present the duck on a heated platter, surrounded by the truffle ragout. Serve the sauce prepared for the duck in a sauceboat.

(Note: The fact that a chef indicates in a recipe the use of a "bottle" does not always mean that he uses the whole bottle to prepare the dish. Since there are no proportions here you may want to try these: Roast the

duck at 500°F. for 15 to 20 minutes; it should be rare. To make the duck sauce, sauté 2 tablespoons shallots in 2 tablespoons unsalted butter; add 2 cups Haut-Brion blanc and reduce to 1 cup; blend this reduction again with 1 cup of demi-glace sauce and reduce by at least one third. You may, if you want, reduce the sauce by two thirds and blend into it the red juices escaping from the duck cavity (gather those juices into a cup as soon as the duck is done). In either case, correct the seasoning and strain the sauce through a muslin.

For the ragout of truffles, try to buy the truffles called in France une cuisson; they are canned especially for professional kitchens and are the best thing next to fresh truffles.

For the sauce of the ragout, use ½ cup white port, blended with ½ cup demi-glace sauce. Ed.)

PURÉE OF CORN WITH FOIE GRAS

To serve 4 persons

You need 4 ears of corn, ½ cup heavy cream, 3½ ounces fat goose liver, salt, cayenne.

Preparation:
Poach the ears of corn in salted simmering water for 40 minutes. Drain them and scrape off the corn kernels. Strain the kernels through a sieve to retain only their meat and milk; discard the skins. Let the obtained creamed corn cook over high heat to evaporate the excess moisture. Add the heavy cream and give a few good boils. Remove from the heat; strain the goose liver into the corn purée, correct the seasoning, and serve in small gratin dishes.

(Note: Corn is a relatively new vegetable in France; up to the early 1960s, it used to be reserved for the feeding of poulardes and de luxe poultry. The long cooking time given by the author may very well be justified by the quality of the French corn kernels used. Ed.)

FRUIT BASKET "DES DIX"

Make a basket out of pulled sugar. Decorate with cherry blossoms also made of sugar. Inside the basket, place large scoops of fresh-pear sherbet and decorate with wild strawberries.

Celebrating April Fools'

I have never celebrated either Christmas Eve or New Year's Eve since those dates mean nothing at all to me. Besides, I don't like the idea of having a good time on a specific made-to-order day with everyone there. For, as my grandmother used to say, " 'Everyone' also means anyone at all."

Most of my actor friends don't celebrate those occasions either, because on such days they work to amuse others. Indeed, now and then they work even harder than usual.

That is why one day, for the Christmas issue of the review *Cuisine et vins de France,* I asked a few stars the following question: "If you could celebrate Christmas Eve or New Year's Eve, what would you like to eat and where?"

The playwright Marcel Achard, *enfant terrible* of the French Academy, was very clear about it: "Caviar (from Iran by the ladleful), with a very dry Muscadet wine; buntings in puff pastry; truffles (with a bit of young turkey around to justify them); Roquefort cheese (with a Château Latour wine to wash all that down), and chocolate mousse."

And the author of *Do You Want to Play with Mee?* added, really playing with *me:* "And, if possible, the celebration should be held at the Hostellerie in Pérouges, in musketeer costumes."

The director Marc Allegret suggested: "Lots of caviar with vodka; lots of Brie cheese with a Mouton-Rothschild, and exotic fruit."

As for the devilish *chansonnier* Pierre-Jean Vaillard, he softened up just thinking of the following menu:

Cancale oysters

Lobster with morels

Baron of lamb Henri IV

Ballottine of pheasant

Salad Dauphinoise

Cheeses

Fresh pineapple Chantilly

Le Grand Véfour
Réveillon du Premier Avril

Huîtres de Cancale
Homard aux morilles
Baron d'agneau Henri IV
Ballottine de faisan
Salade dauphinoise
Fromage
Ananas frais crème Chantilly

Having added his choice of wines: "Meursault '59, Haut-Brion '59, Richebourg '61, and champagne," he concluded, "Naturally, one would have to taste it all at the Grand Véfour, with Raymond Oliver!"

My piece was published and I forgot about it.

Then, one fine day in March, I received two formal invitations. The first asked me to a buffet for the wedding of the *chansonnier* Jean Rigaux at Maxim's on April first.

April first? I thought it was a joke. No *chansonnier* is going to get married on April first.

The second invitation asked me to a luncheon for Pierre-Jean Vaillard on that same April first at the Grand Véfour.

Again I thought it was a joke. A plot to make a fool of me, I thought. Let's wait and see. . . .

But the next day Raymond Oliver called me to check on a detail concerning the lobster.

"What lobster?"

"The lobster with morels!"

"What morels?"

"The morels of Pierre-Jean's lobster!"

Although Raymond Oliver is from Bordeaux, he is a man one may have confidence in. He assured me that Pierre-Jean's celebration was indeed taking place on April first, at one o'clock in the small *salon* of the Grand Véfour. If that were true, perhaps Jean Rigaux was really getting married.

With the aroma of the pineapple with whipped cream still in my mouth, combined with that of a Davidoff cigar (the French government's brands are unspeakable!), I arrived at Maxim's just in time to kiss the bridegroom (and the bride as well, given the occasion), and to greet Maurice Chevalier, the singer Tino Rossi, President of the Senate Gaston Monnerville, and a few other men of goodwill.

Having, however, for the first time waived my principles and celebrated a specific occasion!

True, it was an April Fools' Day hoax. All the more because Pierre-Jean confessed to me that his menu which I had given in my article wasn't his at all. He had taken quite a while to answer my question the previous November, and then one day he said to himself:

"Damn it, I have to send him a menu . . . But which one?"

Just at that moment he noticed, in one of the daily papers, an account of a reception for some African notable given by the President of the Republic at the Elysée Palace (we were then receiving lots of black kings, to give them both money and a lofty image of the French President). Pierre-Jean cynically copied the menu out as given.

And that is how, three months later, we had the same lunch they had had at the Elysée. But it was even better. And among friends!

Recipes of Raymond Oliver
Le Grand Véfour

LOBSTER WITH MORELS

The only ingredients to consider for the preparation of this dish are live lobsters and true fresh morels (*Morchella esculenta*). Do not use the lesser type of morel known as *Helvella esculenta*.

This dish is very simple and, as a result, difficult to prepare properly. I will not give any proportions here, for proportions depend on too many exterior factors.

Use for each person: 1 live 1½-pound lobster, 3½ ounces morels, butter, oil, cream, salt, cayenne pepper, Fine Champagne.

A rice pilaf may be served as a garnish.

Procedure:
Shell the lobster while it is still uncooked. Cut it into large dice which you will let color quickly in a mixture of hot oil and butter in a *sauteuse*. As soon as the lobster has turned bright red, drain and reserve the oil and butter mixture from the *sauteuse*. Quickly flambé with Cognac or a young Armagnac. Remove to a china dish.

Return the mixture of oil and butter to the pan; use it, mixed with a bit more butter, to sauté the carefully cleaned morels. Mix the lobster meat and all the juices it will have rendered with the morels. Season well, cover the pan, and coddle together for 3 to 5 minutes, *not more*.

Bind with heavy cream and serve.

BARON OF LAMB HENRI IV

Choose a *pré-salé* lamb (lamb that has fed in salt-marsh meadows). The best come from Mont-Saint-Michel, but those from Pauillac are not to be disdained. A baron from a Pauillac lamb will serve 8 persons. The baron consists of the two legs and the saddle of the lamb. For 4 persons, one can use only half a baron, which consists of one leg and half of the saddle. Bone the hip and saddle; salt and pepper the inside of the meat. Sprinkle with fresh thyme leaves (if possible) and tie.

Bard with fatback, season, and lay on a bed of celery, garlic and onion. Bake in a hot oven. Let rest for 20 to 30 minutes before carving and serving.

Garnish with artichoke bottoms slowly cooked in butter in a covered pan and filled with béarnaise sauce. There should be very little gravy. Do not serve the fatback covering.

(Note: This recipe can be executed with American Colorado lamb, provided the meat is genuine Prime spring lamb. The baron should be allowed to hang in a cold room for at least 1 week after being purchased for essential aging purposes. If no cold room is available, the baron can stay refrigerated on the lowest shelf of the refrigerator, but it should rest on a rack and be protected by a tent of foil that does not touch the surface of the meat and is open at both ends.

The roasting time is 8 minutes per pound for a baron, 11 minutes per pound for a single leg with the boned saddle attached. The 20 to 30 minutes of rest before carving mentioned by M. Oliver remains essential. Ed.)

BALLOTTINE OF PHEASANT

To serve 4 persons

1. Take a fine young pheasant hen. Remove the nerves from the legs either with a special gadget or with a metal bar. Although this operation makes the boning easier, it is not essential.

2. Bone the hen, taking care to preserve the skin whole. Remove the nerves in the thighs very carefully.

3. Marinate in port or Madeira for several hours.

4. Prepare a forcemeat with 1 boned pheasant breast and wing *(Note: Presumably from a second pheasant; see below under 5., where the author again uses the breast meat, on both sides of the bird, Ed.)* and the same quantity of pork meat and fat from a dry cured ham (Bayonne ham in France, prosciutto in the U.S.). Season with paprika, salt, pepper and truffle juice; just before using the forcemeat, mix in the port or Madeira in which the pheasant marinated. The forcemeat should be rather soft.

5. Lay the pheasant (skin side down) flat on the work table. Remove the two small breast fillets, the remaining breast meat and the meat from the thighs; dice it. Dice enough truffles to obtain the same volume of truffles as of diced meat and blend the mixture evenly into the forcemeat.

6. Spread the forcemeat evenly on the pheasant skin. Fold both flaps of the skin carefully over the forcemeat and sew the skin closed with a small trussing needle.

7. In a large *cocotte* color lightly some coarsely chopped onions with

some white turnips and carrots. Add a large *bouquet garni*. Place the *ballottine* at the center of the bed of vegetables. Add a few chicken feet or a boned calf's foot. Cover the *ballottine* with dry white wine; add salt and pepper and let cook for 2 hours.

Let cool to lukewarm. Remove the *ballottine* from the pot and let it cool completely. Strain the cooking juices, defatten them completely. Add some port and pour into a deep china dish. Let jell in a cold place or in the refrigerator.

Slice the *ballottine* into 8 even slices and present them on the bed of jelly. Do not overchill.

(Note: Chicken feet can quite often be obtained from kosher butchers. Chicken feet and boned calf's foot should be blanched before using in the cooking of the ballottine. *The cooking technique here is braising. When the pot is covered, a large sheet of aluminum foil should be put flush on the surface of the meat and shaped to form an inverted lid; then the pot cover should be put on. If you do not use the foil, the* ballottine *will boil in the white wine instead of the wine reducing properly and the* ballottine *braising; with the foil tent, the* ballottine *will be succulent with juices after the cooking is finished. Ed.)*

SALAD DAUPHINOISE

Shell some English walnuts and peel them. Choose small heads of Boston or garden lettuce and cut them lengthwise into halves. Arrange the lettuce halves side by side on a platter and sprinkle them with the walnut halves.

Prepare a sauce with Dijon mustard, lemon juice, salt, cayenne pepper and heavy cream. Coat the lettuce hearts with the dressing and sprinkle with paprika.

FRESH PINEAPPLE CHANTILLY

Peel some nice ripe pineapples. Slice them. Put the slices on a china platter or in a crystal dish.

Gather the juice of the pineapple in a mixing bowl and mix it with some heavy cream. Split 2 vanilla beans open and mix their inside seeds with a bit of Kirsch. Add the vanilla-Kirsch mixture to the cream; add sugar to your taste and beat the cream with a large hand whisk until fluffy.

Serve the pineapple in one dish and the cream sprinkled with a few candied violets in another serving dish.

My Own Dinner, All Mine

It was an excellent idea. Those gastronomes who write regular columns spend the whole year judging menus that have been not only prepared but also decided upon by others. Why, from time to time, shouldn't others judge dinners devised by the gastronomes?

Therefore, in the fall of 1970, a restaurant keeper from Rungis offered his customers a series of meals composed by each of us and prepared by a chef of our own choice.

I had decided to use a "Parisian menu" as my theme, so I asked Jacques Manière, of the restaurant Le Pactole, to come to cook the dinner on his colleague's stoves.

A hundred informed readers of *Le Monde* made it their business to participate and judge our creations. I was very happy indeed. I would have been even happier if the event could have taken place elsewhere than in Rungis, a kind of glacial ersatz of our good old markets of the past, where the buyers and sellers now act like robots controlled by computers. Moreover, I should add that the hash-house kitchen brigade was not really willing to help our invited chefs. Jacques Manière, who scarcely has the patience of an angel but, rather, a hot head under his chef's hat, confessed to me later that if he hadn't been doing this for me, he would have given up the whole affair!

I consider Jacques Manière one of the very great chefs in France.

That is probably why there is no mention of his restaurant in the *Guide Michelin!*

Actually, it's better to be strong-willed than good-willed, and I am pleased to note that the three most ornery men in French cuisine—in my opinion, Jacques Manière, Pointaire, and Lucien Sarrasset—are exceptionally good chefs as well, and not one of them is mentioned in that famous guidebook, which claims to provide honest information to its readers! No matter.

Here, then, is the menu I had proposed:

115

Cold consommé with sherry

Lobsters Demoiselles de Cherbourg à la nage
with Echiré butter façon Manière

(Pinot de Chardonnay Pol Roger 1961)

Chicken Père Lathuille

(Domaine de Chevalier: red Graves)

Pink champagne granité

Jellied beef cheeks

Curly chicory and walnut salad with
Fourme d'Ambert cheese dressing

Pierre Androuet's selection
of goat cheeses from the farms

(Santenay, Domaine des Hautes Cornières)

Floating island with pink pralines
and warm mousseline brioche

(Magnums of champagne Pol Roger 1964)

Coffee

Strathisla Scotch (pure malt)

Perhaps I should explain. My French readers know well that, to my mind, the most successful way of preparing lobster, crawfish, or scallops is *à la nage*. And that I find pasteurized butter unthinkable, and Echiré butter one of the best in France. And that I like cold dishes, and consider Fourme d'Ambert one of the great French cheeses.

Furthermore, chicken Père Lathuille delights me. It's a historic dish, quite ordinary, of the type that a classic chef doesn't want to hear about, probably because it's simple and flavorful.

I numbered this chicken Père Lathuille among the Hundred Wonders of French Cuisine. It was the glory of the bistro at the Clichy tollgate, which heroically rose to stardom in 1815, when the Cossacks arrived. Actually, Père Lathuille's heroism probably consisted in merely distributing the best bottles of wine from his cellar to French soldiers before the enemy troops could get there to drink them. But a few beneficent shells hit his inn and made it famous. Thereupon, artists and writers made their way to it, replacing the little jades and bad apples of the neighborhood. Manet did a painting of it, and old Goncourt nostalgically recalled his escapades there.

While the quality of the dishes and Jacques Manière's skill were unanimously appreciated, there were some doubts with respect to the menu,

Le Pactole
Le Dîner de Robert Courtine

...

Consommé froid au sherry
Demoiselles de Cherbourg à la nage
au beurre d'Echire façon Manière
(Pinot Chardonnay Pol Roger 1961)
Poulet Père Lathuille
(Graves rouge, Domaine de Chevalier)
Granité au champagne rosé
Joue de boeuf froide à la mode
Salade de chicorée à l'huile de noix
et à la fourme d'Ambert
Sélection Pierre Androuet de fromages de chèvre fermiers
(Santenay, Domaine des Hautes Cornières)
Île flottante aux pralines roses
et brioche mousseline tiède
(Champagne Pol Roger 1964 en magnum)
Café
(Whisky pur malt Strathisla)

and a lively discussion ensued. I love that! The most serious reproach, however, was directed at the whiskey, which concluded the meal. So, for the grumblers, I ordered a compensatory Armagnac, which was unfortunately rather banal (ah! if it had only been a Laberdolive 1904!), although I remain convinced that, since grain alcohols do not produce esters, they are a better ending to this type of meal and that pure-malt spirits are very great Scotches when they are twelve years old, like the Strathisla.

Recipes of Jacques Manière
Le Pactole

COLD CONSOMMÉ WITH SHERRY

To serve 4 persons

Ingredients for basic stock:
1½ pounds plate beef
1¼ pounds beef shin, bone in
1 whole veal leg or shoulder shank
4½ quarts cold water
4 carrots
3 leeks (keep the green part)
salt and pepper
2 large onions
3 cloves
1 large bouquet garni
1 large celery sprig with leaves

Ingredients to clarify consommé:
parsley stems
green part of 3 leeks (see above)
2 tomatoes, peeled, seeded and finely chopped
1 pound lean ground beef
2 egg whites
1 eggshell, crushed
1 large glass of dry sherry
1 sprig of fresh tarragon

Procedure:

Put the meats in a stockpot; cover with the cold water. Bring slowly to a boil. As soon as the boiling point is reached, start skimming. Add 3 carrots, white part of leeks, salt, pepper, 1 onion stuck with the cloves, the *bouquet garni* and celery.

Simmer gently and steadily for 4 hours, skimming at regular intervals. The resulting stock will be kept to prepare the consommé. Note that the meats and vegetables may be served warm or used to make a salad.

To prepare the consommé, chop coarsely the parsley stems, green part of leeks, tomatoes, the remaining onion and carrot. Mix those with the ground beef, egg whites, crushed eggshell and the glass of sherry. Whisk in 2 generous quarts of lukewarm beef stock and bring back to a boil still whisking; the constant whisking keeps the egg whites in equal distribution around the meat and vegetables.

As soon as the boiling point has been reached again, add the tarragon and regulate the heat to obtain a steady simmering. Boiling the consommé too fast would cause breaks in the crust of egg white which will form at the surface of the pot. Let cook for 1½ hours. Remove from the heat and let stand; the crust will fall to the bottom of the pot by itself.

Ladle the consommé delicately into a clean vessel. Let it cool completely and chill it for 24 hours. Remove the thin layer of fat that will have formed at the surface of the consommé.

This consommé can be served either jellied or hot according to personal taste.

CHERBOURG BABY LOBSTERS IN COURT-BOUILLON

Choose preferably female lobsters; they should be active and lively.

For the court-bouillon, also called nage:
> *4½ quarts water*
> *3 carrots, sliced*
> *3 onions, sliced*
> *1 sprig of thyme*
> *3 Mediterranean bay leaves*
> *1 large bunch of parsley*
> *2 sprigs of fresh tarragon (1 teaspoon dried)*
> *2 springs of fresh sweet basil (½ teaspoon dried)*
> *salt*
> *¼ ounce peppercorns (half white, half black)*
> *pinch of cayenne*
> *2 generous cups Muscadet or Pouilly*

Bring the water to a boil. Add all the vegetables and the herbs without their stems. Add the white wine. Let cook for 1½ hours; taste the *nage* to make sure that it is highly seasoned.

Immerse the live lobsters in the *nage* and poach them for 10 minutes. *(12 minutes when using 1¼-pound Maine lobsters. Ed.)*

(Note: True Cherbourg baby lobsters, Demoiselles de Cherbourg *according to their local name, are very small lobsters weighing 8 to 10 ounces each. Lobsters of this size are in the United States called "shorts" and their sale is forbidden by law. Replace them by 1¼-pound Maine lobsters. Ed.)*

ECHIRÉ BUTTER

> *1 finely chopped gray shallot*
> *½ pound less 1 tablespoon first-quality grade AA butter*
> *6 scissored small leaves of basil*
> *½ cup Muscadet*
> *2 tablespoons heavy cream*
> *salt and pepper*

Procedure:

In a tin-lined copper or enameled cast-iron pot (avoid an aluminum pot which would blacken the sauce) melt and heat a nugget of butter; add the finely chopped shallot and the basil leaves and sauté together, taking care not to burn the mixture. Add the Muscadet and let gently reduce until almost dry. Add the cream, salt and pepper. Bring to a high boil and add the remaining butter cut into small dice, whisking constantly. Keep adding while you whisk; the butter emulsifies and becomes a sauce identical to a white butter, but very fragrant.

Serve with the lobsters cut into halves with their claws and articulations cracked open.

(Notes: Echiré butter is an excellent butter produced in the town of Echiré, department of Charente. Echiré butter from Charente and Isigny butter from Normandy are considered the two best butters in France, if not in the world, by chauvinistic French gastronomes. Few butters in the United States will be able to compare to those truly outstanding dairy products. One brand of unsalted butter from the Middle West can be found in most supermarkets and sometimes bears a small resemblance to the flavor of Echiré butter; but the pleasant nutty taste of Echiré is difficult to replace.

There are different types of shallots; the gray shallot M. Manière recommends using in this recipe is rare in the United States. The shallot skin is dirty white and the taste of the vegetable is much more subdued than that of the red shallots usually found for sale in almost all groceries. Ed.)

CHICKEN PÈRE LATHUILLE

To serve 8 persons

1 chicken, 2½ to 3 pounds
salt and pepper
¼ cup flour
oil
butter
1 scant pound Red Bliss potatoes, finely sliced
4 uncooked artichoke bottoms, minced
2 garlic cloves
2 tablespoons chopped parsley
2 large onions, sliced thick and separated into rings
a few bunches of parsley leaves, washed and dried
½ cup (1 ladleful) of meat juices from a roast, or the same amount
     of excellent meat glaze

Procedure:

Cut the chicken into 8 pieces; salt, pepper and flour them. Brown the chicken pieces to a golden color in a mixture of half oil, half butter. Drain the pieces of chicken well and set them aside on a plate for later use.

In a large frying pan, sauté the potatoes rapidly so that they start cooking superficially. Immediately add the artichoke bottoms, the 2 garlic cloves finely crushed and the chopped parsley. Toss two or three times around the pan and remove from the heat.

Arrange half of the potatoes on the bottom and the sides of a heavily buttered 10-inch cake pan *(or well-seasoned 9- to 10-inch cast-iron skillet, Ed.)*. Top the potatoes with the 8 pieces of chicken; cover the chicken with the remainder of the potatoes and the artichoke bottoms. Using the bottom of another cake pan of a diameter smaller than that containing the chicken and potatoes, push down on the potatoes to pack them well. Dot with butter.

Bake in a medium oven (375°F.) for 50 minutes to 1 hour. The potatoes molded by the baking dish should be golden and crusty.

Garnishes:

Flour the onion rings and deep-fry them in very hot oil for just a few minutes; they should just turn golden and crisp; drain them on a napkin.

Deep-fry the parsley tops and drain them on a napkin.

Presentation:

Unmold the chicken onto a serving platter. To do so, invert the platter over the chicken mold and turn both over at once. Surround the potatoes and chicken with bunches of fried parsley and onion rings.

Coat the top of the potatoes very quickly with 4 tablespoons *noisette* butter blended with the meat juices or meat glaze (see pp. 261 and 248).

JELLIED BEEF CHEEKS

(Note: If beef cheeks cannot be located, a rump of beef can be used instead. Ed.)

To serve 4 persons

2½ pounds beef cheeks, trimmed
½ cup spring peas
15 silverskin onions
15 baby carrots, trimmed
half of a boned calf's foot
½ cup dry white wine
2 tablespoons chopped parsley
1 bouquet garni
a few ladles of strong homemade beef stock

Procedure:

Lard the beef cheeks with little sticks of fresh fatback rolled in salt, pepper and mashed garlic. Salt, pepper and flour the meat.

Brown the pieces of meat until they are golden. Remove them to a cast-iron *cocotte*. Deglaze the pan in which you browned the beef with the white wine. Add the deglazing of the pan to the *cocotte* with enough beef stock to barely cover the meat. Add the *bouquet garni*. Add the carrots, onions and peas, presautéed and cooked in butter for a few minutes.

Bake in a 300° to 325°F. oven for 4 hours. The beef is cooked when a fork penetrates each piece easily.

Presentation:

Let the meat cool to lukewarm. Cut the calf's foot into tiny pieces. In a terrine, arrange the beef cheeks and the vegetables mixed with the calf's foot in alternate layers. Sprinkle the layers with a bit of the cooking liquor. Fill the terrine and top it with the remainder of the cooking juices. Chill for 24 hours. Cut into slices which you set on a serving platter. Serve with chicory and walnut salad.

CURLY CHICORY AND WALNUT SALAD

(Note: Fourme d'Ambert is a blue cheese made from cows' milk in the département *of Puy-de-Dôme; should you be unable to locate it, use instead 2 ounces of Bleu de Bresse, left to dry at room temperature for 3 hours. Ed.)*

To serve 6 persons

Ingredients:

2 ounces Fourme d'Ambert, finely grated
¼ cup wine vinegar
salt and pepper
½ garlic clove, finely mashed
½ teaspoon strong Dijon mustard
¼ cup heavy cream
2 tablespoons walnut oil
3½ ounces walnut halves
1 head of curly chicory

Procedure:

In the salad bowl, put first the cheese, then the wine vinegar, salt and pepper, then add the garlic and strong mustard. Whisk well to obtain a thick cream. Add the heavy cream and the walnut oil, whisking well, and you will obtain a sauce looking somewhat like a mayonnaise.

Quickly dip the walnut halves into a frying pan filled with hot walnut oil; drain. Rub the walnuts in a towel; the skins will fall off and the fragrance of the nut will be enhanced by the heating process.

Toss together the walnuts, the chicory and the prepared sauce.

PINK CHAMPAGNE GRANITÉ

To serve 2 persons

½ bottle of pink champagne (Pol Roger)
⅓ cup sugar
2 tablespoons water
juice of 1 lemon

Cook the sugar and water to 240°F. Add the lemon juice and champagne and freeze in an ice-cream machine.

FLOATING ISLAND WITH PINK PRALINES

(Note: The pralines used in this recipe are French candies which were created by the chef of the Duke of Praslin during the reign of King Louis XIII. Pralines are almonds coated with cooked sugar, some pink, some brown. The flavor differs with the color and the manufacturers. The praline mixture for which a recipe is given on p. 271 can be crushed and used instead of pink pralines, which are almost impossible to locate in this country. The flavor will be slightly different but very good also. Ed.)

To serve about 6 persons

English cream:
*   2¼ cups scalded milk*
*   6 egg yolks*
*   ¾ cup sugar*
*   ½ vanilla bean*

a) In a mixing bowl, work sugar and egg yolks until the mixture forms a heavy ribbon when falling from the whisk.

b) Pour the scalded milk, in which the vanilla has been allowed to infuse, into the sugar-yolks mixture, whisking well to homogenize it.

c) Stir constantly over medium heat until the cream coats the spatula. Strain rapidly through a fine conical strainer into a deep dish. Let cool.

Floating island:
*   4 egg whites*
*   ⅔ cup sugar*
*   3½ ounces pink pralines*

Butter a cake mold of a diameter slightly smaller than that of the dish into which you strained the English cream. Crush the pralines with a rolling pin. Sprinkle the bottom of the cake mold with some of the crushed pralines *(one third of their volume, Ed.)*.

Beat the egg whites into a firm snow, gradually adding the sugar toward the end of the beating. Fold in the remainder of the crushed praline and turn into the prepared mold. Bake in a hot-water bath in a 300°F. oven for 30 to 40 minutes.

Unmold the hot meringue on the chilled English cream. Serve cold.

A Racinian Meal

David did finally beat Goliath . . . By which I mean that tourists will, one day, finally understand that the seventy-year-old *Guide Michelin* has become sleepily ossified and is on its way to senility, whereas year after year the *Guide Kléber* is improving, coming into its own, and gaining recognition.

The competition between the two guidebooks, which is all to the good of the tourist, can hardly leave the gastronome unmoved. When the *Michelin* took a star away from the Tour d'Argent a few years ago, there was an interpellation in the House of Lords, because Princess Margaret had just tucked away her *n*th duck there. I've been told that when the *Kléber* took its crown away from Maxim's, there was something of a panic on Wall Street. For the French this was not only a Parisian event but also this time the judgment of anonymous inspectors (and when one knows them, one is set to dreaming)—a group whose doings one might not necessarily approve of, but whose standards are pleasing.

That is why a number of us agreed to become members of the Académie Kléber-Colombes, which, some ten years ago, was founded by the director of the *Guide Kléber,* Monsieur Jean Didier.

This academy of gastronomes (the only real one) gives its verdict each year, based on a varying theme, and names a prizewinner after classifying the restaurants that most closely correspond to the personal criteria provoked by the theme. A symbolic cock—a very beautiful objet d'art, by the way—is awarded to every prizewinner in the Kléber-Colombes challenge during a ceremony that includes the previous and the present winner.

In 1971 the theme chosen by Monsieur Didier was the following: to discover new talent among provincial restaurateurs.

Each of us was to draw up a list of ten candidates, classified in order of preference. I personally headed my list with the Moulin de Mougins, run by Roger Vergé, a very great chef. Incidentally, it was he who won the challenge match!

A few weeks later we went in a body to award the prize to the winner. But Vergé had made a mistake: he had invited too many people to dinner and then prepared a menu that was not up to the occasion. For example, claiming to be able to serve 120 tournedos with a sauce is indeed accepting a challenge. Moreover, there were too many wines that were too badly chosen, for our friend had allowed himself to be influenced by a dealer who, to increase his sales, called himself an "oenological specialist." Oenological specialist my ass-Bacchus, as Queneau's Zazie might say!

Vergé is no less worthy for all that, and as gourmet to chef, one must go and challenge him at his Moulin de Mougins. He might then, according to his mood of the moment, create admirable and unexpected dishes. I remember an absolutely sensational chicken fricassee with mussels.

But I am wandering from my subject. For lunch on that official day Jean Didier had invited the members of the Academy to La Réserve in Beaulieu. Taking into account the rather copious dinner that was awaiting us, he had suggested that our friend Potfer, manager of La Réserve, plan a light, simple meal.

"Strike your heart; that is where genius lies," said a poet. Strike your stomach; that is what reveals a chef's genius, the gourmet might say. Monsieur Pernet, chef at La Réserve, subtly guided by his boss, did wonders. And that simple, vanguard meal—that snack, which is what we had thought it would be—proved to be one of the most truly flavorful and successful meals I ever ate in my entire career as a gastronomist.

Roger Vergé, who is understanding and not the type to get angry, did not hold it against me when I told him the story a few days later. On the contrary, he answered wittily, "I owe you a revenge!"

However, let us return, if you will, to the lunch and its "background."

The small *salon,* directly next to the large dining room at La Réserve in Beaulieu, was a kind of nave bordering on the sea that sunny day—that "sea forever recommencing," as Paul Valéry wrote in his poem "Graveyard by the Sea." Yes, we seemed to be sailing on that "tranquil roof"—over a horizon of ever-changing water flecked by a few dazzling sails. There were twelve of us, no more, almost too many according to the Golden Number of guests—more than the Graces, less than the Muses. But they were all good company and knew when to be silent so that we could hear ourselves eat.

And, quite simply serving a local wine from Nice, Potfer shared the following menu with us:

"Vagabond" raw-vegetable salad
Mixed seafood fry Cap Ferrat
Rack of lamb from the Alpilles, garnished
with small stuffed vegetables Niçoise
Strawberry soufflé

La Réserve de Beaulieu

Déjeuner

Salade de crudités vagabondes

Petites fritures du Cap sauce tartare

Carré d'agneau des Alpilles
garni de petits farcis niçois

Soufflé aux fraises

When I speak of Racinian cuisine (as opposed to other types that might be called Cornélian), some people scoff. Ah! how I would have liked them to have been there that day, sharing our meal at La Réserve in Beaulieu. How I would have liked them to take their first cool bath in the raw-vegetable salad, as Phèdre wished to do in Hippolyte's eyes. How I would have liked them to taste the alexandrine precision of the tiny fried local seafood. Among them—dipped in milk, rolled in flour, then deep-fried separately—were little *mostelles "en lorgnette"* (a fish of the gade family), *nonats* (the springtime whitebait of the Riviera), *supions* (little squid), baby sole, and sardine fritters in a pretty green thicket of parsley, sparkling with lemon halves, and with a brisk tartar sauce on the side.

Yes, it was a great meal, and I thought of Joseph Delteil's saying to me one day: "Cuisine is in the nature of things."

Recipes of Jean Potfer
La Réserve de Beaulieu

SALADE DE CRUDITÉS VAGABONDES (a mixed salad)

(Note: When a French chef or cook writes about lettuce, he or she always means the soft-leaved Boston-type lettuce; any other type of lettuce will be called by its botanical name. A mesclun *is a mixture of wild greens which is very popular in the Midi-Mediterranean area of France. It includes, among many others, wild watercress, wild dandelions and wild sorrel. If you can find some of those and add some lamb's lettuce and a few fresh basil leaves, you will obtain a mixture resembling a little the true* mesclun. *Ed.)*

Prepare a salad bowl of lettuce hearts, *mesclun,* finely diced avocados, grated carrots, finely minced raw white mushrooms.

Add fresh *fines herbes* such as tarragon, chervil and chives. Serve with a vinaigrette (p. 260) containing some Dijon mustard.

SPIT-ROASTED RIB RACK OF LAMB

(Note: The part of the rack of lamb to use is that called "hotel rack" or "collar" by butchers; it consists of 7 to 10 ribs and includes the first shoulder chops and the tip of the shoulder blade which must be removed

for easier carving. The ribs must be "frenched," that is to say, the fell and fat covering of the rack are to be removed almost entirely down to the bare muscle; to give the roast that elegant French look, the meat between the ribs must be cut off carefully to a length of about 2 to 2½ inches, from the tip down. Such a roast cooked at high temperature by the concentration method produces only a minimal amount of natural gravy; you may want to deglaze the gravy with some brown veal stock to increase its volume to serve 6 persons. Ed.)

Spit the roast for about 25 minutes, keeping it red. Then, brush it with a layer of strong Dijon mustard and sprinkle it with a mixture of chopped parsley and bread crumbs. Finish roasting the rack in a 400°F. oven for another 20 minutes to brown it lightly.

Serve the rack surrounded with the stuffed vegetables. Spoon a bit of *noisette* butter (p. 261) over the meat and vegetables before serving.

Serve the pan juices in a sauceboat.

STUFFED ZUCCHINI NICOISE

Use small zucchini. Cut them lengthwise into halves; empty them of their meat with a teaspoon to obtain boats. Keep the zucchini meat.

Poach the zucchini boats in lightly salted water for about 5 minutes. Drain them, line them on a buttered baking sheet, and bake them in a hot oven for a few minutes.

To prepare the forcement:

Chop finely the inside meat of the zucchini and 1 onion. Slowly cook the onion (in butter, olive oil or half and half); add the chopped zucchini and let cook for about 10 minutes, then remove from the heat.

Add a chicken leg cut into fine *brunoise,* a whole egg and a bit of grated Parmesan, and flavor with Provençal herbs. Season with salt and pepper from the mill.

Fill the zucchini with this mixture. Sprinkle them with a bit of grated Gruyère mixed with dry bread crumbs; spoon some melted butter on each half and finish cooking in a medium oven (350°F.).

(Note: The Parmesan used should be real Parmigiano-Reggiano, not just any cheese of the grana type.

Here is the formula for Provençal herbs, which are not to be found already prepared in this country. Note the dominance of the rosemary taste.

Mix together in a small mixing bowl:

1 tablespoon each of dried thyme, chervil, tarragon, marjoram
1 teaspoon each of dried orégano and summer savory
½ teaspoon dried mint
1 teaspoon dried rosemary
2 Mediterranean bay leaves, very well crumbled

Store the well-mixed herbs in a glass jar and keep tightly sealed. Use sparingly; the mixture is very fragrant. Ed.)

STUFFED EGGPLANTS NIÇOISE

(Note: The eggplants used in Provence are very small ones. These can be located in Italian neighborhood vegetable markets. Ed.)

Cut the eggplants into 1½-inch-long chunks, and deep-fry them in a very hot oil bath.

Once cooked, cool the eggplant chunks and hollow them with a teaspoon so as to obtain small containers. Chop the eggplant pulp; mix it with a shallot sautéed in butter, 2 good tablespoons of very thick tomato essence (p. 258) and a pinch of marjoram.

Fill the eggplant containers with the mixture and bake in a 350°F. oven for another 10 minutes.

(Note that the amount of tomato essence applies to each whole eggplant. Ed.)

STUFFED MUSHROOMS NIÇOISE

Choose large white mushrooms. Remove the stems, which you will chop with a bit of garlic and parsley and mix with a bit of fresh bread crumbs.

While you prepare the filling, salt and pepper the empty mushroom caps. Bake them on a lightly oiled baking sheet. Fill the caps with the prepared forcemeat. From 5 to 6 more minutes of oven baking will be sufficient to complete the baking.

PROVENÇAL TOMATOES

Use small or medium-size sun-ripened tomatoes. Cut them into halves; remove all the seeds. Flour the cut sides of the tomatoes and fry each half in hot oil. Salt and pepper each tomato half and garnish it with a mixture of fresh bread crumbs, chopped parsley and garlic. Brown in a 350°F. oven.

SPINACH SUBRICS

Blanch ¾ pound leaf spinach in boiling water. Refresh it under running cold water; drain it and squeeze the spinach between your hands to extract all the excess moisture.

Sauté the spinach in butter. Add 2 or 3 tablespoons heavy cream, 2 whole eggs, 2 ounces diced Gruyère cheese and the same volume of diced boiled ham.

Butter 6 to 8 small baba molds; fill them with the mixture. Bake in a hot-water bath in a 350°F. oven for about 30 minutes.

Unmold and use as another garnish around the rack of lamb.

A Double Dinner Chez Bocuse

Despite the fact that *café crème* and bread and butter are the classic breakfast for Frenchmen, some do know how to live better than that. They revert to the straight and narrow—the path of the peasants, who, having been in the fields since dawn, take a break in the morning and eat a hearty snack. In the past it was said to be "greasing the knife." In Lyons they call it a *"mâchon,"* something to munch.

I love Lyons—a secret, gourmandizing, and hungry city.

Ashen Lyons, Lyons of my heart, Lyons of the three rivers: Rhône, Saône, and Beaujolais; Lyons, the birthplace of the writer Henri Béraud, who was tried for collaboration and was assassinated by de Gaulle.

And I love the fact that people from Lyons, at a time of "les drugstores," salesmanship, frozen foods, and other claptrap, still conform to the morning "munch" ritual.

That is why, when my friend Henri Clos-Jouve, author of *Promeneur lettré* and militantly attached to Lyons, got the idea of creating *l'Ordre des Francs-Mâchons* ("Free-*Mâchons*," shall we say), I was one of the people who instantly raised my hand and answered "Here."

Thus, that year we were in Lyons for the first meeting of the Free-*Mâchons*. It was, properly, to be held in the morning—all of us with forks in hand. But we arrived the evening before and dined, naturally, at Bocuse's.

Paul Bocuse is a curious food man, a real character, as they say. With a chef's hat full of wit, a sparkling eye, a light hand to lift his glass, he is a swashbuckler of the drip pans, a juggler of pots, and a poet of stews. He had prepared a perfect menu for us, in his own image. Here it is:

Crawfish-tail salad with caviar

Mediterranean bass in puff pastry

Cardoons with chicken livers

Roast woodcock on croutons

Fresh duck foie gras with truffle salad

Cheeses

Desserts

Personal commentary: Crawfish, those "little red fish that walk backwards," as we are assured by a nineteenth-century textbook, are—when served in their shells—somewhat difficult to sample with any equanimity. Shelling them is rather too feminine a sport, so I myself prefer them prepared beforehand, in an acidulated and shimmering "environment" to which caviar lends a patrician touch. I imagine that Lucullus, dining at Lucullus's, would have ordered the same type of appetizer.

On the other hand, I am not all that fond of Mediterranean bass, a fish which swims in a calm, overcivilized sea. To me it is somewhat fallacious fare, lacking in joy and tonicity. With all due respect to the illustrious chef Fernand Point, who taught Bocuse and who, I think, created this dish, the puff pastry added nothing to the bass, and the bass added nothing to the gourmet's dinner. But that's purely a personal opinion.

Cardoons, civilized and perhaps degenerate artichokes, are little known even to the French. Lyons, which grows them, knows their secret, and this way of preparing them, with chicken livers (chickens from Bresse, whose livers are pale and have a fine, subtle aroma), is a masterpiece of exquisiteness. Hunters and game fans know that the woodcock (a short moment in the hunter's year) without any question is in the epicurean lead. These plump, profound birds languish on their *canapés* like midnight beauties. And the *canapés* must be spread with the beast's entrails and its juice. The roasted bird on its roasted *canapé* admired itself, like Narcissus, in the scented mirror of itself.

Woodcock season is also the season of fresh liver. No gourmet would, obviously, ever expose himself to canned liver. But his affection might swing between the honest and distinguished livers of geese and the muskier, rustic, monolithic livers of duck. What we had was duck's liver, carved in its own lustrous marble, and the truffle salad proved a supple escort. It was the jeweler's stamp on the engraver's stone.

The cheeses . . . But the whole story actually begins here, because up to that point the dinner might have been better than it was, though that would seem impossible; still, it could have been one of the thousands of meals signed Bocuse.

So we were indulging our tastebuds in the gustatory rhapsody of the Black Princess's crackling flavors and the unctuous languor of the liver, when one of us—Christian Guy—summed up the situation as follows: "That seems like a lot to eat; yet it's so light . . . For two bits, I'd start all over again!"

Christian Guy is the Porthos of the gastronomic press—a giant with both an athlete's appetite and an epicurean's subtlety. A log fire was sparkling in the big fireplace. With my eyes half closed, attentive to that delicate, harmonious after-dinner pleasure, I had just emptied my glass. Francis

Amunatégui, whose culinary prose was like witty lacework, murmured dreamily:

"What a magnificent log for a side of beef!"

That was indeed playing with fire—a wood fire—but one doesn't play with Paul Bocuse. It took only one discreet gesture for zealous acolytes, dressed like scullions, to march in, carrying on their shoulders a whole string of ribs of beef, as well as a board and a big knife. A second later the master of the house was cutting two thick ribs, which were brought over to the flames.

We had just time for a green salad and a little mineral water (the wise man's *trou du milieu,* or "hole" between courses) before the meat was done to a turn, carved, and served. It could not have been equaled. The beef came from neighboring Charolais, and its mother, out of empiricism, had probably learned from its female ancestors the secret of being marbled yet not fatty, tender yet not tasteless, and extraordinarily juicy. It was then, out of pure malevolence, having just refused a third slice, that I dared say:

"Personally, I prefer lobster grilled that way!"

Malevolence it was, for, in fact, I spend most of my time extolling lobster *à la nage.* But what had I said? The lobsters were suddenly there. Alive. And kicking. Ready for the sacrifice.

And we feasted on lobsters—with a Dom Pérignon, prince of champagnes.

To speak of Dom Pérignon, and to drink it in Lyons, is to indicate that Georges Évrard, eternal playboy, pipe-smoking angel of Moët et Chandon, was there with us. It was he who, pouring a last spoonful of melted butter over his last bite of lobster, stated:

"In 1900 this meal would have ended with crawfish."

The turn of the century was the great period for crawfish, which were inseparable from flirtatious dinners and from the ladies of Maxim's or of anywhere else. As I mentioned earlier, a woman's hands—jewels that drive us mad, as in the songs of Mayol, the Frank Sinatra of the times—seem made for such cardinalesque craft:

> *Il eut fallu que tu les visses*
> *Éplucher les écrevisses*
> *Au Café des Ambassadeurs . . .*

> You'd have had to see them
> Peeling the crawfish
> At the Café des Ambassadeurs . . .

Bocuse is not a man of 1900, nor is he a man of today. He is a host of eternity, a kind of Medici of food. He pushes a button, and presto: the

Paul Bocuse
Double Dîner des Francs-Mâchons

.

Salade de queues d'écrevisses au caviar
Loups de la Méditerranée en feuilletage
Cardons aux foies de volailles
Bécasses rôties sur canapés
Foie gras de canard frais avec salade de truffes
(Fromages)

.

Salade verte
Côtes de boeuf charolaise
grillées au feu de bois
Homards grillés
Buisson d'écrevisses

.

Desserts
Oeufs à la neige
Mousseline de reinettes aux noix
L'orange à l'orange

crawfish *à la nage* are there, the burning bush, spicy, stimulating our appetites and our conversation, acidulating everybody's mood.

Then back we were at the time for desserts, which, there, are like an infinite stroll through the gardens of the Sugarplum Fairy's Castle.

We had not yet heard from Clos-Jouve, a well-brought-up boy who was probably taught by his mamma not to talk with his mouth full. It was then that he chipped in. "Please excuse me," he said, "but we haven't yet had the cheese!"

Although the night was short, our digestion was successful. On the morrow (*l'endemain,* as Anatole France would have us write) we founded the Free-*Mâchons* with forks in hand as nine o'clock sounded on the rue du Garet.

Recipes of Paul Bocuse

CRAWFISH-TAIL SALAD WITH CAVIAR

(Note: Please use only Louisiana crawfish. Ed.)

To serve 4 persons, use 4½ pounds live crawfish. Cook them in a *nage* (p. 251). Shell the tails. Prepare a light, lemony mayonnaise (p. 260). Fold in ½ cup heavy cream, whipped, a pinch of paprika, and salt and pepper. Toss the crawfish tails into the sauce.

Fill the bottom of a salad bowl with a chiffonnade of lettuce lightly seasoned (with a mild vinaigrette, p. 260); top the lettuce with the salad of crawfish tails; crown the crawfish salad with a generous spoon of caviar. Serve.

(Note: It would be a good idea here to use exclusively Beluga or Sevruga Malossol caviar, not domestic caviar, and to steer clear of any artificially colored caviar, for obvious reasons. Ed.)

SEA BASS IN PUFF PASTRY

To serve 6 persons, use a 6- to 6½-pound sea bass.

Skin the sea bass; do not remove its head or tail. Slit the fish along its back and down to its center bone to make a pocket; sprinkle chopped chervil and tarragon, salt and pepper into the pocket on each side of the backbone. Press the fish closed.

Roll out the puff pastry (see below) so that it is as long as the fish; cut the pastry (lengthwise) into 2 equal-sized sheets. Put the fish on one of the sheets and cover it with the second. Press all around the fish with the fingertips to outline the fish shape including the tail.

With a small sharp paring knife, cut off any excess pastry all around the fish, shaping a 1-inch-wide dorsal fin close to the head and a 1-inch-wide abdominal fin just before the tail, as you go along. Trace some longitudinal lines on these fins. Out of the excess pastry, cut a thin (¼-inch wide) strip of dough which you will use to suggest the gills by applying it in a curve between the head and the body of the fish. Cut out a small ball of dough which you will place at a suitable location on the head to suggest the eye of the fish.

With the sharp edge of a plain round pastry nozzle or a melon baller, cut halfmoon-shaped slits on the body of the fish; they will represent the scales. Do not cut too deeply into the pastry; proceed carefully.

Bake the fish in a preheated 350°F. oven. The baking time is 1½ hours, but you should take regular checks. The fish may be stuffed with a lobster mousse; in this case, allow for an additional baking time of 15 minutes.

Serve with melted butter.

(Notes: In the United States a striped bass is the best fish to use. To skin the fish, lift one corner of the skin by the head and while you gently pull the skin with your left hand, slide your right thumb back and forth between meat and skin; the skin comes off easily.

You will need one recipe of the puff pastry given on p. 268. For the nonprofessional who does not work with the speed and efficiency of a chef, it may be advisable to proceed as follows:

Cut the pastry into 2 portions. Roll out one portion to obtain a 1/6-inch-thick sheet of pastry, which will become the bottom of the pâté. Transfer it to a baking sheet immediately while it is cold. Put the fish on the bottom sheet of pastry. Roll out the second sheet of pastry ¼ inch thick, put it on the fish, and finish building the pâté, cutting it and shaping it directly on the baking sheet. This way of proceeding prevents the slower cook from experiencing the frustration of seeing the pâté lose its shape during the transfer from the work table to the baking sheet.

Brushing some dorure (p. 270) all around the fish on the bottom layer of pastry will make it seal better to the top layer. M. Bocuse assumes that his readers will know that the surface of the pâté should be brushed with dorure before the pattern of scales and fins is traced on the pastry. Ed.)

CARDOONS WITH CHICKEN LIVERS

To serve 4 persons

Cardoons resemble giant artichoke plants; when they reach maturity, they are tied and laid to rest in a dark place so they whiten and tenderize as they wilt. The variety grown around Lyons is the best. Only the center rib of each leaf is usable. A plant weighing 6 to 6½ pounds yields no more than 2 pounds of edible vegetable. Whatever their final culinary mode of preparation may be, the cardoons must undergo a unique preliminary treatment:

1. Discard all the hard, wilted outer leaves. Then one by one detach the tender center leaves. Cut the center ribs into pieces 6 to 7 inches long, starting at the root; discard the leafy part, which is hard and stringy. Keep only the thick part of each rib; it is the only tender part.

2. Peel all the pieces of vegetable to remove all strings and rub each with a piece of lemon to keep it from darkening; soak the vegetables in water acidulated with some vinegar and lemon juice.

3. Prepare a *blanc,* a mixture of 1 generous quart of water mixed while still cold with 2 tablespoons flour, ¼ cup vinegar, the juice of ½ lemon and 2 teaspoons salt. Bring to a boil, stirring constantly. Add the cardoons to the boiling *blanc;* they should go from their acidulated water bath to the *blanc* without delay. To protect the vegetables from contact with the air, which would alter their whiteness, add to the pot ¼ pound of butter divided into small pieces for each quart of water used to prepare the *blanc.*

Simmer gently, covered, for 2 hours. Check the doneness; the cardoons should give under the pressure of your fingers. Pour the contents of the pot into a large mixing bowl in which you will keep the cardoons before seasoning them.

For the dish described below, start by preparing an 8-pound cardoon exactly as I just explained.

In another pot, heat well ½ pound butter; add 4 chicken livers, finely diced, and 1 tablespoon flour; stir frequently and keep cooking gently until the *roux* turns a beautiful Havana brown. Whisk 2 generous cups of heavy cream into the *roux* and let cook for 20 minutes. Mix with the very well-drained cardoons; sprinkle with some grated Gruyère and brown quickly in a hot oven.

ROAST WOODCOCK ON CROUTONS

Pluck the bird just before cooking it. Do not remove the entrails; only the gizzard should be discarded. Singe the bird lightly, remove the eyes, intertwine the legs into each other, and tie them; turn the head backward and spear the beak into the body just above the legs.

Season the bird with just a bit of fine salt and wrap it with a thin sheet of fresh pork fatback. Spit-roast the woodcock on a lively fire, or oven-roast it in a very hot oven (450°F.), brushing it well with melted butter.

The roasting time varies from 18 to 20 minutes, depending on the size of the bird. Keep the bird rare. Set the bird on a crouton 6 by 4 inches and ⅓ inch thick cut out of white bread and fried in the butter used to roast the woodcock. If at all possible, spread the crouton with 1 to 2 table-spoons of purée of foie gras.

Carve the bird in front of the guests; put the entrails on a warm plate, grind over them a good pinch of fresh pepper, and add a nugget of butter or foie gras; mash the mixture with a fork, adding gradually 3 teaspoons of Fine Champagne. Spread this purée over the crouton, and divide the crouton into two if the bird is to serve 2 guests.

Deglaze the cooking juices with 2–3 tablespoons of brown veal stock or hot water and serve them in a sauceboat.

(Note: One woodcock usually serves 1 person, but in an elaborate menu only one half of a bird might be served to each guest. Ed.)

TRUFFLE SALAD

To serve 4 persons

Use 1 scant pound uncooked fresh truffles. Peel the truffles very care-fully (the peels can be used for the making of a sauce); shave the truffles into thin slices. Just before serving, season them with the juice of 1 lemon mixed with 4 tablespoons virgin olive oil. Toss carefully and serve imme-diately.

BROILED LOBSTER

Split the lobster lengthwise into halves; break the claws open; season with salt and pepper. Sprinkle well with oil and broil slowly for 15 minutes. Serve with plain melted butter or melted butter blended with mustard.

(Note: When you split the lobster, it should rest on the board shell side up, or the shell will curl up badly when you broil it. Remove the sand sack just below the eyes. Ed.)

CRAWFISH "BUSH"

Preliminary remarks:

I would like to stress an important observation concerning the bitter taste of undeveined crawfish. The vein of each crawfish can be removed by gently pulling the center tail fin; the operation is not easy and requires patience and skill.

Some are bothered by that bitterness and will not eat crawfish that have not been deveined; others are of a diametrically opposed opinion and prefer to run a risk, saying that if one pulls the vein off, the crawfish loses its juices and with them its flavor and taste. This discussion among gourmets of varying opinions has brought about a very successful experience which makes everyone happy; here it is, as suggested by Monsieur Bocuse:

Do not devein crawfish; immerse them in a cold milk bath for 2 hours. The little shellfish do not enjoy the taste of milk and wiggle around in the bath; cover the container with a wire rack to prevent them from escaping. While they wiggle around, they purge themselves and they disgorge their bitterness without losing any of their taste. Thanks to this 2-hour-long milk bath, they are positively delicious. The season is also most important: crawfish tastes really good from April to September only.

Court-bouillon:

Make sure that your crawfish are lively and healthy. After purging them in milk as described above, wash them and let them drain well.

To cook 25 crawfish for a *buisson* (a bush), put in a pot: 1 large parsley sprig, 3 garlic cloves, a thyme sprig, 10 to 12 peppercorns, 1 large onion, sliced, 1 medium-sized carrot, sliced thin, about 1½ teaspoons salt, ½ glass—that is to say, ½ cup—dry white wine and 2 to 2¼ cups water. Bring to a violent boil and let cook for a few minutes. After a few minutes, throw the well-drained crawfish into the court-bouillon. Cover the pot and let cook, still on high heat, for 10 minutes, not more, but taking care to toss the crawfish every so often.

(Note: A buisson, *or a bush, can be obtained by hanging the crawfish, cooked as described above, upside down from a wire cone made especially for this purpose. A* buisson *is usually a presentation piece; the red color of it interspersed by dots of very green parsley makes an attractive decoration on a buffet table. The crawfish is usually eaten cold with a light mayonnaise; see page 260. Ed.)*

SNOW EGGS (Oeufs à la Neige)

To serve 12 persons

Avoid the two mistakes generally made when preparing snow eggs: the first one is to oversweeten the egg whites and the milk and yolks used to prepare the custard, the second to poach the egg whites in milk—it makes them heavy and flabby.

Have ready 6 whole eggs, 1 small cup of sugar, 2 cups scalded milk, some vanilla extract or orange-flower water, a pinch of salt.

Also gather the following implements: an egg-white basin and a whisk, a small saucepan, a wooden spoon, a large shallow sautéing dish, a slotted spoon, a sieve, a serving spoon and a large round deep dish to put under the sieve.

Procedures:

Separate the eggs; put the whites in the basin and the yolks in the small saucepan. Add the salt to the whites and start beating slowly so the whites fluff up gradually into a light foamy snow; then beat faster until they become stiff and dull. Remove the whisk and fold in half of the sugar. Keep ready to use.

Add the remainder of the sugar and the chosen flavoring to the yolks. Gradually add the milk and stir over medium-low heat until thickened. Remove from the heat and whisk very fast to prevent curdling. Set aside for later use.

Fill a shallow sautéing dish or other equivalent container with natural unsweetened boiling water; keep barely simmering over low heat. With the serving spoon, shape an egg out of the meringue waiting in the basin; tapping the handle of the spoon sharply on the edge of the dish, drop the egg into the water. You can poach 6 eggs at a time, for 6 egg whites yield 12 snow eggs. Flip the eggs upside down with the slotted spoon to poach the snow eggs on their second side. Drain the eggs on a sieve *(tamis)* set over a shallow dish. Let cool.

Float the eggs on the beautiful golden custard, piling them into a pyramid. This is a dessert which children like and which is good for them.

One can very the sauce by adding either coffee or chocolate or even in the summer using a natural fruit sauce made with raspberries, strawberries, red currants or a mixture of any two of them.

With this method, one always prepares impeccable snow eggs.

(Note: The amateur chef who does not work as fast as a professional may want to prepare the custard before whipping the egg whites to avoid

having them collapse, which they will do if they wait too long after having been whisked to a meringue. Ed.)

MOUSSELINE OF RUSSET APPLES AND WALNUTS
(Mousseline de Reinettes aux Noix)

To serve 6 persons

1. Peel, core and thinly slice 8 russet apples. Cook them slowly in a covered pan with about 2 tablespoons butter, 6 tablespoons sugar, 1 teaspoon vanilla sugar and a bit of finely grated lemon rind.

2. Peel and core 3 more russet apples and cut each into 8 slices. Poach them in a syrup made with ¾ cup water and ½ cup sugar and flavored with a vanilla bean. Poach very slowly and carefully, making sure that the fruit is barely tender. Remove 15 slices of apple at this stage and continue cooking the others until they are completely done. Drain them and reserve the syrup.

3. As soon as the apples described under 1. are cooked through, mash them with a fork and reduce the purée over high heat, stirring with a spatula, to evaporate the excess moisture and obtain a true fruit paste.

Remove from the heat. Bind the apple paste, while it is still hot, with ⅓ cup heavy cream, whipped, 3 whole eggs and 3 additional egg yolks, well beaten, ½ cup coarsely chopped blanched walnuts and the half-poached slices of apples.

4. Butter heavily a charlotte mold. Pour in the prepared apple mixture; pack it lightly and bake in a hot-water bath at 300° to 325°F. for about 40 minutes. Check the doneness by pressing lightly with the tip of a finger. The mixture must feel like an upside-down custard.

5. Remove from the oven. Let rest for about 10 minutes before unmolding onto a warm round serving platter. Coat the dessert with the following cream:

Reduce the poaching syrup of the apples to about ¼ cup. Away from the heat add about 3 tablespoons fresh unsalted butter and ¼ cup whipped cream. Flavor with some Noyau liqueur.

Serve with a plate of *langues de chat* or other dry *petits fours* of delicate texture.

(Note: Use a 4-cup charlotte mold. Noyau liqueur is the fine French almond liqueur known as Noyau de Poissy. None of the almond liqueurs made in the United States can truly replace it. The Bols Crème de Noyau made in Holland, not the U.S. version, can be considered an adequate replacement. Ed.)

L'ORANGE À L'ORANGE

To serve 6 persons

Peel 6 oranges to the pulp, and cut out each section without leaving any skin on it. Cut the rinds of the oranges into a fine julienne; cook the rinds in ¾ cup water mixed with ½ cup grenadine syrup. Sprinkle the orange slices with a spoonful of sugar and add the candied rinds as soon as they have cooled completely.

Empty another 6 oranges of their pulp. Strain the pulp and keep the obtained juice to make sherbet; keep the orange skins to use as serving cups.

To make the orange sherbet, melt ¾ cup sugar in 1 quart orange juice mixed with the juice of 2 lemons. Freeze in an ice-cream machine.

Put some sherbet at the bottom of each orange shell. Top the sherbet with the orange sections and the candied rinds and serve.

(Note: Lift the rind of the orange in long strips with a potato peeler before peeling the oranges to the pulp; it will be easier and no white skin will remain attached to the strips of rind. To cut the rind strips into a julienne, put the skin upside down on the board and use a very sharp thin-bladed knife; cut the julienne ⅛-inch wide, across each strip if you want a short julienne, along each strip if you want long curly julienne strips. Ed.)

The Inscrutable Orient

Curnonsky, our Prince of Gastronomes, used to say: "France and China are the only two countries that have both cuisine and courtesy." "Nay," as said Rabelais's Panurge! Mao's courtesy seems questionable to me and his cuisine even more so. In sum, I am not very fond of Chinese cooking. Or, more precisely, it amuses me now and then in the same way as an avocado or hearts of palm tickle the surface of the tongue. Besides, I don't at all like being threatened with sticks, even when they involve only my appetite.

Doubtless, such celestial cuisine has its harmonious inventions that are new and strange. But it appears to me more likely that it comes to us from the devil. All that flesh shredded with a scalpel makes me think of the torturers some thousand years ago. Perhaps they were also cooks! The great philosopher Lao-tzu once said: "Govern the Empire as you would cook a little fish." I shall let the exegetists deduce some political theory from that comment or, at any rate, an art for using up scraps.

In other words, I am not a faithful customer of the nearly two thousand Chinese (or Vietnamese or Sino-Vietnamese) restaurants in Paris. For, in addition, we have an occupation army of scullions, a yellow peril in pots and pans, and a multiplication of shrimp breads and phony lacquered ducks.

Before the last war, at the Halles, Paris's central market, one would see crates of *langoustines* on their way to rot and absolute unsalability, and hear, "Leave those aside; they're for the Chinese." Deep-frying and a spicy sauce would hide the poisonously fishy nature of the fish. True, at the time there were no more than a handful of Chinese restaurants in Paris—two or three more or less decent ones in the elegant neighborhoods, and the rest in the Latin Quarter, a cheap blessing for penniless students.

We have changed all that, as Molière's doctor would say. Molière, in the likeness of his bourgeois personage Chrysale, surely preferred to live on good soup rather than on the esoteric language of Parisianized foreign cuisine.

For the fact is, this cuisine is strictly "made in Paris." Travelers who were captivated by Chinese cuisine on the spot (Curnonsky was among them) guarantee that there is no comparison between it and its exported versions.

So enough of passing judgment.

The very honorable Paul Luong Lap is a friend of mine. Roly-poly, well-padded, smiling, and skillful, he managed to reconcile me to his cuisine. But I must add that it is the *ne plus ultra* and that his restaurant, the Tong Yen, is the Tour d'Argent of Chinese cuisine in Paris.

It was actually with Curnonsky that I'd first discovered it, near the Sorbonne. He had initiated me in Cantonese cooking (the best, they say) and in lacquered duck, really lacquered—the kind one must order in advance because it takes forty-eight hours to prepare. In return for that favor I had informed Paul that sauerkraut was of Chinese origin. Straightaway he concocted a *choucroute* from behind the bamboo curtain. We washed it down with beer.

Yes, I know . . . Jasmine tea is a most pleasant drink and perfectly suited to Chinese cooking, which it allays, scents, and refines. But a Frenchman feels awfully unhappy when there's no wine to drink—indeed, when there's no drinking—and in China one doesn't drink while eating; one drinks afterward, and then just a small glass of wine, which in fact is rice alcohol and not wine at all. So Chinese restaurants in Paris offer their customers . . . rosé!

In my opinion rosé is not wine. Or, at the very most, a bastardized wine. And the rosé in Chinese restaurants is generally still worse—the refuse of wine factories.

The best one can do, if one wants to drink and disapproves of tea, is to have a light and fresh Beaujolais.

And that leads me to the Chinese dinner organized by Paul Luong Lap at the Saint-Nom-la-Bretèche golf club to conclude a lecture on love given by Marcel Achard of the French Academy, a gourmet from Lyons and a joyful companion.

Why a Chinese dinner to illustrate the lecture on love? I have no idea! Why had Paul Luong Lap gone out and found a Chinese chef from London for the occasion? I couldn't say. In the old days elegant people thought it good form to have their laundry bleached in London. Did Paul believe that Parisian gourmets would find it pleasant to have this strange meal yellowed by London?

In any case, there were at least a hundred of us, scattered at small tables, chopsticks in hand, to light into this Anglo-Sino-*tout*-Parisian dinner. I was at the table of the good Achard himself, and as we ate Tsin Tchao pâtés, we meditated on the culinary supremacy of truffled sausages with pistachio nuts, served hot with steamed potatoes. Lyons was far away, although the former French silk capital had always had business ties with China. And the mention of business to a merchant of Lyons implies a gastronomic meal.

The next dish had a wonderful taste.

"What a pity," said Marcel Achard sincerely, "that we don't know what it is."

"The menu guarantees that it has to do with fillets of sole."

"But perhaps the menu is in Chinese!"

We drank.

Extra help had been brought in to ensure good service. And since my appetite and I are in the habit of wandering from place to place, I know a number of waiters and, generally, at an occasion of that type, I see a few familiar faces. At this dinner it was an old maître d'hôtel who, as barman at cocktail parties, with a wink of complicity, never failed to serve me the best Scotch or more caviar canapés than to others. It didn't take long for us to come to an understanding. He himself brought all the fresh teapots to our table. Marcel Achard and I emptied our cups often. When we got to the lacquered duck (a beauty), we were very gay indeed. Everyone watched our group enviously. The great playwright's conversation must be constantly sparkling, thought our jealous fellow guests. There was, in fact, no lack of good spirit at our table, but I daresay it was the spirit of wine . . . We were the only ones there who had had teapots full of Beaujolais.

Recipes of
Paul Luong Lap – Restaurant Tong Yen

PÂTÉS TSIN TCHAO

To serve 4 persons

Prepare a forcemeat with about 20 chopped medium-size shrimps, 2 grated carrots, 3 scallions and 4 mushrooms, both chopped, 6½ ounces cooked lean salt pork, chopped, 8 coriander seeds, ground, 3 pinches of Five Spices, salt and pepper. Mix all these ingredients well.

Purchase some rice pancakes in a specialty store. You will find that they resemble white crêpes and are almost translucent. Buy 4 crêpes per guest or 16 crêpes altogether. Moisten them lightly.

Put 1 crêpe on top of another; spread with some forcemeat and roll like large cannelloni. Put the rolls on a baking sheet and bake in a medium oven for 10 minutes; then immerse the rolls in a hot oil bath and cook for 3 minutes. Drain on a clean napkin. Serve surrounded with fried parsley or fried onion rings.

(Note: The Five Spices or Ng Heung Fun *is a mixture consisting of fennel, anise, pepper, clove and cinnamon.*

Rice pancakes—it is not clear here whether the author is speaking of wonton skins or meat wrappers (Sao Mai); *in France, egg-roll skins and meat-dumpling wrappers are effectively both white and translucent with a thickness somewhere in between an American-made wonton skin and a sheet of Greek* phyllo *pastry. Close the dough over the filling as you would for an egg roll.*

The oven baking here seems to replace the steaming done by many Chinese cooks before deep-frying. Ed.)

FILLETS OF SOLE CANTONESE (Filets de Sole Cantonais)

Use 2 fine fillets of sole per person; trim them well. Sprinkle the inside of each fillet with a bit of coriander, cinnamon, Five Spices (above), nutmeg and chopped onion. Add 2 very thin slivers of ginger root and fold the fillets in half over them. Sprinkle the fillets with oil and dust them again with a bit of the spices mentioned above. Steam the fillets for 20 minutes.

Put the cooked fillets on a warm platter; salt and pepper them.

Prepare a sauce as follows:

Stir-fry in ½ cup oil over high heat, 2 chopped scallions, 4 thinly sliced mushrooms, 8 lardoons of smoked bacon, a good slice of ham slivered, 3½ ounces cooked and chopped shrimps, the well-drained contents of a small can of crab. Cook for 5 minutes, stirring constantly.

Break 2 eggs over the mixture and add 1 tablespoon of pepper sauce, stirring with a wooden spoon to scramble the eggs. Remove from the heat. Add 1 teaspoon of soy sauce *(the author does not mention which one. Ed.)*.

Stir a bit of stock and 3 to 4 tablespoons of strong tomato sauce into the resulting sauce. Add some cooked peas and slivers of bamboo shoots. Pour over the fillets of sole.

LACQUERED DUCK PEKING STYLE (Canard Laqué)

To serve 6 persons

one 5-pound duck
1¾ quarts water
½ cup honey
4 slices of peeled fresh ginger root, each 1 inch in diameter
*   and ⅛ inch thick*
2 scallions with their green tops, each cut into 2-inch pieces

For the sauce:
*   ½ cup* hoisin *sauce*
*   2 tablespoons water*
*   1 teaspoon sesame oil*
*   2 teaspoons sugar*
*   12 scallions*

Preparation:

1. Wash the duck under running cold water and dry it inside and outside with paper towels. Tie one end of a 20-inch string around the neck of the duck. Should the neck skin have been cut up, tie the string in a bow under the wings. Hang the duck in a well-aired place for 3 hours, or let an electric fan blow on it for 2 hours.

2. In a large pot, mix 6½ cups water, ½ cup honey, the ginger root and the scallion pieces, bring to a boil over high heat. Holding the duck by the string, immerse it in the boiling liquid. Holding the string in one hand and a spoon in the other, turn the duck from one side to the other until the skin is well soaked with water. Remove the duck from the liquid and discard the liquid. Hang the duck in the same well-aired place as before, but put a container under it to collect escaping liquids. Count from 2 to 3 hours to dry the duck again (or 1 hour if you use an electric fan).

3. To prepare the sauce, mix *hoisin* sauce, water, sesame oil and sugar in a small pan and stir until the sugar dissolves. Bring to a boil, then reduce the heat and simmer, uncovered, for 3 minutes. Pour the sauce into a small boat; let cool and keep until ready to use.

4. To prepare the 12 scallions, cut them into 3-inch pieces and discard the roots. Stand each piece of scallion on one of its ends and cut 2 parallel incisions 1 inch down into the scallions. Turn the piece of vegetable upside down and repeat the same operation at the other end. Immerse

the scallion brushes in ice water and refrigerate until each end of the scallion pieces fans out like a brush.

Roasting the duck:

Preheat the oven to 400°F. Untie the duck and cut away the flabby part of the skin around the neck. Place the duck breast side up on a rack and set the rack in a deep baking dish just large enough to contain the duck. Pour 1 inch of water into the baking dish and roast for 1 hour. Lower the temperature of the oven to 325°F., turn the duck over, and roast for another 30 minutes. Raise the temperature of the oven again to 400°F., turn the duck again on its back, and roast for another 30 minutes. Place the duck on a carving board.

Using a sharp paring knife and working with your fingers, remove the crisp skin from the breast, sides and back of the duck. Cut the skin into rectangles 2 by 3 inches. Place them in a single layer on a heated platter. Detach the wings and drumsticks and cut the meat of the breast and carcass into pieces 5½ by 1¾ inches. Arrange them with the wings and thighs on another heated platter.

To present the Peking duck, place both the platters containing the duck skin and meat, the pancakes (below), the dish of scallions and the sauceboat at the center of the table. Each guest will unfold a pancake on his plate, take a scallion, dip it into the sauce, and brush some of the sauce on the pancake. He will then put the scallion at the center of the pancake together with a piece of crisp skin and a piece of duck meat. He will fold the pancake over this filling and roll it so as to be able to hold it between his fingers.

Mandarin pancakes:

To make 24 pancakes

2 cups sifted flour
¾ cup boiling water
1½ tablespoons sesame oil

Sift the flour into a mixing bowl; make a well in the center and add the boiling water. With a wooden spoon, mix the flour gradually into the water until you obtain a homogeneous dough. Knead the dough on a lightly floured surface for 10 minutes, until smooth and elastic. Cover it with a moist cloth and let it rest for 15 mintes. Then, still on a floured surface, roll out the dough to form a large circle about ¼ inch thick. Using a cutter or a glass 2½ inches in diameter, cut as many circles as you can. Knead the excess dough again, roll it out, and again cut new 2¼ -inch circles. Put these circles side to side and brush half of them with a thin layer of sesame oil. Top each oiled circle of dough with an unoiled one. Using a rolling pin, flatten these sandwiches to obtain circles 3½ to 4 inches in diameter; to do so, as you flatten with the rolling pin, turn the dough 90 degrees to the right. Turn the crêpe over to flatten it on the other side.

Heat a pan over high heat for 30 seconds. Over moderate heat, cook the pancakes one at a time, without greasing the pan, and turn them over as soon as they show bubbles at their surface.

(Note: The author means to have one cook a double pancake each time and to pull the two layers apart after cooking. Ed.)

A Dinner Behind Closed Doors

Sacha Guitry, who added a nice touch of appetite to his pen and who also understood the spirit of the dining room, wrote of him: "This man will have spent two-thirds of his life dressed either all in black or all in white. As head cook for the Czar and then for the Emperor of Austria, for twenty years he wore his white robes and his chef's hat, shaped like a brioche, which were tranquilizingly clean and pleasing to glimpse between two doors. At the age of forty he exchanged his white clothes for tails, and from forty to sixty he lived in black. Moving from table to table, advising sole, suggesting partridge, recommending a dessert, keeping an eye on everything, salting this, and sugaring that, he might well have said that he had All Paris at his table."

Him? Who is that him?

All right, Édouard Nignon!

Don't trouble to search your mind. You've never heard of him; you won't find his name in cookbooks; he isn't known in hotel schools, and no clubs have been founded to honor his name. Yet he was a great chef, a great writer about food, and all the Escoffiers and Montagnés are merely little boys compared to him. That's how life is. . . .

But it doesn't matter. Way up there, at the eternal banquet, if the serene Nignon leans over slightly to glance down upon us, he probably fastens his eye on Levallois-Perret, on a very ordinary little restaurant there, and on the owner-chef of that little restaurant.

Thus he is repaid, as it were, for all the disdain and the forgetfulness. For he, Nignon, is way up there.

And here, with us and with him, is Pierre Pointaire.

No one is considered a prophet in his own country. Pointaire is omitted from the *Michelin* and is little known to gourmets or so-called gourmets. Initiates know the happy way to his small restaurant, but the initiates of initiates are aware that behind the kitchen is the Pointaires'

152

special dining room—a provincial dining room, a lower-middle-class dining room that would have delighted the Naturalist novelists—such an ordinary dining room that it has its own juicy savor. That is where one goes to become truly acquainted with Pointaire's cuisine, having ordered the meal in advance.

There are two equally good ways of ordering a meal from a great chef: either one asks him for such and such a dish, prepared precisely as one would wish it to be, or one leaves the entire menu up to him. I have tried both possibilities with Pointaire on several occasions, and the results were always admirable.

Because I have talked endlessly about him, explaining that he, like me, admires Nignon to the point of fanaticism, and that he also has the kind of standards and precision that make true chefs, I have often been asked to organize dinners at Pointaire's.

I remember . . . No, I would rather describe the last meal I had there with four colleagues—three American friends and a friend who is a reporter for Radio-Geneva. They came there as explorers, somewhat as innocents.

"We're the barbarians," one American kept repeating, with a little smile that belied his words. . . .

The Swiss woman admitted that she was only one-quarter Swiss to one-quarter French to two-quarters Russian, which, she felt, lent a certain nobility to her appetite.

The Frenchwoman (for there was one with us!) admitted quite simply that she was a gourmand, exactly like the American, who proved it even more by constantly digging into each course with a pioneer's enthusiasm.

My good friend Martin Wess, perhaps more blasé—a friend of the dance and of bel canto—escaped the foods of this earth, at least in conversation. But valiant, nevertheless, in his use of his fork and his glass, he from time to time came out with some basic truths that clearly emerged from his soul as well as his stomach, and Madame Pointaire can now say how the word *extraordinaire,* pronounced with an American accent, is music to the ear of a good hostess!

I had ordered the following menu:

Souffléed sea urchins
Beuchelle à la Tourangelle
"Rosettes" of lamb Bordeaux
Frozen charlotte Sophie

Chez Pointaire
Dîner

Oursins soufflés
La beuchelle à la tourangelle
Rosettes d'agneau de Bordeaux
Charlotte glacée Sophie

The souffléed sea urchins, a creation of Pointaire's, were a Racinian masterpiece. The *beuchelle* and the lamb rosettes were adapted from Nignon.

I say "adapted" because that is how, with all honesty, one must describe the reconstruction of dishes of another period—for various reasons that would be too complicated to go into or even to outline here, but which are quite natural. In any case, cooking is almost always a rediscovery. Nignon himself, when perfecting his *beuchelle* (which he called "Tourangelle" because it was euphonious), admitted that he got the idea from an Austrian folk dish named *beuschell*. It was, in fact, a stew of common viscera: hearts, spleens, lungs (we have similar dishes in the French countryside—for example, *la sauce de pire* in Charentes, or the Basque *tripotcha*), which the imperial cook transposed, using noble viscera (sweetbreads and veal kidneys) and adding the nobility of truffles.

The charlotte Sophie, made with tangerine juice, was also one of Pointaire's creations. Thus both chefs' hats got equal points!

No matter. My guests stated categorically that not in Calvin's city of Geneva, or in New York, city of eight million inhabitants, or in the epicurean city of Paris, had anyone ever seen this! Had ever dined like this!

While we'd been drinking our apéritifs before the meal, I had heard the telephone ring and Madame Pointaire answer:

"Hello? So sorry, sir; we're booked for tonight."

"Hello? Yes, this is the Pointaire Restaurant. No, no, Madame, not tonight; we're all booked."

Those customers would have been very surprised had they come there to see. For as we left the dining room, I noticed that no one had sat at any of the tables in the empty restaurant. And when I asked why, I was told, "Sir, you see, a meal like that requires the chef's complete attention. The others wouldn't have been served properly. No, we refused all customers tonight and kept the kitchen for your friends."

That brought to mind a hairdresser in Castelnaudary who once had a sign on the door of his shop which amused Curnonsky. It read, "Closed because of a cassoulet."

So might Pointaire have hung a sign on his door reading, "The restaurant is closed because of a meal."

Recipes of Pierre Pointaire
Restaurant Chez Pointaire

SOUFFLÉED SEA URCHINS

To serve 4 persons

You need 12 large very fresh sea urchins, 1 live 1¼-pound lobster, 4 eggs, separated.

Prepare and cook the lobster *à l'américaine* (p. 263). Shell it completely.

To make the lobster sauce rather thick, bind it with 4 egg yolks. Dice the meat very finely and add it to the sauce. Keep for later use.

Open the sea urchins. Drain their water and lift the "tongues" with a teaspoon. Wash the shells, drain them well, dry them well, and butter them.

Beat the 4 egg whites into a firm snow. Fold this into the lobster sauce. Pour some of the resulting soufflé batter into each of the urchin shells so as to half-fill each of them. Top the batter with the urchin "tongues" and cover the tongues with more batter. Bake in a 400°F. oven.

(Notes: This beautiful recipe must unfortunately remain for the use of people living close to the seashore since the urchins must be consumed absolutely fresh and they do not take gracefully to freezing. Sea urchins are prevalent on all rocky coasts. The best are the green and black ones. If you cannot gather them yourself, there are specialized fish stores that will order them for you and open them for you. The tongues are the little coral-colored masses of roe that line the bottom of the shell. This is indescribably delicious eaten raw with the very light rye bread that the French bake especially for oysters and shellfish. When cooked, the tongues will taste somewhat like freshwater crawfish.

When you make the lobster à l'américaine, *reduce the sauce to 1 cup before adding the egg yolks; then cook the sauce as you would a custard, without boiling. Ed.)*

BEUCHELLE À LA TOURANGELLE

To serve 4 persons

You need 2 veal kidneys, 3 "heart" (the large lobe) sweetbreads, 5 ounces button mushrooms, 6 ounces dry Bordeaux wine (that is to say, ¾ cup Graves Blanc), ⅓ cup Fine Champagne or Armagnac, 1 table-spoon cornstarch or arrowroot, ⅔ cup heavy cream.

Blanch the sweetbreads very well in salted water containing a bit of lemon juice. Rinse under cold water. Dice the blanched sweetbreads.

Remove the outer membranes and all the fat from the veal kidneys.

Clean and wash the mushrooms, leaving them whole.

Have 3 different frying pans ready. Sauté the kidneys and flambé them with the Fine or Armagnac. Remove from the heat; keep ready for later use.

Sauté the sweetbreads without letting them take on any color.

Sauté the mushrooms without letting them color.

Drain all 3 ingredients very well and mix them in a bowl. Keep the deglazing of the kidneys; mix it with the white wine and bind with the starch diluted in 2 tablespoons of the cold cream. Add the remainder of the cream and, if at all possible, 1 fresh truffle very thinly sliced.

Coat the mixture of meats and mushrooms with the sauce and serve piping hot in a timbale.

(Notes: These remarks are for amateur chefs. As soon as the kidneys are cooked, remove them from the frying pan to a colander, but keep the juices in the frying pan to make the sauce. If the kidneys are left to wait in the pan, they continue cooking and ooze blood into the Armagnac used for flambéing. The end result is a grayish sauce which is too loose.

Also, since the mushrooms are apparently not to be browned, they will exude moisture; add it to the Armagnac. Add the mushrooms to the colander containing the kidneys. Proceed in the same manner with the sweetbreads. Finally assemble all the juices from the kidney and mushroom frying pans into the sweetbread frying pan and add the wine. Although M. Pointaire does not say to reduce the wine, probably it is obvious for him; it is recommended to reduce the mixture by half before adding the cream to eliminate the taste of raw natural wine in the finished sauce. Ed.)

"ROSETTES" OF LAMB BORDEAUX

To serve 4 persons

You need 1 saddle of lamb, 2 chicken cutlets, poached, 4 eggs, finely chopped *fines herbes,* a generous ½ pound of very fresh fine green beans, ⅔ cup heavy cream, 6 ounces dry Frontignan wine.

Lift the fillets and *filets mignons* from the saddle; cut the fillets into 12 *noisettes* which you will flatten slightly. Keep the *filets mignons* whole; remove all traces of fat and gristle.

Cut the poached white meat of chicken into a fine julienne (⅟₁₆ to ⅛ inch wide). Butter very generously a small savarin mold. Line it with the julienne of chicken. Beat the eggs as for an omelette with the *fines herbes*; pour the mixture into the mold. Cook, set in a hot-water bath, in a 300°F. oven, keeping the eggs soft. While the eggs cook, sauté the *noisettes* of lamb in butter; keep them aside until ready to serve.

Sauté the cooked green beans cut into 1-inch pieces in some butter and bind them with the cream.

Unmold the eggs onto a serving platter. Garnish the inside of the ring with the green beans. Set the *noisettes* on the border of the dish. Discard their cooking butter and deglaze the *sauteuse* with the wine (dry Frontignan or Banyuls). Add ¼ cup very fresh butter, shaking the pan back and forth over the heat to obtain a juice that will coat the meat lightly. Spoon over the meat. Sprinkle the meat with a touch of chopped parsley and serve very hot.

(Note: American heavy cream will not bind the vegetables unless it has been allowed to reduce by half first, or unless it is thickened with a pinch of potato starch. You may want to reverse the order of procedure given here and have the beans ready before you finish cooking the lamb since you want it to remain juicy pink. Ed.)

FROZEN CHARLOTTE SOPHIE

(Note: This is a large-quantity recipe, as made in the restaurant. Ed.)

You need 2 pounds sugar, 2¼ cups tangerine juice, 1 generous cup lemon juice (juice of 6 to 7 large lemons), 30 egg yolks, 2¼ cups heavy cream, a few peeled tangerines, 1¼ cups English cream (see p. 271).

Prepare a syrup by melting 1¼ pounds sugar with the tangerine juice. Add the grated rind of a few tangerines. Let cool, then mix with 20 egg yolks and thicken over medium heat as you would an English custard. Let cool again and fold in two thirds of the unsweetened heavy cream whipped to the "Chantilly" stage.

Prepare an identical custard with the remainder of the sugar dissolved in the lemon juice and the remaining 10 egg yolks; let cool, and fold in the remainder of the cream beaten as indicated above.

Freeze both parfait mixtures until frozen but still soft enough to handle. Freeze an ice-cream mold and line it evenly with the tangerine parfait mixture. Fill the center of the mold with the lemon parfait. Keep in the freezer overnight.

Peel the tangerines and remove all traces of white skins or membranes. Sugar the tangerine slices and macerate in Grand Marnier overnight.

Unmold the parfait. Coat with the chilled English cream. Decorate with the slices of tangerine and a few sliced toasted almonds.

(Note: Use a 5-quart ice-cream mold. Read the techniques of English cream on page 271 before setting out to make the parfaits. Creams made with 10 egg yolks per cup of liquid thicken much faster than the usual cream with only 3 egg yolks. Ed.)

The Battle of the Bouillabaisse

That year Marcel Pagnol's well-known play, *Marius,* had just been revived at the Théâtre Sarah Bernhardt (which has since been debaptized by a bunch of stupid apes). A. M. Julien, the director, had asked me to organize a dinner for the whole company and a few fellow journalists.

They simply *had* to gather around a bouillabaisse, I thought. And since Lucullus enjoyed dining at Lucullus's, I told myself that Pagnol's Marius ought to dine at . . . Marius's—in other words, at Marius et Janette's, since that was—and, Comus be praised, still is—the name of the most Provençal of all restaurants. It is located in the Alma district of Paris.

Alma . . . mater: that too was a kind of symbol, since Marcel Pagnol had at first been an insignificant English teacher.

So one evening at Marius et Janette's I awaited the actors who were playing in *Marius,* as well as its father, Marcel Pagnol—of the French Academy, the son of a gun! It was 7 o'clock.

At 7:05 the first of the actors arrived, the play's Caesar. He informed me that he was born in Marseilles, and that down there, to tell the truth, one ate bouillabaisse with potatoes.

At 7:10 the second arrived. He was conclusive: "A bouillabaisse, my boy, is a dish made to be eaten among friends!"

"Okay . . . But how do they prepare it where you live?"

"What do you mean? For friends, how else?"

At 7:15 Milly Mathis arrived, decked out like a schooner sailing into the old port of Marseilles, and told me: "I was born in Marseilles and I hope there'll be lots of croutons rubbed with garlic in the soup, because we real natives of Marseilles won't eat anything but the bread, understand? We like fish too much to eat it boiled."

At 7:22, interrupting an absolutely fascinating lecture by Milly Mathis (the play's Honorine) on true tomatoes *à la provençale* (which got us a little off the subject), there appeared Pagnol's Marius and Fanny. As both were native-born in the ancient Phocaean city, it goes without saying that on the question of bouillabaisse each had a final and quite diifferent opinion.

At 7:40 the last of the actors came in, Escartefigue, who assured me: "Like all true Marseilles actors, I'm from Toulon."

That complicated things, but it broadened my horizon to a point that young Marius would have envied. For if all the true Marseilles actors were actually from Toulon, where and how are true Marseilles bouillabaisses made?

Fortunately a gastronomist is never unprepared, and from my pocket I took Charles Monselet's little book entitled *La cuisinière poétique*. In it there is a long poem by the Marseilles poet Méry, which begins as follows:

> For fasting on Fridays, one day, an abbess
> From a convent in Marseilles invented bouillabaisse.
> And people have never since then been ungrateful . . .

It is a rich rhyme and would have been even richer had Méry written that the epicurean ecclesiastic had invented a *bouille-abbess*. But on to more of the poem:

> Indispensable to that flawless Phocaean dish,
> Indeed, it *must* include the savory hogfish,
> Which always feeds in each syrt and bog
> On the laurel and myrtle around bays clear of fog,
> Or on the blossoms of thyme that cover the rocks
> And flavor the flesh as well as the stocks.
> Then there are fish that feed far from the ships
> In the cracks of the reefs as they pucker their lips:
> Red mullet and breams in all their delicacy,
> The Saint-Pierre, the dorado, and the bass of the sea.
> Finally, the *galinette* with its wide popping eyes . . .

"Bravo, bravo!" applauded the thirsty guests. "Bravo, sir, you can read poetry without whining. But wouldn't we do better with a bit of real wining? Isn't it time for a white wine from Provence?"

It was produced.

After which, at 8:30, the hero of the evening, the smiling and witty Marcel Pagnol, arrived with his wife. We started with seafood. We talked warmly. In fact, I was as surrounded by Marseilles accents as a flower sweetened by bees in the summer sun. Then, finally, we were served the bouillabaisse.

"Horrors!" exclaimed the author of *Marius*. "There's spiny lobster in it!"

No gastronomist is caught short, even by an Academician. From another pocket I took another book, *La cuisine simple et anecdotique,* by someone whose name is very dear to me (my own, you can bet!), and read yet another poem (quoted on page 124, to be precise), this one by a certain Jacques Normand and entitled "La Bouillabaisse":

> Garlic . . . It needs a bit, if only for the principle of the thing,
> But very little, I tell you . . . Just a touch, a chime's ring.

I very nearly had to stop right there. All Marseilles and all Toulon lit into me by way of my guests, who indignantly assured me that that Normand was a foolish Norman, that we understood nothing at all about it, and that, really, garlic was as necessary to their national dish as air to living beings.

Once they had quieted down, I continued:

> Fish one must have, but fish of delicate zest,
> Spiny lobster, Saint-Pierre, and what's surely the best:
> Hogfish . . .

Never, no, never again, will I talk about bouillabaisse to natives of Marseilles. It's too dangerous!

Finally Marcel Pagnol agreed to explain to me how bouillabaisse originated as a fishermen's dish. The catch of the day was thrown into a cauldron, either on the beach or in their boats, and once the soup had boiled *(bouilli)*, they would ladle it down *(abaisser)* to their plates . . . Whence *bouille-abaisse*.

"You can well imagine, my dear fellow, that poor fishermen don't have the means to eat lobster. When they catch them, they sell them."

That was how I learned that bouillabaisse with spiny lobster is a Parisian dish.

But who cares? Parisians may sometimes have good taste. And, besides, that lobster . . . *They* ate it. All of them.

Recipes of the Restaurant
Marius et Janette

LA BOUILLABAISSE

You need 10 to 11 pounds of small fish for soup, 2¼ pounds conger eel, 2¼ pounds rockfish or wrasse, fennel flowers, powdered saffron, powdered ginger, powdered basil, 2¼ pounds fresh sun-ripened tomatoes, 6 heads of garlic, peppercorns, ⅓ cup olive oil, shallots.

Cooking times:

fish soup, 30 minutes
marination, 2 hours
bouillabaisse, 15 minutes over high heat

Prepare the fish soup first:
     In a copper kettle, sauté 4 finely minced shallots and the unpeeled
and crushed cloves of 3 heads of garlic. Add 5 seeded, crushed, very ripe
tomatoes, a few sprigs of fennel and a large *bouquet garni*. When all these
are nicely sautéed, add the small fish, the conger and the wrasse. Cover
with water; bring to a boil. Add a small tablespoon of saffron and let
cook. When the fish is well done, strain the soup through a sieve, pressing
on the fish remnants *until they are positively dry.*

Marinade:
     In another vessel, put some black hogfish, red mullets, gurnards,
weevers, a John Dory, red hogfish, conger eel, small squids cut into strips,
blue crabs, large black mussels and 2 thinly sliced potatoes. Sprinkle the
whole with coarsely grated pepper, coarse salt, chopped parsley stems,
thyme, laurel, fennel flowers with their stems, olive oil and a bit of saffron.
Mix well and let marinate for 2 hours.

Final cooking:
     In a large kettle, mix the marinated fish and the fish soup. Correct
the seasoning and cook over high heat for 15 minutes.
     Set the cooked fish on a large platter and pour the stock through a
fine strainer. Serve with slices of toasted bread rubbed with garlic and with
a large bowl of *rouille.*

P.S.—Rouille
     Mix crushed garlic, egg yolks, salt and pepper; thicken with olive oil
and flavor with saffron.
     *(Note: The recipe is a faithful reflection of the marvelous physical
and emotional heat, of the disorder and happiness, and of the color present
in a Marseilles kitchen when bouillabaisse is in progress. It is difficult, due
to lack of Mediterranean fish and herbs, and maybe also of temperament,
to prepare anything on our side of the Atlantic that will be the real bouillabaisse; an imponderable little something always seems to be missing.*
     *To make the fish soup, you may want to try a mixture of 5 pounds
ocean perch heads and bones; 2 pounds whiting heads and bones, 2 pounds
sea bass heads and bones and 2 pounds of gray sole or winter flounder*

heads and bones; use 2 whole heads of garlic, the cloves being left unpeeled but crushed under the flat of the knife blade.

The rouille should be made according to the mayonnaise recipe on page 260. Mix the egg yolks with 2 to 6 mashed garlic cloves according to personal taste. A solid pinch of cayenne will do no harm either. The reddish color is obtained by a solid addition of a purée of spicy peppers cooked gently in olive oil. The oil to use for the rouille should the virgin olive oil, greenish and fruity. Ed.)

OMELETTE NORVÉGIENNE (Baked Alaska)

To serve 6 persons

You need 4 egg yolks, 8 egg whites, 1 quart vanilla ice cream, ¼ pound homemade ladyfingers (see p. 23), Kirsch.

Beat the egg yolks and the egg whites separately and fold into each other. On an ovenproof platter, place a layer of ladyfingers well permeated with Kirsch. Put the ice cream on the ladyfingers and cover it with more ladyfingers also dipped into Kirsch. Coat the preparation with the Kirsch-flavored soufflé mixture; smooth with a spatula. Decorate with the remainder of the soufflé mixture elegantly piped through a pastry bag fitted with a rosette nozzle. Bake in a moderate oven until golden.

(Note: The author does not use any sugar in the soufflé mixture and does not specify how much Kirsch to use to flavor it. It may be a good idea to beat ⅓ cup sugar with the egg yolks and to flavor them with 2 to 3 tablespoons Kirsch. Beat the mixture until it spins a very heavy ribbon when falling from the beaters before folding in the egg whites. Ed.)

Lyons Chez Lasserre

I have already mentioned how faithful I am to Lyons, the capital of Good Eating.

I had just returned from Bocuse's restaurant and felt like seeing Lyons' ambassadors in Paris—by that I mean to say, her famous children. For some of them did "come up" to conquer the Capital.

If one wants to get natives of Lyons together, it must be around a table. So I chose Lasserre's.

There was the painter Touchagues, who decorated the well-known sliding roof of Lasserre; Michel Duran, the playwright and scriptwriter; the young actress, Julia Dancourt, and Mick Micheyl, singer and painter, mistress of ceremonies of the Casino de Paris revue, trapeze artist, and television producer—Mick Micheyl, I need say no more.

Lasserre had composed a remarkably Parisian menu for these natives of Lyons:

Seafood platter

Fillets of sole Walewska

Roast pheasant en volière

Pineapple "Club de la Casserole"

As he started to feast, Touchagues declared, "Personally, I'm for very simple Lyonese cuisine—in other words, hot sausages with steamed potatoes."

"Donkey-meat sausages or not donkey-meat sausages?"

"Ah, no! Pure pork sausages. Half-aged, three-quarters aged, or something like that. I don't remember exactly. It was the pork butcher's wife who said that. My mother used to send me out to market: 'Get a three-quarters sausage . . . ' "

Apropos of the pork butcher's wife, Touchagues liked to tell the story about the Lyonese shopkeeper who had been taken to see the Mediterranean by her pork-butcher husband. For the first time! When she saw

165

Chez Lasserre
Dîner Lyonnais à Paris

———

Plateau de fruits de mer

Filets de sole Waleska

Faisan rôti en volière

Ananas Club de la Casserole

that vast expanse of sea, she admitted that she was disappointed. "So *that's* the sea? But it's nothing but water!"

They returned to Lyons.

Then Touchagues came back to the hot sausages: "With steamed potatoes, not potatoes in oil, which in Paris they try to make us believe is Lyonese custom!

"What I also like is carp in red wine, with croutons rubbed with garlic. And boiled chicken. Or country-style *pot-au-feu,* the magnificent potful as they cook it in Saint-Cyr at the Mont d'Or, with veal knuckle and short ribs and as many carrots as you can get in. That's terrific!"

But I insidiously asked my question again: "Answer yes or no. Are sausages from Lyons made of donkey meat or aren't they?"

"Yes," said Mick Micheyl.

"No," guaranteed Touchagues.

"Uhh," muttered the others.

"I protest," continued Touchagues. "Sausages from Lyons are not what they think they are in Paris . . . Ah! There's also that big long sausage in silver paper, red, with little squares of fat in the middle. It's more or less eatable, by the way, but, no, it's not made of donkey . . ."

"Now, listen to me," argued Mick. "I know all about sausage. When I got my start in Paris, I couldn't give fancy presents, but still I wanted to thank my friends who'd been so great to me. So I'd bring them sausages from Lyons. But they were made of donkey."

"No," said Touchagues, "it was pork."

"Pork or maybe beef," someone said, to be conciliatory.

In any case, when people talk about Lyonese cuisine, the first things that come to mind are: sausages. And *quenelles!* Still, there are other things, thank God. There are *paquets* with cracklings and pig's tails and ears, and sautéed tripe, ideal of morning snacks. And cardoons!

"Cardoons in cream, they are good!"

"And in people's gardens they all have mufflers on, did you notice?"

"*Mufflers,* Mick?"

"Yes, yes, they have mufflers on. All the cardoons have mufflers on until . . . they're taken down to the cellar to be blanched, and after that they're cooked up with beef marrow . . ."

"Oh!" exclaimed Michel Duran, who is bald. "*I* put beef marrow on my head to make my hair grow."

"It's certainly better used on cardoons," said Touchagues with a sneer.

"You could put it on your head and then on the cardoons," said Mick Micheyl, who is practical. "Not many people know about cardoons, it's true, but still, they're wonderful. What about blood sausage?"

"Blood sausage comes from nearer the Beaujolais region. Beaujolais and Bresse make us very fancy presents," replied Touchagues.

"What about the *frites* on Mont Cindre?"

They all looked at Touchagues, who was born at the foot of that hump which the Lyonese climb for their Sunday stroll. On top of it there is a very beautiful chapel painted by Touchagues. It is mostly at Easter time that people go up there to eat the *frites,* french-fried potatoes cut in very thin strips.

The true *frites* are the Rhône fish fries. Those are good, too. . . .

"That's not true! They're the Saône fish fries!" proclaimed Mick Micheyl. "To fish for gudgeon, you walk in the water, then you scrape the bottom with your feet—like that—and the gudgeon come."

"The Rhône gudgeon are far more nervous," someone said.

For a moment there I thought I would have to separate the adversaries. Donkey meat or not donkey meat, Rhône gudgeon or Saône gudgeon . . . René Lasserre, in turn, took the floor.

"I don't quite agree with all of you, and especially not with Touchagues when he says, 'I see Lyonese cuisine as absolutely simple.' Because Lyonese cuisine deserves its title of nobility. It's *the* great classic cuisine, par excellence. . . . The chicken 'in half-mourning' is itself permeated with subtlety."

Touchagues broke in, "Yes, but the great Lyonese restaurants were first run by women. In other words, our cooking is above all home cooking, cooked by women and not by chefs, with all their rules and things like that. . . ."

"In fact, it's the kind of cooking you watch other people do." That was the case with Mick Micheyl. She doesn't know how to cook except for a few specialties. "Eggs in red wine, for instance. Ah! There I can hold my own as well as anybody!"

A new argument began. Touchagues thought the dish had to have onions in it. Mick put in garlic. I, again insidiously, asked if she added chocolate to it to thicken the sauce (that's been done).

"Chocolate? But it's not a dessert!"

"It's scrambled eggs in wine."

"No, not at all, it's . . . it's a kind of jugged eggs, that's it!"

"Then you put blood in it?"

"No! I don't put blood in it. Where in the world would I find eggs' blood?"

"But you put blood in jugged hare, you cluck . . ."

"But I didn't say I knew how to make jugged hare," Mick said angrily. "I said I made eggs in wine. And they're very good, so there!"

With the roast pheasant *en volière* we were drinking a Château Cheval Blanc of a great year. Naturally we talked about Beaujolais, the blood of the Lyonese. Again I thought of Henri Béraud: "When we were a bunch of brats in Lyons, we drank Beaujolais, as is the venerable custom, in a small café where the empty glasses remained on the table, so that, between them and the green bottles, we were behind lovely bars, through which the drinkers exchanged handshakes, swore friendship, and made remarks filled with wisdom."

Because in Lyons one not only drinks the lightest possible wine of the year, but drinks it very cool, which in itself is wisdom. Lasserre then told us the story of the mayor of Lafayette, Indiana, who would put ice in a great red wine. "Since that's how you drink it, I'm going to give you some Beaujolais!" he told his customer. And the mayor had a real treat. He even commented, "You drink it very cool and then you get very hot, don't you?"

And to think that there are still wine stewards who are proud of their profession and dare serve warm wine to tourists!

"Were you a gourmand when you were little?" Mick asked Touchagues.

"I was very much of a gourmand and I loved my grandmother's soup. She made Lyonese soup. Every Thursday I'd race over to her place to eat her soup. It was a feast. . . ."

Mick immediately started extolling bread soup: "Oh! Bread soup, that's what's good! Not all that elegant, but it's good. . . . I'm not much of a gourmand, but when I go to Lyons, I try to spend a few days with my parents. Some time ago I said to Mom, 'Why don't you make me pigs' feet?' Fine. Mom was delighted to please me and served me pigs' feet. Once, twice, three times, four times. . . . After ten days of them—it was rare, but that time I stayed two weeks because I was doing some painting there. I say that with my eye on Touchagues, but it's true; I was preparing my exhibition—anyway, after ten days of them I told Mom, 'Listen, I love pigs' feet, but enough is enough!' It was true! Counting them up, it made ten plus ten—twenty pigs' feet that she served me!"

On that conclusive statistic we finished our coffee, but not before Touchagues took the responsibility of giving the following definition, worthy of a gourmand painter: "Lyonese cuisine is very golden, isn't it? Very golden . . ."

Recipes of René Lasserre
Chez Lasserre

FILLETS OF SOLE WALEWSKA

To serve 4 persons

Fillet 2 soles each weighing 1¼ to 1½ pounds. Flatten the fillets; season them with salt and pepper from the mill; fold them.

With the heads and bones of the fish, prepare a classic fish *fumet* (p. 250). Put the fillets in a heavily buttered *sauteuse*; add the prepared fish *fumet* and ½ cup dry white wine. Cover with a buttered parchment paper. Bring to a boil over direct heat, then finish cooking in a 400°F. oven for 12 to 15 minutes.

Drain the fillets of sole; remove them to a round platter, arranging them in a crown. Keep warm. Top each fillet with a small slice of cooked lobster lightly sautéed in butter.

Strain the cooking juices of the sole into a saucepan containing a scant cup of heavy cream mixed with ½ cup of sauce Mornay (p. 257). Reduce over high heat, stirring constantly with a spatula until the sauce coats the spatula to a thickness of ⅙ inch; remove from the heat. Spoon the sauce on the fillets of sole and glaze in a very hot oven. Fill the center of the platter with a ragout of diced lobster, shelled shrimps and minced mushrooms bound with a cardinal sauce (p. 257). Just before serving top each lobster slice with a slice of truffle coated with melted butter.

(Note: After making the fish fumet, *there will be much more than is necessary to prepare this dish. To cook the soles, use the same amount of fish* fumet *as you should use of white wine, that is to say ½ cup. Also, even if the fillets of sole have been well drained, they will lose more moisture while waiting for the sauce to be ready. Absorb it with paper towels before you spoon the sauce over the fillets or your beautiful sauce will become thin and flat. The best shrimps for the ragout in the United States are Maine Red shrimps, or the San Francisco Bay tiny shrimps. All elements of the garnish should be sautéed lightly in a bit of butter before being added to the cardinal sauce. Ed.)*

ROAST PHEASANT EN VOLIÈRE

To serve 4 persons

You need one beautiful young pheasant weighing 3 to 3¼ pounds and with a pretty plumage, ⅔ cup butter, 5 ounces unsalted fatback sheets to tie around the bird while roasting it, 2 ounces liver mousse, 1 bunch of watercress, 4 croutons cut out of white bread and fried in butter, 1 tea loaf of white bread with crust completely removed, salt and pepper.

Keep the feathers from the pheasant's tail and its head. Use the tea loaf of white bread to simulate the body of the bird. Take small wooden sticks (strong food picks); spear one end of the sticks into the bread and the other into the feathers and the head of the bird so that the whole construction resembles a pheasant; this is called a *volière*.

After you pluck, clean and singe the pheasant, season it inside and outside; wrap it in sheets of fatback; tie the sheets of fatback around the bird with 2 kitchen strings placed 2 inches from each other

Put the pheasant in a roasting pan with the butter and roast in the oven for 40 minutes; baste often with the cooking butter.

As soon as the pheasant is cooked, remove the strings and fatback. Spread the butter-fried croutons with the liver mousse; heat the croutons briefly in the oven, then set the pheasant on the croutons at the center of a large serving platter.

Defatten the cooking juices of the bird and deglaze them with a few tablespoons of water. Decorate the dish with bundles of watercress and the *volière*. Serve very hot with the plain cooking juices of the bird.

PINEAPPLE "CLUB DE LA CASSEROLE"

The pineapple "Club de la Casserole" is a sherbet served in the shells of the pineapple itself. Each pineapple should be cut lengthwise into halves; spoon out the pulp, leaving a thickness of about ¼ inch of pulp attached to the shell.

To serve 4 persons

Use 2 small very fresh pineapples. Remove the leaves.

Weigh the pulp; you should have about 1 scant pound of it; set aside one quarter of that pulp, dice it very finely, and macerate it in Kirsch or Maraschino.

To the remainder of the pineapple pulp, which should be about ¾ pound, add the same weight of sugar (1¼ cups), the juice of 1 lemon and a bit of warm water, just enough to allow the sugar to melt.

When the sugar has melted, pound the mixture to obtain as fine a texture as possible. Strain the mixture through a fine sieve or a fine conical strainer, pressing as much as possible to squeeze all the juices out. The juices should now present the appearance of a rather heavy syrup.

Bring the syrup to measure exactly 17 degrees on the saccharometer by adding again and very gradually a bit of hot water; mix well. Put the syrup in the container of an ice-cream machine and let the machine work until you obtain a light sherbet which is neither thick nor granular.

Spoon the sherbet into the pineapple half shells. Spoon over each portion an equal amount of the macerated diced pineapple and a few brandied cherries. Slide 3 *langues de chat* between sherbet and shell on one side of each shell.

(Note: A pineapple sherbet closely resembling that of Lasserre's can be obtained by using 1½ cups sugar melted in 1⅓ cups warm water mixed with the juice of 1 lemon and 2 cups of fresh pineapple pulp blended in the electric blender to a uniform purée. Ed.)

With Maurice at the Meurice

It was through the writer Paul Léautaud that I first met Florence Gould. In his *Journal littéraire,* under Monday, November 22, 1943, he wrote:

> Well! I don't at all regret having gone to that lunch at Mme. Gould's. She clings to you when she talks to you; she's pretty—about thirty-five, brown hair, tall, slim, supple, gracefully slender, in an old-fashioned long skirt, more elegant than today's styles—she has curious eyes. At one point during coffee, she was sitting next to me, and since I was talking about cats, my favorite animal, she said, with her face close to mine, "*I* have cats' eyes, look." Curious eyes, as I said before, which resemble a cat's, a female cat's; they have a kind of languor and amorous warmth. . . .

From that date on, the admirable misanthropist Paul Léautaud was a devoted guest at the lunches given by Florence Gould, who received "all of literature" at her apartment on the avenue Malakoff. He used to feast on a "sublime" chocolate cake, and since I wanted the recipe for it, I wrote to the lady. And, although I still do not have the secret recipe for that sweet so dear to Léautaud, I was her guest on at least several occasions.

Originally from Bayonne, she married an American, Frank Jay Gould, who was the heir of a pioneer in American railroads. (It is said that he fought a duel with a rival, also in railroads, each one standing atop a locomotive.) A millionaire and a widow, Florence Gould divided her time between the spa La Roche Posay, where she took the waters, and the Hôtel Meurice in Paris, and her villa, Le Patio, near Cannes, surrounded by her collection of Dresden china, Italian Renaisssance vases, and paintings by Toulouse-Lautrec, Corot, Gauguin, Van Gogh, Bonnard, Sisley, etc. She is still a kind of adorable patron of letters. Carrying her literary salon around with her (as Proust's Madame Verdurin carried her "little nucleus"), using the charming majordomo Jean Denoël as a Father Joseph, Florence Gould has received for thirty years.

She had her "Wednesdays" at the Meurice. I shall long remember the last lunch I went to, on October 13, 1971, not that the menu was more astonishing than the others, but because it was Maurice Chevalier's last lunch "in town."

When I arrived at Florence Gould's apartment, there were a few of her "regular" Academicians on duty: Marcel Jouhandeau ("Jouhandeau, who never leaves the house," noted Léautaud even back in 1944), the actress Arletty, Maurice Escande of the Comédie Française, and *the* Maurice—Maurice Chevalier. The latter, sitting in an armchair, was chatting with the wonderful Arletty, while Félix Paquet—his devoted friend right to the end—kept a fond eye on him, although it seemed to me that his gaze was tinged with anxiety.

Monopolizing the elevators, we all went down to a small dining room, where the following menu was awaiting us:

Spiny lobster en Bellevue

Noisettes of venison grand veneur

Chestnut purée

Artichoke bottoms Clamart

Shepherdess salad

Peach Melba

I was seated next to Félix Paquet, but Jouhandeau, who was on the other side of Maurice Chevalier, had to admit later on, over a Radio-Luxembourg microphone, that he had found his old friend (they had known each other for half a century) less sparkling than usual, conversing without much verve. Perhaps he thought, seeing the spiny lobster *en Bellevue,* that the word sounded somewhat like Belleville, his native village, and that the dish is also called *à la parisienne.* A dish from home, as it were!

In the great culinary quarrel between those who support lobster and those who support spiny lobster, it would seem that spiny lobsters are the best when prepared as a cold dish, as these were. Perhaps because their long, thin legs and even longer antennae lend themselves more effectively to decoration. Or is it because chefs sometimes enjoy overdecorating them, playing with truffles, tomato skins, parsley curls, and heaven knows what?

As for the shepherdess salad, I looked it up in vain in the dictionary *Répertoire de la cuisine.* When I consulted the Meurice's chef, he at first got someone to tell me very stupidly that it was a "mixed salad." I had to persist in order to discover (and I must admit I hadn't remembered it) that it was a mixture of lettuce, escarole, corn salad, and . . . watercress. The watercress, it would appear, is what made it a "shepherdess" salad.

Déjeuner offert par
Madame Florence Gould
à l'Hôtel Meurice
le 13 Octobre 1971

••••

Langouste en Bellevue
Noisettes de chevreuil grand veneur
Purée de marrons
Fonds d'artichauts Clamart
Salade bergère
Pêche Melba

But here are a few useful bits of advice concerning the chestnut purée.

To begin with, one has a choice between *marrons* or chestnuts, which must be well curved on the two main sides (whereas the other variety, *châtaignes*, are flat and also far more difficult to peel). And one chooses chestnuts with shiny, light brown, very taut skins.

Then comes the peeling. I recommend one method which takes longer than some but is by far the most reliable. Make a gash in each chestnut. Place ten at a time in a large pot, cover them with cold water, and boil them over a high flame for one minute. Remove the pot from the burner and quickly peel the chestnuts while they are still boiling hot; both skins are thus easily removed. Continue the process until all the chestnuts are peeled.

Now this is how to prepare the purée: You need about two pounds of chestnuts for every four servings. Once they are peeled, place them in a pot with one quart of bouillon, one pint of water, and a stalk of celery. Put over a high flame, and when the mixture comes to a boil, lower the flame, cover, and simmer for forty-five minutes. Force through a food mill. Place the purée in a skillet and, over a low flame, stir with a wooden spatula until smooth, while it thickens through evaporation. Then keep the purée warm in a double boiler.

Just before serving, while it is still in the double boiler, add two tablespoons of butter, small bits at a time, and stir with the spatula. Remove from heat, add salt, pepper, and about three ounces of cream, and serve.

Everyone knows that artichoke bottoms Clamart are garnished with peas, in memory of the days when admirable peas were grown in that suburb of Paris.

Last came the peach Melba, named after Madame Melba, the Australian opera singer to whom, after a performance of *Lohengrin* at Covent Garden in London, Escoffier served poached peaches over vanilla ice cream, covered with fresh raspberry purée, presented on a swan of carved ice. The poached peaches were also fresh and came from Montreuil, near Paris. Melba's was surely the peach that Victor Hugo described in the following rhyme:

> Its charms richly pleased one's sight
> And everyone knew its taste was right.
> Such skin, as to be beyond one's reach,
> Like rose and lily joined in bliss
> It might have been proud Philis
> If, indeed, it hadn't been a peach.

But what a pity the Meurice's chef, highly improperly, added slivered almonds to that simple and great dessert.

Recipes for Florence Gould's Luncheon at the Hôtel Meurice

SPINY LOBSTER EN BELLEVUE

To serve about 4 persons

Immerse a 2¼-pound spiny lobster in boiling salted water and let cook for 25 minutes. Let it cool in the cooking water. Drain the lobster.

Remove the meat from the tail without damaging the shell. Cut the tail into medallions. Set the empty shell on a large platter, the feelers pointing backward at a 45-degree angle. Set the medallions on the tail of the lobster; decorate each medallion with a small triangle of truffle and coat it with aspic (p. 253). Surround the lobster with 4 hard-cooked eggs cut into halves and filled with Russian salad (p. 266) bound with mayonnaise and the mashed hard-cooked egg yolks.

NOISETTES OF VENISON GRAND VENEUR

The *noisettes* should be cut from the fillet of the venison saddle. They should be thickish (¾ inch) and weigh around 2½ ounces each.

Marinate the *noisettes* for 3 to 4 hours. The marinade consists of white wine, oil and vinegar, and is flavored with a carrot, a thinly sliced onion and parsley stems (see the complete list of ingredients and procedure on p. 265). Drain the *noisettes* after marination, pat them dry, season them with salt and pepper, and panfry them in butter, keeping them rare.

Serve them on a hot platter coated with the Grand Veneur sauce and present the remainder of the sauce in a sauceboat.

Grand Veneur sauce:

Heat ⅓ cup oil; add 1 carrot and 1 large onion, each cut into fine *brunoise,* a few chopped parsley stems, a sprig of thyme and 1 bay leaf. When these ingredients have browned to a nice golden color, add 2 finely chopped shallots and let cook over low heat for another 3 minutes without letting the shallot color at all.

Discard the cooking oil; add a good ½ cup of wine vinegar and ⅓ cup of dry white wine. Bring to a boil and reduce by half. To the reduction add a brown sauce prepared with 2½ tablespoons each of butter and flour cooked to a brown *roux* and moistened with 2½ cups brown stock. Bring to a boil and simmer for 1 hour, skimming from time to time. Strain the sauce through a fine sieve or conical strainer. Add ⅔ cup of the marinade and continue reducing the sauce over low heat until about 2 cups are left.

Whisk into the sauce ¼ cup unsalted butter divided into small nuggets and 3 to 4 tablespoons of hare blood mixed with the same amount of marinade. Cook together for 5 minutes. Strain and serve.

(Note: Only hunters would be able to use the blood of a true hare. They should proceed as follows. Hang the hare for 2 days in a cool place, not a very cold or freezing one. Skin the hare, then rupture the upper abdominal membrane and collect the blood in a cup containing ½ teaspoon of vinegar to prevent coagulation on contact with the cold air. Some hares have no available blood; this is due to the fact that they were shot through the lungs instead of the head or heart.

Cooks who would not for diverse reasons use hare blood can transform the sauce into a simple poivrade sauce by adding a scant teaspoon of coarsely cracked fresh black peppercorns to the sauce during the last 10 minutes of cooking after the ⅔ cup of marinade has been added. The addition of butter should be 6 tablespoons instead of 4. Ed.)

CHESTNUT PURÉE

Peel a generous pound of chestnuts. Blanch them to remove their second skin. Cook them slowly in salted water seasoned with 2 sprigs of fresh celery for 40 minutes. Drain. Strain through a sieve. Lighten the resulting purée with 2 tablespoons or so of heavy cream. Salt and pepper.

ARTICHOKE BOTTOMS CLAMART

Cut the stems and remove the outer leaves of small very fresh artichokes. Peel their bottoms as you would a potato and leave the straw at the center. Rub each artichoke with a slice of lemon.

Moisten 2 tablespoons flour with 1 generous quart of cold water; season with salt, pepper and the juice of 1 lemon. Bring to a boil, add the artichoke bottoms, and cook them until the straw can be easily pulled off.

Remove the straw and fill the artichoke bottoms (one or two per guest) with peas *à la Française.*

Peas *à la Française* are cooked covered with just a bit of water, butter, small white onions, a head of soft-leaved lettuce and a *bouquet* of fresh parsley and chervil.

PEACH MELBA

To serve 4 persons

Melt ¾ cup of sugar in ⅔ cup of water; bring to a boil and reduce the heat to keep the syrup at a simmer.

Choose 4 large beautiful white peaches; peel them very carefully. Poach the peaches in the syrup, keeping them a bit firm. Let them cool in the syrup.

Put 4 large scoops of French vanilla ice cream in 4 champagne goblets. Top each scoop of ice cream with 1 peach, drained and pitted.

Mash ⅓ pound of fresh raspberries and add a bit of Kirsch. Coat each peach with 3 or 4 tablespoons of the mixture.

A Weird Meal

To begin with, what—in regard to cuisine—does "weird" mean? (The word in French, weird in itself, is *insolite*. Ed.)

"My child," said the writer Jacques Chardonne to me one day, "all dishes have seemed weird to me." And to Joseph Delteil peach Melba is weird because "a peach on the tree is so good!"

All the same, to anyone accustomed to swallows' nests or caiman stew, steak and french-fried potatoes are perhaps weird.

When I asked a friend, he answered, "Weird—anything that is unusual, against the rules. I keep away from it!" Whereas another friend, a great traveler, assured me, "China got me in the habit of never finding anything on a plate weird."

Yet Chinese cuisine has come to seem less weird (perhaps because these last years it has become so widespread) than other types, and I personally have never tasted dog-meatballs on tobacco leaves, dipped in the Ganges at Benares, which seemed so to delight Paul Guimard, author of the novel *Les choses de la vie*.

But is there any need for going so far away?

We all know the saying: "In 1870 the French were compelled to eat rats, because in '69 they had gobbled up all the cats!" In fact, during the siege of Paris, weird meals were almost a daily occurrence; one has only to read the Goncourts' *Journal*. The Little Culinary Museum on the ground floor of the Tour d'Argent exhibits the following menu, dated December 25, 1870—the ninety-ninth day of the siege—which is a whole digest of them:

Stuffed donkey head
Elephant consommé
Roast camel English style
Jugged kangaroo
Roast ribs of bear with pepper sauce
Haunch of wolf with venison sauce
Cat flanked by rats
Terrine of antelope with truffles

Menu parisien du 25 Décembre 1870
au Petit Musée de la Table
à la Tour d'Argent

◆

Tête d'âne farçie
Consommé d'éléphant
Chameau rôti à l'anglaise
Civet de Kangourou
Côtes d'ours rôties sauce poivrade
Cuissot de loup sauce chevreuil
Chat flanqué de rats
Terrine d'antilope aux truffes

That was because all the animals in the Bois de Boulogne Zoo had just been sold to the English butcher, Roos, on the Boulevard Haussmann. Roos had put (according to the Goncourts) "lots of onions in a blood sausage made of the bounteous blood of Polux, the Zoo's elephant."

But in 1972 anyone who feasted on bear, crocodile, or elephant did so not out of hunger but out of eccentricity. And thanks, most particularly, to Paul Corcellet.

Around 1780 Hilaire Germain Chevet, a gardener in a suburb of Paris, created a rose: the *chevette*. Madame de Lamballe, at the Court of Versailles, used them to adorn her headdresses, and Marie Antoinette, who noticed them, became the gardener's patron. She entrusted him with the planting of all the flowers around her Trianon, and later on, when she was imprisoned in the Temple, those who hoped to help her escape hid their messages in Chevet's bouquets.

The Revolution ruined Chevet, though it left him just enough to buy a little shop on the Palais Royal gardens and to become a greengrocer. Under the Empire and then the Restoration, the House of Chevet, specializing in fancy foods, was very fashionable. Talleyrand got his sturgeon and truffled pâtés there, Balzac his exotic fruits.

In 1850 a son of the Chevets married a Mademoiselle Corcellet. A descendant of that young woman, herself a native of Savoie, founded the House of Corcellet at 46, rue des Petits-Champs, to which gourmet enthusiasts came with the idea of reliving the splendors of the House of Chevet.

Paul Corcellet is a curious man. I shouldn't be at all surprised if he were even a bit mad! What else can one think these days of a businessman who would rather give his merchandise away to those who appreciate it than sell it to a bunch of dimwits?

Paul Corcellet began by stocking his shop with all the best products: spirits, seasonings, fruit, etc. . . . It was quality that interested him above all. That led him to launch into very rare products, which is not a far step from very weird products. In France an elephant's trunk prepared *en daube* and a simmered python stew are not readily available. Just procuring the basic ingredients used to be difficult. Preserving them was even more so. A passionate researcher, Corcellet immediately became interested in the process of freezing food. To put the world in our plates, he made use of the most modern techniques. From that time on, although depending on distant hunting possibilities and unreliable deliveries, one was able to buy extremely rare dishes on the rue des Petits-Champs and to prepare rather unexpected meals.

It was to a meal of that sort that I invited a few friends one evening. Among them was a young actress who, a few hours later, was to perform on stage with Pierre-Jean Vaillard. Albert Simonin was also there.

I had chosen a restaurant and had brought Paul Corcellet's products, along with instructions for preparing them. The menu included the following:

Bear pâté

Python stew

Caiman tail à l'américaine

Hippopotamus daube

Elephant's trunk

Chocolate-covered termites

"I wouldn't eat snake for anything in the world!" wailed the actress Josyane Lonzac when I had described the meal.

She therefore watched one course after another with a suspicious eye. Still, the bear pâté went over very well.

"What now?" asked the blond child as the python stew was being served.

"It's shark from Tananarive!" I answered.

She tasted it. We all tasted it. She swallowed with difficulty, although she admitted that it wasn't "so bad as all that!" Then we went on to the caiman.

"Actually," said Josyane, "it's crocodile, isn't it?"

"Unless," said Simonin, "it's alligator."

"Who cares!" said Pierre-Jean Vaillard. "Alligator or crocodile, it's surreptiliously the same thing!"

Nevertheless, the saurian did not go over all that well. Nor did the hippopotamus *daube*. On the other hand, the elephant's trunk provoked great enthusiasm from the group: "It tastes like beef tongue!" It did indeed seem almost a normal thing to eat, which shows how taste is purely a matter of habit.

As for the termites, at first no one would believe they weren't just chocolate candies. I'd offered them as such. Still, no one was really feasting on them, and Josyane did comment that my chocolates must have been bought on sale. When I confessed that they were ground-up termites, rolled in a chocolate covering, my guests were willing to agree that they were "different" and that, after all, my candies were pretty good. They had seconds, but then their imaginations went to work and put a stop to both their appetites and their gluttony. "We'll give what's left to the stagehands!" said Josyane sweetly.

Un Repas Insolite
(Produits de la Maison Paul Corcellet)

—

Pâté d'ours
Ragoût de python
Queue de caïman à l'américaine
Daube d'hippopotame
Trompe d'éléphant
Termites au chocolat

—

A half-hour later, when she was standing behind the set about to walk on stage to confront Pierre-Jean Vaillard, I whispered to her: "You know, that shark we ate . . . Well, it was really python!"

Then I returned to my seat, hoping for a real drama.

There was none. Nevertheless, the audience found the young actress a bit pale that evening, and her partner, watching the odd contractions of her throat, wondered for quite a while whether she was going to throw away her lines or throw up her python stew.

Afterward I asked Paul Corcellet for his weird recipes. He sent me the following text. It is not altogether clear, but he probably wanted to keep some of his secrets. And besides, I doubt that you would have much opportunity to serve such food to your guests.

Recipes of Paul Corcellet

BEAR PÂTÉ

Marinate the meat from several days in good-quality red wine with the spices usually entering the composition of a marinade. Proceed then as for a hare pâté.

PYTHON STEW

Remove the skin. Cut the snake into chunks and flour them lightly. Brown in a frying pan; flambé with Armagnac. Add a generous amount of smothered onions, shallots and tomatoes flavored with thyme and bay leaf. Add a bit of cayenne. Cook for about 6 hours.

ALLIGATOR TAIL

Prepare as you would a lobster *à l'américaine,* the only difference being that it should be floured before being braised.

HIPPOPOTAMUS

It is a curious animal. All its flesh is surrounded by a tight net of nerves resembling piano wires. It should, as a consequence, be carefully denerved. Hippopotamus is to be prepared as a *daube*. Brown the meat. Moisten with sherry wine; add lardoons, onions, mushrooms, thyme, bay leaf and a few Málaga raisins. Cook in a slow oven for 6 hours.

ELEPHANT'S TRUNK

Wash the skin very carefully. Cut the trunk into chunks.

Start cooking in cold water with the herbs usually used to cook turtles or terrapins. Add salt and pepper. The cooking time is 16 (sixteen) hours.

The meat can be enjoyed with the strained bouillon flavored with a glass of sherry or with a mustard sauce or a green sauce. The skin, of course, must be discarded.

TERMITES

I purchase them toasted. I blend them into some praline and coat them with chocolate.

Meet Me at the Archestrate

Raymond Castans, author and adapter of many plays, is also a poet. Poetry, in real life, may sometimes be called "uncertainty."

We had agreed to dine together. He'd told me the day he was free. The evening before, he had someone ring me up to cancel the dinner. We had a great deal of trouble arranging another date, but finally we managed it.

"Next Tuesday, the eighth, at eight-thirty. I absolutely guarantee it!"

At the time, *Plaza Suite* (translated into French as *Rendez-vous au Plaza,* or *Meet Me at the Plaza*), the Neil Simon comedy, adapted by Castans, was being performed in Paris. Just for local color, I could easily have invited him to the new Régence restaurant at the Plaza. But the cuisine there is so insipid, and the service so stiff and strained, and the atmosphere so terribly anti-epicurean, that I'd preferred the Archestrate.

Archestratos was a Greek cook, none of whose writings are extant. That is perhaps fortunate, since he may therefore be given credit for every talent you can name.

The talents of, for example, the young chef Alain Senderens!

Senderens is a cook of great imagination and intelligence, which is rather rare in his profession. Moreover, he knows how to read! His peers, and more especially his elders, have never gone beyond Escoffier and Montagné and have read only the comic strips (mind you, I didn't say they understood them). *He* reasons. *He* does not believe that cuisine got its start with Carême. *He* told himself that between Archestratos, who perhaps cooked for Lucullus, and Talleyrand, who feasted on Carême's cuisine, there were surely gourmets and gourmands, as well as chefs to make them feasts. So he consulted all the books on the subject. And he realized that if one has arrived too late in a world that is too old, one can no longer "invent" cuisine; one must rediscover it, re-create it!

As a result, Senderens came to the conclusion that Solomon's *Nil novi sub sole,* like the humble truth of the French Legion's marching song

187

("When you take to the highroads, don't ever forget / That your elders did it before you, on that you can bet"), could be applied to recipes in the most ancient of works, headed up by *Le viandier,* or *The Meat Book.* The exact title of that well-known *Viandier* reads: *Hereinafter Follows the Meat Book, Showing How to Dress All Manner of Meat, which Taillevent, Chef in the Service of the King, our Sire, Wrote, with Instruction on Trimming and Dressing Boiled Cookery, Roasts, Fish from the Sea and from Sweet Water, Sauces, Spices, and Other Things Conceivable and Necessary as Hereinafter Shall Be Said* . . . It was first printed in 1490.

Astonishing cuisine at a time known for its obscurantism. And one soon comes to realize that, on the contrary, the cooks then were inspired, bold, and had genius, and that their cuisine, as compared to ours, was revolutionary! Senderens had only to read (again, one must at least know how to read, gentlemen), transpose, adapt, and draw inspiration in order to bridge the gap and serve us, in 1972, a cuisine far in advance of our time because it was centuries old!

It was to that man and to that cuisine that I wanted to introduce Castans—and to perform for him my "Meet me at the Archestrate."

We arrived at eight-thirty.

At eight forty-five we ordered a glass of port for her, a glass of sherry for me. Just waiting.

At nine o'clock Senderens came to our table. "Would you like to see the menu while waiting?"

We would. All the more so because Senderens' menu is a little master-piece of typography.

"Well, well," I said, "there are snails in chicken fricassee."

"What's that?"

I explained that Senderens had picked up the recipe from Menon's *Souper de la cour,* which had been published in 1755. It was thus a more than bicentennial dish that rejuvenated the menu of the perceptive young chef: one no longer creates cuisine; one re-creates it.

"Yes, but the turnips braised in cider are tempting . . ."

"Obviously!"

"Mmm, it makes one hungry!"

In fact, what was making us hungry was the time—nine-thirty. And still no Castans! Had he misunderstood? Did he think in terms of his play and believe I had said, "Meet me at the Plaza"?

"What would you say," I suggested, to change the subject, "to a zephyr of sole?"

"I've heard of that. It's one of Édouard Nignon's creations, isn't it?"

It was indeed a dish of Édouard Nignon—the great chef of the nineteenth century who is so little known today. Whereas everyone extols the Escoffiers and Montagnés, those gravediggers of French cuisine, they forget that brilliant and subtle master chef who is quite rightly admired by Pointaire and Senderens. But they are (almost) alone in their admiration!

Nine forty-five!

Senderens took pity on us and brought us a beautiful slice of foie gras with toast, a way of verifying the old saying that "if you sit down at the table, the latecomer will arrive."

The adage lied. Castans never came that evening (he had quite simply noted down the wrong date).

And it was ten o'clock when we finally began the following meal:

Stuffed turnips braised in cider

Zephyr of sole Édouard Nignon

Courtinandise

Grandmother's desserts

Actually, since our hunger had been appeased by the foie gras, we'd ordered only the turnips and zephyr of sole. But then Senderens mysteriously brought us a huge stewpot.

"What's that?"

"That is the Courtinandise!"

"Wouldn't you say it was more a matter of courting to please?"

"Not in the least. I had an idea; then I told myself that you'd like my dish. I was daring enough to name it after you, but not to put it on my menu without your permission."

After I tasted it, my permission was given. The Courtinandise is precisely the kind of dish I like: simple, hearty, yet carefully conceived, refined, and ennobled by the chef's creative intelligence.

I might add that the dish is made with champagne and that I am among those who believe that champagne adds wit to cuisine.

So from then on, I knew that when I said, "Meet you at the Archestrate," I was meeting not only a friend but a dish: the Courtinandise.

L'Archestrate
Dîner

———— · ————

Navets farcis braisés au cidre
Zéphir de sole Edouard Nignon
La Courtinandise

Les desserts de grand-mère :
Brioche mousseline
Mousse au chocolat
Oeufs à la neige crème anglaise

Recipes of Alain Senderens
L'Archestrate

STUFFED TURNIPS BRAISED IN CIDER

To serve 4 persons

Use about 1½ pounds round white turnips. Peel and blanch the turnips. Hollow them out with a melon-ball cutter. Cook the turnip balls in salted water to make a purée. Purée them through a fine strainer and set aside for later use. Sauté the hollowed-out turnips in a mixture of half olive oil and half butter until they turn light golden; salt and pepper them.

Meanwhile reduce ½ bottle of dry cider. Add the turnips to the pot and add enough veal stock to cover. Bake in the oven for 15 minutes or longer depending on the quality of the turnips. Add the turnip purée to the braising stock to thicken it. Correct the seasoning and thicken the sauce further by fluffing in some butter. Keep warm.

While the turnips cook, prepare a forcemeat. To 3½ ounces sausage forcemeat, add 5 very finely chopped mushrooms and 1 large shallot, both sautéed in butter until the mushrooms have lost all their moisture. Grate and render 1 ounce of fresh pork fatback. Stiffen 2 beautiful chicken livers in the resulting lard. Mash and strain chicken livers and fatback and mix them with the sausage and mushroom mixture. Add a bit of basil, rosemary and thyme flowers. Shape small meatballs out of the mixture and cook them in butter. Stuff 1 meatball into the hollow of each turnip. Coat with the sauce and serve very hot.

ZEPHYR OF SOLE ÉDOUARD NIGNON

To serve 4 persons

Fillet 2 Dover soles. Spread the fillets with a classic pike forcemeat. Fold the fillets in half. Poach them in a mixture of half fish *fumet* prepared with mushrooms (p. 250) and half dry white wine.

Serve the fillets coated with a *coulis* of crawfish mixed with a bit of vegetable *brunoise* cooked in butter (see pp. 261 and 267).

The zephyr mousse served with the fillets is prepared as follows:

Reduce 2 cups of fish *fumet* to a thick glaze. Add 4 egg yolks, one at a time, whisking over low heat until the mixture is thick, pale, yellow and foamy. Whisk in ½ pound of clarified unsalted butter. Whip 4 egg whites and fold them into the finished sauce. Bake in a hot-water bath.

COURTINANDISE

To serve 6 persons

Use 1 calf's head, 6½ pounds calves' tails. Soak the head and tails in cold water in 2 different vessels.

Blanch the head; rub it with lemon. Cut it into pieces of identical size which should be about the same size as the cut pieces of the tails.

Sauté the pieces of tail in a mixture of half oil, half butter. Season and brown well. Transfer the pieces of tail to a braising pot with a *mirepoix* of vegetables (p. 267) and a *bouquet garni*. Add a bottle of champagne, flambé, and reduce by half. Add just enough good lightly thickened veal stock to cover the meats. Cook in a low oven. When the pieces of tail are almost tender, add the pieces of head. Cook for another 30 minutes.

While the meats are cooking, cut and trim some carrots, turnips and celeriacs into olive-shaped chunks; blanch them well; glaze some silverskin onions.

When the calf's head and tails are completely done, remove them from the pot and strain the cooking juices. Correct the seasoning. Add the prepared vegetables. Seal the pot with a paste of flour and water and let cook in a hot-water bath for another 30 minutes.

Grandmother's Desserts consist of:

BRIOCHE MOUSSELINE

2 cups sifted flour
3 eggs
1 envelope dry yeast
½ teaspoon salt
2 tablespoons sugar
¾ cup unsalted butter

Make a well in the flour. Add the yeast and dissolve it with 2 tablespoons of lukewarm water. Add 3 eggs, mix well. Mix salt, sugar and butter and divide into 4 equal parts. Gradually work each part of the butter and sugar mixture into the egg and flour paste. Work until the dough gathers a certain elasticity. Let rest for 1 hour; then refrigerate the dough for 2 hours; it will be easier to mold.

(Note: The chef's recipe has been divided by four to prevent the home cook from having a kitchen full of brioche dough. Fresh yeast can be used instead of the dry granular product. With American yeast, either fresh or dried, it may be a good idea to let the brioche rise for 1 hour, then punch it down and let it rise again as much before refrigerating it. To mold this brioche, you will need a 1½-quart brioche or charlotte mold. It should be buttered lavishly. Let the dough rise to reach the rim of the mold and bake at 425°F. for 25 minutes. Ed.)

MOUSSE AU CHOCOLAT

> *½ pound semisweet chocolate*
> *½ cup cocoa powder*
> *¾ cup sugar*
> *1¼ cups unsalted butter*
> *10 eggs, separated*

Melt the chocolate over a hot-water bath. Add the cocoa powder. Whip the egg yolks and sugar until they spin a heavy ribbon. Cream the butter. Add it to the ribboned egg yolks. Add the cooled and melted chocolate. Beat the egg whites and fold them into the chocolate mixture. Chill.

SNOW EGGS

Beat the whites of the eggs used to prepare the English cream. Sweeten them with ¼ cup sugar. With a spoon, shape a ball from the egg whites; poach the ball in 190°F. water. Make as many balls as the meringue will let you shape, and drain the meringue eggs on a towel. Pour some light caramel onto the eggs.

(Note: Although the author does not say so, the snow eggs are usually floated on the English cream below before the caramel is dribbled onto them. Ed.)

ENGLISH CREAM FOR SNOW EGGS

2 cups milk
1 vanilla bean
6 egg yolks
½ cup sugar

Split the vanilla bean lengthwise and steep it in the scalding milk. Beat egg yolks and sugar until white. Gradually add the scalded milk. Thicken over low heat without boiling. Strain into a cold bowl as soon as the cream coats the back of a spoon.

Publisher's Lunch, Deluxe Edition

My friend Louis-Ferdinand Céline never failed to call his publisher "My Vampire." In that short but descriptive phrase he summed up the eternal dispute between writers and those who profit from making them known.

When a writer and publisher lunch together in a restaurant, who generally foots the bill?

"The publisher!" one may well exclaim.

"Yes, perhaps, but . . . with our money!" the writers reply.

Even if they haven't got Balzac's knack for sucking money from their vampire! Everyone knows the story. Balzac had just finished a novel. He rushed out to take the manuscript to Werdet, his publisher; and, to induce him to sign the contract, Balzac invited him to lunch at Véry's, a restaurant run by one of the great chefs of the time. Werdet, who was suffering from a liver ailment, made do with a potage and a chicken wing. As he talked, Balzac had himself served one hundred Ostende oysters, a dozen lamb chops *pré salé,* a duckling with turnips, a pair of roast partridges, a sole *normande,* some side dishes, and fruit. Accordingly he drank the finest wines. And he left with his contract in hand but with Werdet holding the check. Ah! The good man, the sweet writer! He avenged us all!

I don't know whether one would dare do the same thing today. I shall have to ask Garin.

I have often met publishers and writers Chez Garin in Paris, so he must know which of them pays the check most often.

I myself entertained the representatives of a French publishing house there. I am somewhat ashamed to admit it, but it was I who invited them. Still, who cares? Balzac had consoled me beforehand . . .

A strange man, that Garin! With a beard like one of the Three Kings', more salt in it than pepper; a huge head somewhat leaning to one side, as if he were listening to mysterious and discreet voices; a gentle, muffled, velvety voice; a soothing hand . . . He somewhat resembles the stone saints one finds in cathedrals—very close to the earth, but with heaven in their

195

Chez Garin
Déjeuner

———— ◆ ————

Chiffonade de homard
Bécasse
Ragoût de truffes
Les crêpes du Chapitre

eyes. Yes, a curious man whom one would hardly notice were he dressed like you or I, but whose white chef's costume lends him a kind of purity. Then one imagines he might be dressed like those thousands of bourgeois who made up the aristocracy during the Middle Ages. Or else one imagines him with the light of glowing embers sculpting his bleak face, like an attentive alchemist in the secret recesses of an ancient tower. Even the name Garin evokes millennial memories and resounds as if the soil were being marched over by armies from beyond the grave. One would like to say—familiarly, but also respectfully—"my old Garin," as one says "my old hometown."

And there he was, perhaps weary and a bit disillusioned, talking of emigrating because he'd discovered a foreign land, which means to him the sun and Provence, and had bought a house there. Mind you, I am not saying that Provence isn't France or that there is no sun in Burgundy, Paris, or wherever. But the Provence sun is something else again. And the cooking as well! Garin, an alchemist of sauces and skillful worker in the culinary art, discovered, near Solliès-Pont, quite another art of living to which he nearly succumbed. After some hesitation he chose to remain with us a while longer. We were delighted, because one of the great restaurants of Paris thus continued. I personally was doubly delighted, because I believe deeply that the tones of northern France should endure and that the language of the south should be spoken only by its sons. (However, one cannot begrudge Garin the pleasures of Solliès-Pont, where he did later settle and continue to work.)

Wherever one has read it, the menu of Chez Garin is a wonder of concision, precision, and clarity which culminates in the following inscription: "When reserving your table, inform Garin of the dish you would like to taste." One is therefore not at all surprised to find that he prepares classic dishes. But classics of "purity," as it were. The lobster, for example (and of course they are small, blue Breton lobsters, admirably fresh and of the best quality)—the lobster is offered *en chiffonade* (that is, cold), *à la nage,* or as a fricassee with port. When cold, it is served with a variety of sauces, all of which are eloquent, but one of them—a mousse of fresh tomatoes—leads us, with *suavissimo,* to ecstasy. And I am weighing my words! As for the roast woodcock, the scrambled eggs, the fresh truffles, the stuffed pigs' feet, the ribs of beef *à la vigneronne,* they are quite simply what they should be. These days, isn't that the highest of compliments? The vegetable purées (celery and string bean) are as much a tribute to the garden as the wine menu is to the vineyard.

And that Larousse lunch was a masterpiece. One of the thousand masterpieces signed Garin, day after day.

Recipes of Georges Garin

LOBSTER EN CHIFFONADE

To serve 4 persons

Two lobsters, 1 pound each, cooked in court-bouillon for 12 to 15 minutes and cooled in the court-bouillon.

When the lobsters are cold, separate the heads from the tails. Shell the claws; keep them whole.

Split the tails into halves; remove the meat. Split the heads into halves, remove tomalley and coral, and strain both through a fine sieve.

To 2¼ cups very firm mayonnaise, add the tomalley and coral purée, 2 tablespoons ketchup, 1 dessertspoon Cognac, ½ teaspoon Worcestershire sauce (preferably Lea & Perrins), 3 to 4 drops of Tabasco.

Presentation:

Put 1 head of Boston lettuce or 1 head of curly chicory cut into chiffonade on the bottom of a silver or other platter. Return the half lobsters to their half shells, putting them in upside down so their red part is visible on the top; top each half tail shell with a claw.

Put all the lobsters on the dish, alternating tails and heads. Fill with the prepared sauce or serve the sauce in a boat, and fill the lobster heads with a mousse of tomato sprinkled with a julienne of truffles.

WINES: White Mercurey, Muscadet in a great year, still wine from Champagne, Chablis Fourchaume, or Pouilly-Fumé.

TOMATO MOUSSE

In season use 2¼ pounds of fresh tomatoes peeled and seeded; off-season use a large can of chopped tomatoes finely chopped and reduced until all traces of moisture have disappeared. Add ½ cup aspic or, if unavailable, 2½ teaspoons gelatin melted over a hot-water bath.

Season with salt, pepper and a teaspoon of paprika.

Strain through a fine sieve or the finest blade of a food mill. Let cool. Measure the same volume of heavy cream as you have of tomato base. Whip it until it starts retaining the imprint of the whisk and fold it into the tomato base.

WOODCOCK

To serve 2 persons

Hang the bird in its plumage for 4 to 5 days in a cold place, not in an ice-cold one, to allow mortification to take place.

Pluck the bird and singe it carefully; do not forget the head. Remove the gizzard without cutting the bird open; keep all the innards inside of the bird. Turn the head to face backward and thrust the beak through both thighs.

Season with salt and pepper. Cook in a hot oven or in a *cocotte* on top of the stove for 15 minutes. Remove the bird to a plate and let rest for a few minutes. Then remove the fillets and the legs and gather the innards into a bowl.

Chop the carcass as finely as possible. Return it to its cooking pot with 2 shallots finely minced. Flambé with 2 ounces of Armagnac or Cognac. Moisten with ¾ cup of a very generous red wine. Reduce by a good half and strain, pushing and pressing on the carcass to extract a maximum of its juices and essences. Return those juices to a pot and bring back to a boil with 2 tablespoons of heavy cream. Add the innards that you will have first mashed with a tablespoon or so of *foie gras* if possible, if not with a chicken liver lightly sautéed in butter. Bring to a boil without letting reduce and strain again through a conical metal strainer. Return to the heat, adding a dessertspoon of fresh butter that you will whisk in very quickly. Bring to the boiling point and keep hot.

Arrange the fillets on 2 toasted slices of French bread. Surround them with the legs and the head split into halves. Finish the sauce with an addition of 1 tablespoon Cognac or Armagnac. Correct the seasoning and coat the woodcock with the sauce.

The garnish may be a purée of celeriac, lentils or onions, or some dry fried potatoes (straw potatoes, potato chips or butter-fried sliced potatoes).

WINES: Musigny, Chambertin, Corton Clos du Roi, or Château Pétrus.

TRUFFLE RAGOUT

To serve 4 persons

Use 8 truffles each weighing 1¼ to 1½ ounces, or the same amount of *première cuisson* truffles. The peels may be used in scrambled eggs. Cut the truffles into 4 to 6 pieces each; season with salt and pepper. Put the truffles in a container with 3 tablespoons port or Madeira or even dry Banyuls and let macerate at room temperature for 15 to 20 minutes.

Reduce by half ¾ cup of a good full-bodied red wine such as Cahors, very dry Banyuls, Côtes du Rhône, Corbières or Mascara in a container that will contain the truffles adequately; it may be an earthenware *cocotte*, a copper saucepan or even a heatproof glass container, but in any case rub it with garlic. Blend 1 teaspoon flour mixed with 2 teaspoons unsalted butter into the reduced wine. Bring to a boil; add the truffles with their marinade. Cover with a sheet of foil resting flush over the truffles and with the pot lid. Or, if you prefer, cover the pot and seal the cover with a paste of flour and water which will preserve all the fragrance. Bake in a medium oven (325°F.) for 10 minutes.

Meanwhile, prepare some croutons about 1 inch thick out of stale French bread. Let the croutons dry, rub them with a bit of garlic, and spread the garlic-rubbed side with goose, duck or poultry fat or, if none is available, with olive oil. Serve on the side at the same time as your truffles. Or, cut a lid into each of 8 round or long dinner rolls and remove their soft centers. Treat the inside of the rolls as described above for the French bread croutons and fill the rolls with the truffle ragout. Cover each roll with its lid.

WINES: Château Chalon, Hermitage, Grand Saint-Émilion, or very dry Banyuls.

(Note: Première cuisson *truffles are not to be found in fine groceries since all the truffle industry reserves them for the finest restaurants. They can be obtained from the Société Alimentaire Guillot, 84, Grillon, France, which answers readily to inquiries and airmails to the United States. Be prepared for a considerable expense but the truffles are well worth it. Ed.)*

LES CRÊPES DU CHAPITRE

To serve 6 persons

Crêpe batter:

Mix 2 whole eggs, 2 egg yolks, ½ cup sifted flour, ⅓ cup sugar and a pinch of salt. Add gradually 1⅛ cups of milk, working the batter until it is homogeneous. Whisk in ¼ cup butter, melted, cooked to the *noisette* stage (p. 261) and cooled, 1 generous tablespoon of olive oil, only if you wish. Strain through a fine strainer and add the finely grated rinds of 2 lemons and 1 orange. Let stand for 2 hours.

Pastry cream:

Mix in a saucepan 2 egg yolks, ¼ cup sifted flour, 3 tablespoons sugar and a small pinch of salt. Add 1 small cup scalded milk and 6 tablespoons praline. Bring to a boil over medium heat, stirring constantly.

Presentation:

Cook the crêpes in a crêpe pan; spread each with pastry cream and fold in half.

Cream ¼ cup butter; add 2 tablespoons each of Grand Marnier and Mirabelle. Rub each side of the folded crêpe in this mixture and fold again in half.

Put the crêpes in a gratin dish; sprinkle them with sugar and bake in a 425°F. oven for 8 minutes. Pour 3 tablespoons Mirabelle into the dish; light the hot brandy and flambé until the flames die out. Add another generous tablespoon of Mirabelle and bring flaming to the table.

(Note: Mirabelle is a brandy distilled from the small round yellow plum of the same name. The plum grows particularly well in Lorraine and Alsace; one very well-known shipper of Alsatian wines prepares it and bottles it under his own name. The brandy should be easy to locate in the leading liquor and wine stores of larger cities. Ed.)

Roger Lamazère,
Conjurer of the Table

Seven towns vied for the honor of being Homer's birthplace. Even more towns claim to be the home of the "true" cassoulet. Among them is Toulouse, capital of the South of France, the pink city, the "red flower of summer," according to a song I was taught in school.

This is not the time to discuss the conflicting or mutual merits of the various cassoulets and their legends (for the cassoulet is a dish that creates legends). But one may say, along with all its enthusiasts, that the main ingredient is goose preserved in its own fat in an earthenware jar, cooked together with dried beans. The rest is a question of latitude, although clearly, between Périgueux, its northernmost point, and Castelnaudary or Carcassonne, its southeastern boundary lines, there may well be a number of variations on the dish.

As far as literature is concerned, I personally prefer the Mère Clémence cassoulet described by Anatole France in his *Histoire comique*—a cassoulet "with those very special warm amber tones like the color of the flesh in the works of old Venetian masters," and at present—in other words, when it comes to our appetites—in the work of Roger Lamazère.

Roger Lamazère, another curious man!

He is from Toulouse and is proud of it.

He is a juggler, a conjurer, and, most of all, a magician. He went from the art of card tricks—to which his *à la carte* menu bears some resemblance —to the art of cuisine. I mean by that that his menu astonishes the customer who comes to the spectacle with the spirit of a child—in fact it raises him to seventh heaven. A sincere gourmet always has—or should always have—something of the child about him.

In addition to the cassoulet, the gems of the region are truffles and foie gras. As well as buntings, which one finds not far from there and which have their fanatic enthusiasts (I must admit that I am not among them) and have, in that devil of a man, their jeweler. Indeed—and it is one aspect of Lamazère's talent as a conjurer—he discovered a boyar's recipe for them and, during the few weeks of the bunting season, offered them to his very rich customers.

Chez Lamazère
Dîner

Truffes fraîches "à la croque au sel"
Cassoulet des cassoulets d'Austin de Croze

(Médoc Château Duhart Milon)

Brie de Melun
Sorbet de prunes à l'Armagnac

In the nineteenth century, Richardin, the well-known culinographer, now forgotten, had published that recipe as the creation of a then current novelist, who is even more forgotten, René Maizeroy. The dish was called "buntings in a coffin"! What a coffin—made of a huge truffle, hollowed out just enough so that the tiny, plump little bird, roasted separately, would fit.

All I can still taste of that romantic dish is the truffle.

Lamazère is a kind of truffle trainer. And when one tells me that the origins of this—this what?—no one even knows whether it is a vegetable, a mushroom, or a mysterious underground beast, which is what the Spaniards believed for a time, just as they believed in the devil—and thus, when one tells me that its existence is due to a miracle and a fairy tale, I then understand why Lamazère made it his specialty.

According to the fairy tale, long ago, in Périgord, there lived a very poor family who had nothing to eat but the few potatoes that grew in their barren fields. One day an old woman, even poorer than poor, walked through the village begging. She was refused by almost everyone but that most down-and-out family, who were willing to share their last potatoes with her. Then, as she thanked them, the old hag turned into a beautiful girl and told them they would find their fortune. The following year the potatoes that grew in their field were black, scented, and altogether unexpected: truffles were born!

Well, at Lamazère's one always has the feeling that truffles are miraculous, illusory creatures. Lamazère arrives with empty hands and empty pockets, and presto! a black diamond sparkles in his palm: a fat truffle.

It is therefore unimaginable that this magician would be stingy enough to scrape the fat truffle like a hazelnut to make it last a week, or carve the diamond into tiny chips to set in junk jewelry! No! Lamazère serves you the whole truffle with salt, as is proper. So we shall start our meal with one: a fresh truffle, naturally raw, huge, and well-brushed. One cuts off a slice, butters it, salts it, crunches it! Curses on anyone who is not piggish enough (and, appropriately, in that region pigs are mobilized to rout out the truffles) to swallow a whole basket of them served that way!

Then that very commendable beginning yields to a cassoulet.

A short war ago, a wealthy gentleman from the South of France, Austin de Croze, had concocted for a publisher (clearly, one *is* well-fed in that profession) a special cassoulet—a mixture of the Castelnaudary cassoulet (the ancestor), the spirited Toulouse cassoulet (something of a Gascon braggart), the Quercy cassoulet (the country cousin), and finally the royal Carcassonne cassoulet. He called it the cassoulet of cassoulets. And that ambitious dish is what I asked Lamazère to prepare for us.

Must I say that once we had eaten it, we were no longer hungry? Probably, but a gastronome always keeps some room for cheese, and there was still some Château Duhart-Milon left in the magnum (for those who have never heard of it, Duhart-Milon is a Médoc wine, a neighbor of the Lafite-Rothschild, and in its good years almost its rival, even though they have the same godfather in Monsieur Elie de Rothschild). So we ordered a perfect Brie cheese from Melun. Then a simple plum sherbet, with some Armagnac. It was Byzantium, as a very dear friend once said—impassioned but very badly informed on the sex of angels.

Recipe for the Cassoulet of Cassoulets by Austin de Croze

The day before cassoulet, soak 1¾ pounds dried white beans in lukewarm water flavored with a shadow of fennel; with the beans also must soak ¼ pound of fresh brisket of pork, ½ pound of pork rinds and a boned pig's trotter.

The next day, blanch the brisket, rinds and pig's trotter. Change the water of the beans. Cook them until they are three quarters done with salt and pepper, but neither too much nor too little of each. Drain and keep warm. Keep the cooking water to make a delicious soup.

Sauce:
Mince 2 or 3 medium-size onions. Brown them, the brisket diced into small cubes and 1 large sliced carrot in 6 tablespoons goose fat. Toward the end of the browning, add 3 finely minced garlic cloves; sprinkle with a large pinch (2 teaspoons) of flour, stir briskly and add 5¼ cups of excellent beef stock. Stir this mixture until it starts boiling, then add a large *bouquet garni* made of an onion or a beautiful leek stuck with 6 cloves, a celery rib broken into 2 pieces, a branch of thyme and 3 bay leaves *(Turkish or Mediterranean only, please. Ed.)* and also the meat of 3 medium-size sun-ripened tomatoes. Let this sauce simmer and skim it as it reduces. Keep the skimmed-off fat for later use. The sauce having reduced by half, strain it through a sieve and keep it over very low heat,

adding a small, very small, almost imperceptible pinch of saffron. Mix well, cover, and keep the sauce warm without cooking it further.

Brown over medium heat a large wing or a beautiful leg of a *confit* goose in ½ pound of its own fat (see note). Also brown a small country garlic *saucisson*. This operation should require 45 minutes altogether. Keep warm and defatten the pan.

Gather the fat from the sauce (par. 3) and from the browning of the *confit* (par. 4) in an earthenware casserole. This fat is better than butter and you are going to use it to brown a small, very small, boned leg of lamb studded with garlic (this is the Carcassonne custom) or a generous pound of breast of lamb which should be as lean as possible. Halfway through this browning add a full glass (½ cup) of very good dry white wine. You will then add (as is always done in Toulouse) the blanched pork rinds, the parboiled pig's trotter and—in season—that partridge or ringdove that the people from the Quercy and the Landes would never forget. Braise until all the meats are three quarters done and keep warm.

Rub with garlic the bottom and sides of an earthenware terrine. In the bottom of the pot, put the goose wing or leg; cover it with a layer of beans which you will sprinkle with a trifle, truly a nothing, of paprika and barely a touch of *quatre-épices* (p. 266), just as much of those as can be gathered on the very tip of a knife. Moisten with all the juices produced while cooking the goose *confit* and the *saucisson*. Add the leg of lamb cut into thick slices or the breast of lamb and, if you have used it, the partridge or ringdove cut into 4 pieces. Surround and cover all this with beans and add half of the sauce prepared under par. 3.

Add the *saucisson* cut into thick slices, the pig's rinds and trotter. Cover with the remainder of the beans, all the cooking juices of the lamb and partridge and the remainder of the sauce prepared under par. 3. The beans should be barely covered by the fragrant liquid. Put the covered terrine over high heat and bring to a boil.

When the contents of the terrine have boiled for 5 minutes, remove the terrine from the heat and sprinkle the cassoulet with fresh bread crumbs mixed with chopped parsley. You can—as is done in Périgord—add a small well-brushed truffle shaved into fine slivers.

Put the uncovered terrine in a well-preheated oven—not too hot though—where you will let it bubble for 45 minutes *(use 350°F. oven, Ed.)*. If you double these proportions, bake the cassoulet for 1 hour; if you triple them, bake it for 1½ hours.

True gourmets use either the bakers' oven or a country oven; in each of those the fire is started with dried blackberry brambles mixed with a bouquet of pine needles. Those using a stove oven will have to put a handful of juniper berries in the oven before baking the terrine for it is from their balsamic fragrance that the cassoulet takes on that special ever so rustic taste which heightens its flavor and charm.

Cover a silver or brightly colored rustic ironstone platter with a napkin; spread a few lavender flowers on the napkin and serve the cassoulet in its burning hot terrine on burning hot plates.

(Notes: 1. Although a confit d'oie *can be sometimes located in fancy grocery stores in large cans, it may be a better idea to make it oneself; a* confit *keeps from November to May before being "renewed," that is to say before being recooked to prevent fermentations. An American goose will make a good* confit, *though, because it is not force-fed, it will not correspond exactly to the French goose.*

To make the confit:

Use a 10-pound goose. Cut it into pieces (2 breasts with wings attached, 2 legs with thighs attached). Remove all the fat you can at the entrance of the abdominal cavity and under the skin of the back and abdomen. Put that fat in a pot large enough to contain all the pieces of goose; add about 1½ cups of water to the fat and let it melt very slowly to prevent it burning. Keep the melted fat for later use.

Salt the pieces of goose (use about 2 teaspoons of salt per pound of meat). Sprinkle them very generously with dried thyme and crushed bay leaf. Pack the pieces on top of one another and keep them in this salt marinade for 2 nights separated by 1 day.

Scrape the salt from the pieces of goose and immerse them in the bath of melted goose fat. Bring to a slow simmer and continue cooking for 2½ hours. Check the doneness of the confit *by spearing a fine skewer at the fattest part of the thigh; if it comes out freely the meat is done. If not, continue cooking longer.*

When the meat is done, remove it to a thick opaque bean pot. Continue cooking the goose fat until the meat juices trapped at the bottom of the pot come floating like scum to the surface of the fat. Remove the scum and let the fat stand for a few minutes. Spoon it over the pieces of confit, *so that the fat covers them completely. Let the fat solidify completely and seal the pot with a parchment and its lid.*

To renew the confit: *melt it in a large pot and bring the fat to a good simmer; 5 minutes of steady simmering are enough to recook the* confit *for another 6 months.*

2. To replace the Cantal saucissons (which are truly not replaceable), you may want to try very good spicy and garlicky Italian sausage.

3. To use juniper berries in an oven, start by crushing them. Put half of them in a shallow container at the bottom of the oven behind the terrine and the other half in another shallow container at the front of the oven just beside the terrine. Ed.)

A Wedding Feast

France's noble child, His Excellency Champagne, was married the other night to young Italian Cuisine.

Young, because there is still something juvenile about that cuisine. It is, if you will, a flighty young thing straight out of Italian comedy. It frolics, toe-dances, capers about, delicately humming a barcarole—as much an intimate of Zampone as of Pantalone, of Harlequin as of Valpolicella, with ruffles of fettucine and ribbons of tomato sauce.

The groom's mother was Madame Odette Pol-Roger, the great lady of Champagne. The bride's parents came from Paris, rue des Écoles—the *trattoria* called Chez Mario. Together they made a lighthearted, gourmand, and happy family. The ceremony took place, as they say, during a series of rituals that were meant to prove, by way of Pol Roger (dated 1966), that champagne is the wine not only for all great occasions but also for every type of cuisine.

Invited to the wedding were French and Italian journalists and actors. I chatted with some as I drank an appropriate americano—that is, a drink with Pinot de Chardonnay replacing the vermouth. We were awaiting not the "future couple," since they were already there, but an important witness, the commercial attaché from the Italian Embassy in Paris.

While promptness is the courtesy of kings, it is probably not spelled out in the little textbook for training diplomats. Seven-thirty, 8:20, 8:30 . . . Signor Tutti-Quanti had still not arrived. On the other hand, all the guests were clinking and reclinking glasses in the pleasant atmosphere of friendship. Voices grew somewhat louder, although joyous. Thirst made everyone thirsty, and drink made everyone even thirstier. Somebody called Signor Tutti-Quanti a series of birds' names which probably can't be found in any French-Italian dictionary.

It was almost time for a *coppa* when, two full hours later, the above-mentioned Tutti-Quanti arrived, undaunted, his missus trailing behind, and without a word of apology. Then we swiftly went on to serious matters— that is to say, the wedding ceremony.

Restaurant Chez Mario
Dîner

———— ◆ ————

Rougets à la livournaise

Médaillons de veau piémontaise

Sabayon au champagne

(Pol Roger 1966)

Would Monsieur Champagne take this child from across the Alps as his lawful wedded wife?

And would she, Signorina Italian Cuisine, take Champagne as her lawful wedded husband?

It was a crucial moment: the red mullet *livournaise* was being served.

For what counted was not only that champagne accompany the fish, meat, cheeses, and desserts, but that it be included in the recipes themselves. Mario and his chef are skillful cooks indeed. But even if they were able to pop a champagne cork properly, they still had to make it across the Alps. It was done very nimbly.

Signor Tutti-Quanti, gobbling down his food, probably to make up for lost time, was willing to admit that it was "a success." A Frenchman told us Italian stories. It was announced that Magali Noël, who had just been chosen by the Italian press as the most attractive French actress, would be there for coffee. What strange tastes they have over there! But the coffee still seemed far away; medallions of veal *piémontaise* were being served.

Helped by the Pol Roger, our seats became warmer and warmer. A number of our Italian colleagues began to juggle with forks as well as with words. Luckily there was no spaghetti planned for the meal! As for Signor Tutti-Quanti, he said little and occasionally looked at his watch, like a man whose own time counts more than the time of others. We had just narrowly escaped the cheese (a pity, since I was convinced that Gorgonzola was perfectly suited to the Pol Roger 1966) and were anticipating the desserts—among which was a zabaglione. It was at that point that Magali Noël arrived, assaulted by flashbulbs and more curdled than the zabaglione.

Finally the champagne *marc* was served. Our Italian colleagues had reached the most cordial of ententes: that of the bottle and the self. Growing more and more talkative, and more and more Latin, they were all holding forth, each one telling his own story and taking no account of the others.

Signor Tutti-Quanti had left discreetly; Madame Odette Pol-Roger had disappeared. We went out into the lukewarm night. Mario was wondering whether he ought to entrust the keys to the last survivor . . .

But no matter. It was a fine wedding!

Recipes of the Restaurant
Chez Mario

RED MULLETS LIVORNO STYLE

To serve 4 persons

Clean and season 4 red mullets weighing 6 to 7 ounces at the most. Brown them slowly in about ⅔ cup of butter in a large frying pan.

Add to the pan a split of Champagne Brut Pol Roger, 4 very finely chopped shallots and 1 sprig of chervil. Bring to a boil, cover the pan, and let simmer over very low heat for 15 minutes.

When the mullets are done, remove them to a plate and blend the cooking juices with 1 tablespoon of brown *roux*. Add 6 fresh tomatoes, peeled, seeded and chopped, or a 1-pound can of whole or chopped tomatoes. Strain the obtained sauce through a fine strainer and let it reduce again until it turns syrupy.

Off the heat whisk a nugget of butter into the sauce and add the chopped leaves of a sprig of tarragon.

VEAL MEDALLIONS ALLA PIEMONTESE

To serve 4 persons

Purchase 4 medallions of veal cut from the fillet or the top of the round; 2 hours before cooking them, marinate the medallions in the following mixture: ¼ cup olive oil, the juice of 1 lemon, salt and pepper, finely chopped tarragon, sweet basil, chervil, ½ cup dry Marsala or port or, even better, Pol Roger Champagne.

Drain the medallions, flour them, and brown them in butter over medium heat. As soon as they are done to your personal taste, remove the medallions to a plate. Deglaze the pan with the marinade and reduce over high heat until the sauce reaches coating consistency. Arrange the medallions on a platter; spoon the sauce over them.

CHAMPAGNE ZABAGLIONE

To serve 4 persons

Put 6 egg yolks and ⅔ cup sugar in a saucepan. Work very well with a whisk until the mixture whitens and spins a ribbon when falling from the whisk. Gradually add 1 cup of Champagne Brut Pol Roger. Place the saucepan over a hot-water bath and thicken the cream, rolling the handle of the whisk between the palms of both hands to obtain a thick and abundant foam.

Just before putting the pan over the hot-water bath, add a vanilla bean and the grated rind of 1 lemon.

Denis Is Denis Is Denis

I must say, I am very fond of Denis.

To my mind, he has the distinction of being intelligent and of having character, which are rare qualities in chefs. He has a good (if evil-tempered) head on his shoulders.

He also has the distinction of not being a professional chef. By that I mean that he didn't go to school and learn Escoffier, Montagné, Pie-Face, or What's His Name—those manglers of true cuisine.

Cuisine came to him by way of his appetite: through eating. Through eating up three inheritances, as he likes to put it. One must admit that, with the help of taste and wit, the best way to learn is by spending.

The delightful quality of women's cuisine is its empiricism, whereas it is precisely empiricism that is missing from a chef's cuisine. This is another type of empiricism, no doubt, patterned on the art-of-living school, but, as such, elegant, subtle, and intelligent. The word is worth repeating, for it is intelligence that has really been missing from cuisine since the eighteenth century.

Therefore, since Denis is Denis, one puts up with a lot from him—to begin with, a kind of haughty curtness, insolent and imperious irony, and a sovereign disdain for anything that is not "his" truth. And when one asks him to be tactful, he quite simply replies, "I'm from Bordeaux!"

Hang it all! When Eleanor of Aquitaine added to her bonnet the sprig of broom from her Plantagenet groom, didn't she also marry British humor? And since Bordeaux currently has the master hardhead of all hardheads, Chaban Delmas, as mayor, why would Denis bother to give him competition?

Come on, dear friend, great man, admirable cook, accept the need to smile.

I know, yes, I know perfectly well. It is difficult to keep one's cool when faced with a nouveau riche who is amazed to be told that it takes twenty minutes to make a *salade niçoise* (the beans and eggs must be cooked at the last minute), or with a minister of state who thinks that Pomerol and Saint-Émilion are "real" Bordeaux wines, when at home, before the war, they were considered ordinary wines because the only Bordeaux were Médoc and Graves. But still. . . !

In any case, Denis is the only cook today who can—and wants to— serve a meal *à la française* according to the traditional rites. You will tell me that I am not being logical, that I extol the simplicity of women's cuisine, that I reproach chefs their useless pomp and display, and that at Denis's I demand (and am delighted with) the whole ceremony of a chef's cuisine par excellence—*le service à la française.* But you're wrong! I approach that kind of meal the way one enters a museum—with a collector's admiration. I see myself as Talleyrand dealing with Carême, and I am set to dreaming!

Le grand service à la française, as Carême practiced it, was merely the continuation in another and already limited form of what, under Louis XIV, was called *le grand couvert,* or "the big setting."

A meal served *à la française* is divided into three parts. Part I: *potage, relevé d'entrée* (or the dish after the soup), and the main course. Part II: a hot roast, a cold roast, a salted side dish, and a sweet side dish. Part III: preserves and pastries. Category by category, the dishes used to be multiplied, and it was not rare for a meal like that to number up to forty-eight courses, the cold dishes on centerpieces, the hot ones in covered metal warmers.

I talked about this to the young owner of a great Parisian restaurant, unquestionably one of the best.

"That would be impossible for us to do," he told me, with a touch of regret in his voice. "For meals like that, you'd have to limit yourself to a handful of customers . . ."

What he didn't add, but implied, was, "You'd have to be an amateur!"

Well, yes! And that is what makes Denis Denis, always Denis, and unable to be other than Denis! He wants to be an amateur. An amateur of great skill, an amateur of genius, from whom the greatest of professionals could learn . . . without ever altogether managing to!

Witness the following meal, a dinner *à la française* to which he, in fact, invited the young restaurant keeper in question. This was the menu:

Iranian caviar canapés
Jellied tomato velouté
Calves' brains in cream puffs
Souffléed brill with shad mousse
Purée of watercress
Lemon sherbet

Chez Denis
Dîner à la française

Premier Service

Caviar d'Iran sur toasts
Velouté de tomates en gelée
Profiteroles de cervelle
Barbue soufflée à l'alose
Purée de cresson
Sorbet au citron

Deuxième Service

Rognonade de veau Chez Denis
garniture de truffes, pommes parisienne
et fonds d'artichauts avec mousse de champignons
Chaud-froid d'ortolans
Flan Bourdaloue aux fraises

Troisième Service

Petits fours secs
Fruits déguisés   Confiseries
Truffes au chocolat

Boned saddle of veal Chez Denis
with its garniture of truffles,
potatoes parisienne, and
artichoke bottoms with mushroom mousse
Chaud-froid of buntings
Strawberry flan Bourdaloue
Petits fours
Glazed candied fruits and sweetmeats
Chocolate truffles

Recipes of Denis

CAVIAR CANAPÉS

Butter the canapés. Spread each of them with caviar and decorate it with creamed butter piped through a very fine pastry tube and with a small piece of peeled lemon.

JELLIED TOMATO VELOUTÉ

To serve 6 persons

Cook 3 very finely minced gray shallots in butter very slowly and without letting them color at all. Add 1 generous pound of tomatoes, peeled, seeded and finely chopped, and continue cooking slowly, still without letting the mixture color at all. Add 2 tablespoons of mixed *fines herbes* (equal parts of chives, tarragon, chervil and parsley); moisten with 4½ cups of beef consommé and ⅔ cup tomato *coulis* or essence (p. 258), a good pinch of cayenne and a *bouquet garni;* let slowly reduce by half. Let cool completely.

Whip ⅔ cup heavy cream. Blend 6 egg yolks into the cooled tomato soup. Pour the soup slowly into the whipped cream, whisking constantly. Correct the seasoning and keep chilled until ready to serve.

CALVES' BRAINS IN CREAM PUFFS

To serve 6 to 8 persons

Cream-puff paste

Put ½ cup each of milk and water in a saucepan. Add a pinch of salt, a pinch of sugar, ½ cup unsalted butter. Bring to a boil. Remove from the heat and add 1 cup sifted flour, stirring with a spatula to obtain a ball of dough. Return to the heat and stir well with the spatula until the mixture does not stick anymore to either pot or spatula. Remove from the heat again and beat in 4 large eggs, one by one. The dough should remain soft but be able to hold its shape when piped through a pastry bag.

Pipe small ½-inch cream puffs or profiteroles onto a pastry sheet and bake in a 375°F. oven for 30 minutes.

Slowly sauté calves' brains in clarified butter. Cut the profiteroles open and fill them with the diced brains. Keep warm.

Sauté gently in butter 1 ounce of truffles and the same amount of poached pickled tongue, both finely diced. Add 3 tablespoons of Madeira and let reduce completely. Add ⅓ cup meat juices or meat glaze, bring to a boil, and add plenty of butter. Spoon the sauce over the profiteroles.

(Note: To bake the profiteroles, butter the cookie sheet, then rinse it under cold water. The steam caught under each puff will keep its bottom from scorching. Also, use either 2 calves' brains or 4 small lambs' brains. The brains must be soaked in acidulated water and skinned and poached before being sautéed. Ed.)

SOUFFLÉED BRILL WITH SHAD MOUSSE

To serve 6 persons

Shad Mousse

Pound ¾ pound shad in a mortar; add one by one 3 egg whites, beating well with a spatula. Strain through a sieve. Season; add some *fines herbes*. Gather into a bowl fitted into a larger bowl containing crushed ice. Beat in 1⅔ cups heavy cream, working thoroughly with a spatula.

Slit the brill open along the center bone; lift the fillets, remove the center bone, and stuff the brill with the shad mousse. Fold the fillets back over the mousse. Put the stuffed fish in a buttered dish. Add to the dish a *fumet* which you will have prepared with the heads and bones of the shad. Bake in a preheated 375°F. oven for about 25 minutes. Serve with pistachio and hazelnut butter.

Pistachio and Hazelnut Butter

Clarify ½ pound of butter; add to it, while hot, ½ cup very finely powdered skinned hazelnuts or filberts. Let stand for 6 hours. Strain and add ¼ cup very finely chopped blanched pistachios. Let stand for 1 hour before serving.

(Note: To make this hazelnut butter, the hazelnuts should be lightly toasted in a 350°F. oven for 10 to 12 minutes; to skin the nuts rub them in a tea towel. Ed.)

PURÉE OF WATERCRESS

To serve 4 persons

Clean 3 pounds of watercress. Blanch the leaves for no more than 10 seconds. Rinse under running cold water; drain carefully and force through a sieve. Put the purée in the top container of a double boiler and heat very gradually, beating in about ⅓ cup heavy cream.

LEMON SHERBET

Mix one third of its volume of Italian meringue into a lemon ice. Fold it into the ice with a spatula and freeze.

(Note: To make a sherbet similar to Denis's, use this formula: Boil together 2 cups water and 1 cup sugar mixed with the grated rinds of 2 lemons. Cool completely. Add 1 cup of lemon juice. Freeze in an ice-cream machine. Bring ½ cup each of water and sugar to a boil with 2 drops of lemon juice. Cook to 240°F. Beat 1 egg white to soft peaks. Pour the hot syrup into the meringue and continue beating until cold. Add the meringue to the already frozen sherbet and churn together until homogeneous. Ed.)

BONED SADDLE OF VEAL CHEZ DENIS

To serve 6 to 8 persons

Use a 3-pound saddle of veal boned and studded with truffles, pickled tongue, and ham.

Prepare a mushroom mousse with ½ pound mushrooms, 1 generous cup of cream, 2 egg whites (see shad mousse), *fines herbes,* shallots, salt and pepper. Defatten completely a beautiful veal kidney; surround it with the mousse and a pig's caul; place the kidney between the tenderloin and the strip and wrap the roast with the brisket. Tie a ¼-inch-thick sheet of fatback around the roast and roast for 45 minutes. Remove to the warmer of the oven.

Prepare a puff paste (use half of the recipe for puff pastry on p. 268). Roll out half of the pastry. Remove the fatback surrounding the roast. Put the roast on the sheet of pastry; surround it with whole uncooked brushed truffles. Roll out the second sheet of pastry and cover the roast. Decorate and glaze with *dorure* (p. 270). Bake in a 425°F. oven for 25 minutes. Serve with the deglazed juices of the roast.

Garnishes: As garnishes use truffles, butter-fried Potatoes Parisienne, artichoke bottoms filled with mushroom mousse.

(Notes: For the amateur chef, the mushroom mousse is best made by chopping the mushrooms very finely or even blending them to a purée in the blender. Sauté the purée in butter; add shallots and fines herbes *and let the moisture evaporate completely. Then add the cream and also let reduce completely. Finally beat the egg whites and fold them into the creamed purée of mushrooms.*

Also, considering the type of veal generally available in the United States, it may be a good idea to consider casserole roasting or even braising the veal in excellent veal stock and letting it cool before wrapping it in the pastry. The potatoes should be fried in clarified butter and the artichoke bottoms cooked in a blanc (p. 249) before being filled with the mushroom mousse. After being filled the artichoke bottoms should be baked at 375°F. to puff up the mushroom mousse, which as described in this note is more a soufflé batter than a true mousse. Ed.)

CHAUD-FROID OF BUNTINGS

(Note: Ortolans are small birds of the bunting family; unless one shoots one's own birds, the recipe will have to remain a description. Ed.)

Bone the ortolans completely through the back. Stuff them with some fresh fat duck liver; close the skin over the filling. Wrap each bird in a piece of pig's caul and a piece of thin muslin or cheesecloth. Poach in aspic flavored with port for 17 minutes.

With the birds' carcasses, a few chicken giblets, some of the cooking aspic and some Chambertin, prepare a strong *fumet* and bind it with a bit of fat duck liver. Let cool, stirring constantly.

Pour some of the semijelled sauce onto the bottom of a serving platter and let cool completely. Set the ortolans on this layer of sauce. Glaze them with some of the cooking jelly and decorate with cutouts of jelly and jelled sauce.

STRAWBERRY FLAN BOURDALOUE

To serve 6 to 8 persons

Coat an 8-inch Savarin mold with some caramelized sugar. Melt ½ cup plus 2 tablespoons of sugar in 2¼ cups scalded milk flavored with a vanilla bean. Mix the milk with 7 egg yolks and 1 whole egg. Strain into the caramelized mold. Bake in a hot-water bath (in a 325° oven) for 30 minutes.

Prepare a classic *génoise* (p. 270) of the same diameter as the Savarin mold. Slice off the top and bottom crusts so as to obtain a 1-inch-thick cake. Unmold the cooled flan on the *génoise*. Garnish the center of the mold with strawberries and garnish the edge of the cake with more strawberries. Glaze the strawberries with cardinal sauce; decorate the flan with candied fruits and slivered almonds. Serve the flan coated with the cardinal sauce (a mixture of raspberry purée, lemon juice and confectioners' sugar).

Thirteen at Table

Because the thirteenth place at the Last Supper was Judas's, men who are otherwise perfectly sane—at least ostensibly—have dreaded sitting at a table set for thirteen. Among them were Victor Hugo, Alexandre Dumas, Alfred de Musset, and Théophile Gautier.

When Gautier was invited to the well-known Restaurant Magny, the glory of the Left Bank, and saw that there would be thirteen guests in all, he wanted to leave. Sainte-Beuve, who was also a guest, suggested that a small separate table be set up next to the large one for the author of the poems *Émaux et camées,* but in vain. Old Théophile growled that they would merely be trifling with fate and that a fourteenth guest had to be invited—the restaurant keeper's young son.

The same thing happened at the Café Anglais, but the writer Paul Déroulède saved the day by going out to the Boulevard des Italiens and finding the driver of a hansom cab, who dined with the group of famous men while the restaurant's doorman kept watch over his horse. . . .

Superstitious people can cite innumerable instances of a thirteenth guest dying (from something other than indigestion), whereas others can cite even more instances proving that thirteen is a lucky number. In New York, before the war, there was apparently a Club Thirteen, whose members gave dinners which consisted of thirteen courses for thirteen people on the thirteenth of every month.

And what about the writer Barbey d'Aurevilly, who, at the Maison Dorée (another famous restaurant on the Boulevards at a time when all of them constituted "The Boulevard"), saw the literary critic Armand de Pontmartin alone at table with a dozen oysters in front of him and asked his permission to sit across from him.

"Sorry," answered Monsieur de Pontmartin, "but I always dine alone."

"But, look, there are thirteen of you at the table," Barbey replied, pointing to the shellfish. "And you know that brings bad luck!"

But down with superstitions. At lunch the other day, at the Vivarois Restaurant, there were thirteen of us at the table—that is, Jacques Bodoin and myself!

Le Vivarois
Déjeuner

...

Consommé au jardin du curé

Ragout d'écrevisses, de morilles, et de truffes

Petit sauté d'agneau au pistou

Foie gras en canard,
glacé aux fruits au gingembre

Brioche aux pralines

Jacques Bodoin is one of France's greatest whimsical entertainers and a true gastronome. The two are not at all incompatible. Like Balzac, he seems to want to compete with the government records of everyone who has ever lived or died, but whereas the author of *La comédie humaine* used his pen, Jacques Bodoin uses his voice. His *Human Comedy* is vocal, and everyone knows his hilarious characters who, from behind the mask of their *papa,* are born and accepted by way of a kind of vocal miracle. Along with Jacques there are always the mocking little Philibert, an insolently fierce Parisian kid right off the streets; Eustache Derouge, a unionized worker; Coldur de la Feuille, a somewhat senile aristocrat from an old and noble family; Lucien Palmiera, a philosopher from Corsica, the Isle of Beauty, and a professional idler; Guy-Louis Guili, a sprightly dress designer; Colonel Du Gland de Surcroit, a military man who does no shame to the collection of great soldiers of straw, from MacMahon to de Gaulle; Monsieur Gamin, a verger; Baronnet Christopher, forever going from tea to whiskey and back again; the two theatrical extras Anodin Masseboeuf and Claudius; and finally, Henriette Mangetout, an old maid who is getting on . . . Add them up and you have eleven, plus their creator and yours truly, which made thirteen at the table!

We lunched at the Vivarois, run by Claude Peyrot, to whom I had given a free hand. Actually, that is far and away the best method.

I had telephoned Claude and said, "Next week, on Tuesday, we'll come and eat . . . anything you want!"

It was a dazzling meal, but also what I'd call a "meal of truth."

Ah! That young chef, not as well-known as others, does not "stand on his head"! He knows how to be reasonable, he innovates only with logic and wisdom, and he cooks only with love.

Our first course was consommé with sherry. Jacques Bodoin commented: "It's like a springtime walk through a priest's garden!" We were then served a stew of crawfish tails, morels, and truffles. Each element had kept its own personality and was covered with the sauce, not drowned in it, not dimmed by it: the crawfish, exquisitely fresh and flavorful, were briskly melded, whereas the admirably supple morels added their elegant dance steps and their arabesques, and the truffle mutedly and occasionally punctuated that rhapsody of essences like a deep-toned gong. Here again, the word "Racinian" naturally comes to mind.

It would seem more appropriate to evoke La Fontaine apropos of the next dish: a kind of *navarin* of lamb with an *arlequinade* of vegetables— a very simple dish but, in fact, probably one of the greatest because of its very simplicity, aside from the practical problem involved in presenting the *arlequinade*—composed in the style of Carême. This properly preceded the final dish, a duck "foie gras" cooked inside a duck, braised and glazed.

It was an entire liver, marbled as if from Carrara, with a strong savor. For an amusing and subtle touch, Claude Peyrot served as a side dish to accompany it prunes with ginger and cherries in vinegar.

The sherbets, crowned with strawberries and served with slices of brioche dotted with pink pralines, as in Saint-Genis; the wines; the excellent coffee; the cigars . . . The whole of it makes "a whole" when it comes to meals of friendship like this one.

Yes, friendship. For Claude Peyrot considers anyone who orders and gives him a free hand a connoisseur. You thus become his friend, and as he puts it: "Cooking is my way of loving you."

Recipes of Claude Peyrot
Le Vivarois

THE RECTOR'S CONSOMMÉ

Prepare a very flavorful beef consommé, well seasoned and carefully clarified (p. 249). Cut into a fine *brunoise* (p. 267) carrots, sweet peppers, celery, tomatoes. Cook this garnish in a bit of consommé. Flavor the consommé moderately with some old sherry. Sprinkle with some chopped parsley, and serve cold, when the consommé starts to gel.

This consommé is always pleasant; it is reminiscent of spring and predisposes the guests to good assimilation of the remainder of the meal.

(Note: To prevent the brunoise *falling to the bottom, put the consommé in which it has cooked in a bowl placed over ice and stir gently, without provoking a tempest of bubbles, until it starts jelling; the vegetables will stay in even distribution in the jellied stock. Spoon equal amounts of this mixture on top of each portion of consommé. Ed.)*

RAGOUT OF CRAWFISH, MORELS AND TRUFFLES

Prepare an excellent court-bouillon; sauté its vegetables in butter first, then add some Chablis, chervil and parsley stems, thyme, bay leaf, a garlic clove, anise and celery (see *nage,* p. 251). Wash the crawfish, devein it (p. 141), and cook it for 10 minutes.

Prepare a crawfish butter with the heads and shells of the crawfish; it will give the sauce its subtle flavor and its color.

Cut some truffles into thick slices so they unparsimoniously crunch under the tooth. Cook them slowly in butter in a small covered pot. Also cook some true morels (see p. 112) in the same manner; real morels have nothing in common with the false, rotund specimens sold in deluxe Parisian grocery stores.

Mix all the elements of the dish with the crawfish butter and simmer gently with some heavy cream.

There is no need to use any type of wine or brandy in this preparation for each of its ingredients has a *sui generis* flavor which will impart to the dish its own marvelous taste and flavor.

SAUTÉED LAMB AU PISTOU

To prepare the basil butter: chop the basil with a bit of fresh unsalted pork fat and a pinch of garlic; whisk some olive oil into the mixture. (I would not mind proposing that mixture to Lanvin as an afterbath lotion for gentlemen *nouveaux riches,* nor would I mind sharing the profits with Lanvin. . . .)

Cook in butter some new vegetables: onions, carrots, white turnips, artichoke bottoms, peas, green beans. All these vegetables are to be cut into the shape of garlic cloves, with the exception—and this precision is for the benefit of the American housewife—the green peas and the green beans. *(This precision is given by the author himself,* not *by the editor, Ed.)*

Sauté in butter some small cubes of lamb cut from the saddle, quickly so as to keep them pink. Let all these elements cook slowly for a few minutes after you add to them some clear and strong-tasting *jus* of lamb (p. 247).

Gradually add the *pistou* butter which will bind the whole concoction. This Provençal dish goes very well with a Château Rayas wine.

(Note: Pistou *is probably well known to our readers as the French version of the Italian* pesto *or basil paste.* Pistou *is a staple of Provençal cookery. Ed.)*

GLAZED DUCK STUFFED
WITH DUCK "FOIE GRAS"

A description:
Choose a large 4½- to 5-pound duck. Clean it through the neck; remove the wishbone and the ribs.

Season a beautiful fat duck liver with salt and pepper and marinate it in port. Stuff the duck with the liver and truss it.

Casserole-roast the duck in a very moderate oven (325°F.); toward the end of the cooking, add the port from the liver marinade and some very strong and tasty aspic prepared with the duck giblets. The cooking procedure requires some care; the duck should be pricked all around with a fine needle to prevent its bursting. Let the duck cool completely; clarify the cooking juices and glaze the duck with them as for a *chaud-froid*.

Put the duck on a platter and surround it with cooked prunes, cherries cooked in aspic mixed with red wine, slices of oranges arranged in pinwheel patterns, green olives stuffed with goose liver or a ham mousse, cooked apple slices sautéed in butter. All these fruits should be flavored with ginger and glazed with aspic.

This dish is very flavorful. The fat duck liver permeates the duck with all its fine fragrances. Serve with a crisp salad with a cream and *fines herbes* dressing.

BRIOCHE WITH PRALINES

(Note: The recipe has been divided by three, as for Alain Senderens' recipe on p. 193, to prevent yet another kitchen full of brioche. Ed.)

Take ⅔ cup of flour to make the starter; make a well in the flour; add 1 envelope of dried yeast and dissolve it with a bit of lukewarm water. Gather all the flour to make a soft dough. Let it rise for 20 minutes.

Take 2 cups more flour and add 1 teaspoon salt, 2 tablespoons sugar and 2 eggs. Mix and knead together to give the dough some body; gradually add ¾ pound of excellent soft butter, bit by bit. Fold the starter into the bulk of the dough; observing a baker while he "breaks" the dough to mix it with the starter is a magnificent experience.

Let the dough rise at room temperature. Mold the brioche and bake in a medium high oven after dotting its top with some good pralines. *(See the note on pralines, p. 124.)*

A Jersey Luncheon

When André Gide was asked whom he considered the greatest French poet, he replied, "Victor Hugo, alas!"

And whereas Jean Cocteau guaranteed us that the author of *La fin de Satan* was a madman who took himself for Victor Hugo, the novelist Claude Farrère believed that he was "as stupid as the Himalayas."

If I were the Himalayas, I should be offended!

But probably once in his life Juliette's little Vic, who was cuckolded, if not every Monday, at least by the author of *The Mondays,* told the truth: "Jersey is a wondrous garden placed on the sea."

I like Jersey. Jersey is good for me. No doubt because, like the Englishman who, when he arrives in Jersey, thinks he is already in Normandy, the Frenchman who so arrives there thinks he is in England.

But without all those Englishmen!

In Jersey I am only superficially irritated. I enjoy finding luxurious bars in all the hotels and drinking good beer and inexpensive whiskey, but I do not enjoy the fact that those bars stay closed until six o'clock. I enjoy finding an orchestra in every hotel, or almost, and dancing until midnight with English women dressed in those curtains they call evening gowns, but it annoys me to have to reckon with the complicated British currency and to drive on the left-hand side of the street. I enjoy, after early morning tea, being served an abundant breakfast of bacon and eggs and poached haddock, but I do not enjoy having a room without a bidet. Et cetera, et cetera . . .

Every year the Jersey Tourist Committee organizes a gastronomical festival. A jury made up of Frenchmen and Britishers is asked to go from restaurant to restaurant and to decide which is the best. I have the honor of being on that jury.

One eats extremely well in Jersey. Or, rather, one would eat extremely well if the chefs were willing to forget that they were French, English, Italian, or German and handled the admirable products of the island (all manner of fish and shellfish, as well as potatoes, spring vegetables, and dairy products) as a Jersey (or Norman) peasant woman would.

The Sea Crest Hotel
Luncheon

———

Melon, jambon de Parme
Homard aux légumes
Steak Diane
Salade d' asperges
Bourdelots normans
Stilton

Alas! The Germans too often contribute their rather strictly routine methods, the Italians their rather Latin flourishes (flames here, flames there, flames, flames everywhere!), the English their rather haughty Oxford disdain, and the French their rather typical ill will.

In the dining rooms themselves one finds more and more of a Portuguese influence, which has followed an Italian period that left its mark.

But apropos of those Italians who came to Jersey as conquerors, there are still Roman Legions that besiege the island with swords (knives) and fire (hearths). Indeed, some of their members have married and become, as it were, full pot-ners in crime . . .

That's true of my friend Vittorio Cornaglia, whose English wife appears to have escaped from a Gainsborough painting. Together they bought a hotel, The Sea Crest, which offers some of the best cuisine on the island.

The jury, which agrees, bestowed its favor upon it last year.

Straightaway, to celebrate the occasion, Vittorio invited us to an Italo-Jerseyan-French lunch, which was truly a delight—harmoniously balanced and brimming over with friendship.

It began with melon and Parma ham (*prosciutto con melone*) in the purest of Italian traditions. But the ham was superlative, as was the fruit—small green melons with luscious flesh, cleverly prepared, cut up in thin slices and served in the rind. We were off to a good start. One of us, inspired by the succulence of all the melons, which had been individually selected, recited the famous quatrain:

> Friends are not all that nifty,
> They're much like melons in the shop.
> You have to go and try at least fifty
> Before you find one that's tip-top.

How many melons had Vittorio tasted before he chose those seven? For there were seven of us—the golden number, as you all know.

Then came little Jersey lobsters *à la nage,* with their vegetables. That morning, at the ceremony announcing the winner, I mentioned that the French consul had assured me there were no lobsters in Jersey and that they came from Guernsey. To which the person next to me added that it was possible to be both a French consul and a fool. No one ever doubted that fact, given the old French proverb which states: "Like minister like consul."

Yielding to the Italo-Jerseyan style, we were treated to a steak Diane. Steak Diane is on every menu in Jersey. But I also encountered it in Portugal (at Algarve) and in Geneva, which would tend to prove that almost everywhere you go it's meant to represent stereotyped French cuisine. Besides, no one in France would ever think of serving this dish, which

—nevertheless—is both amusing and excellent if it is well prepared. As in certain American movies two ruffians wearing caps and red scarves represent Pigalle, steak Diane is supposed to represent French cuisine all over the world. There could have been a worse choice.

So we had a steak Diane prepared by Vittorio himself and, along with it, some excellent boiled vegetables from Jersey: new potatoes, broccoli, and fresh peas.

Then an asparagus salad.

Then some Stilton cheese.

But no, not yet! Since we were "from the other side," and since we respected the culinary customs which, anywhere you go, reflect the local folklore and traditions and even the soul of a people, we first sampled a dessert: Norman apple dumplings, which in Jersey have a right to full citizenship. Apple dumplings covered with the beautiful cream of the island—light, fragrant, and tender.

Only then did we light into the Stilton, one of the greatest cheeses in the world, along with Fourme d'Ambert, Brie, Gruyère, and a few others. . . . And with the Stilton we drank a glass of old port. As was proper!

Recipes of the Sea Crest Hotel in Jersey

LOBSTER AND VEGETABLES

Peel and slice lengthwise, quite coarsely, some carrots and white turnips. Cut a celery rib into slivers. Stick a few cloves into 2 large onions. Prepare a large *bouquet garni*.

Immerse the vegetables in boiling water, add 1 cup of dry Sherry, and boil until the vegetables are tender. Add the lobsters (1 to 1¼ pounds) and let cook for about 12 minutes.

Remove the lobsters from the court-bouillon. Cut them lengthwise into halves; crack the claws open. Cook some green beans cut into ¾-inch chunks in salted boiling water.

Prepare a hollandaise sauce as follows:

Put 3 egg yolks, 1 tablespoon lemon juice, 2 tablespoons of the cooled court-bouillon and a bit of salt in a pot. Work with a wooden spoon over a double-boiler. As soon as the mixture becomes foamy, add gradually 1¼ cups very fresh melted unsalted butter. As the sauce thickens lighten it with a bit of court-bouillon. Correct the seasoning, paying special attention to the pepper. Add 1 teaspoon of lemon juice.

In each warm plate, put a bed of vegetables from the court-bouillon (discard onions and *bouquet garni*) and some green beans. Set 1 lobster on the vegetables and coat with a few tablespoons of the court-bouillon mixed with the hollandaise.

STEAK DIANE

To serve 1 person

Place a *sauteuse* on a burner (in a restaurant steak Diane is prepared in the dining room). Melt ¼ cup butter. Add 1 large onion, finely chopped, and sauté gently with a good tablespoon of chopped parsley.

Add to the *sauteuse* ¼ pound sliced fresh mushrooms and sauté them without drying them at all. Push the mushrooms to a corner of the pan not exposed to the flame of the burner.

Prepare a piece of fillet of beef weighing about 8 ounces by cutting it crosswise into halves and flattening it like an *escalope*. Salt and pepper it highly; add a pinch of English mustard and put it to cook in that part of the *sauteuse* directly exposed to the flame of the burner. Let it cook for 1 minute and turn the meat over. Add a bit of Worcestershire sauce and cover the steak with the mushrooms. Push the meat covered with mushrooms to the side of the pan closest to the handle. Tilt the pan so that only its lip is in contact with the flame of the burner. Add ¼ cup of red Bordeaux wine and bring to a boil. Let reduce; once in a while spoon over the meat and let reduce again. Bring the meat back to the center of the *sauteuse*. Add a dash of raw wine and serve after giving a last boil.

NORMAN APPLE DUMPLINGS

Make a pastry with flour, melted veal kidney fat, water and salt. Roll out the dough; fold it in four. Roll it out again and fold again; rolling and folding should be done six times altogether.

When the dough is finished, roll it out ⅛ inch thick and cut as many 6-inch circles as you have guests.

Peel 1 apple per guest; core the apples and bake them in a buttered dish in a 325°F. oven until they are half baked (25 minutes).

Put an apple on each circle of dough. Garnish the center with a bit of jam or jelly diluted with Calvados. Bring the dough over the apples and seal each apple in a cabbage leaf. Bake in a bread oven (use 425°F. in a regular oven) for 30 minutes. Remove the cabbage leaves and serve the apples bubbling hot, coated with cold heavy cream.

(Notes: The jam or jelly is not specified; either apple or apricot would be suitable.

To make the pastry use 2 cups sifted flour, 1 teaspoon salt, ¾ cup melted veal kidney suet and just enough water to hold the dough together. Ed.)

The Meal I Should Have
Liked to Have

In 1971 we celebrated the one-hundredth anniversary of the birth of Marcel Proust. Does one imagine the author of *Remembrance of Things Past* a subtle gourmet or a man indifferent to the pleasures of the table?

Painter describes him dining at home, at nine in the evening, on three croissants bought at the Gare Saint-Lazare, boiling hot café au lait in a thermos bottle, eggs with Béchamel sauce, fried potatoes in a small silver vegetable dish, and stewed fruit (1910). That was clearly not one of Lucullus's meals. Yet no one who reads his long novel can escape the fact that he is a sensual epicurean, very attentive to the taste of things.

Little Marcel had been to a good school: everyone ate extremely well at the Prousts', where the cuisine was the work of women. Thus it is simple to transpose the details so faithfully reproduced in Proust's novel and to recognize the qualities of Françoise in real life:

> To the permanent background of eggs, chops, potatoes, jams, and biscuits, which she now served without even announcing them, Françoise would add—depending upon the labor in the fields and orchards, the harvest of the tides, the ups and downs of trade, the courtesy of neighbors, and her own genius; and so effectively that our menus, like the quatrefoils that were carved on the porches of thirteenth-century cathedrals, somewhat reflected the rhythm of the seasons and the incidents of life—a brill, because the fish-seller had guaranteed it was fresh; a turkey, because she had seen a fine one in the market at Roussainville-le-Pin; cardoons with marrow, because she had not prepared them for us that way before; a roast of lamb, because fresh air made one hungry and there would be plenty of time for it to "settle" during the seven hours before dinner; spinach, as a change; apricots, because they were still hard to get; gooseberries, because in two weeks there would be none left; raspberries, which M. Swann had brought specially . . . a cream cheese, which I was very fond of in the past; an almond cake, because it had been ordered the night before; and a brioche, because it was our turn to offer it. When all that had been eaten, we were served a chocolate cream, composed expressly

for us but dedicated more particularly to my father, who had a special taste for it—a personal gesture of Françoise's, light and fleeting as a work improvised for the occasion and into which she had poured all her talent.

Yes, Proust simply had to be a gourmet and an epicure to have written those pages, and many more of them, in which he describes Françoise in her kitchen and her delight at asparagus "soaked in ultra-marine and rose," at Gilberte Swann's "Ninevite" cakes, at Monsieur de Charlus's digression on pears from Normandy, and at Monsieur de Norpois's dinners at the home of "the narrator's" parents.

That is why I should have liked to have a Marcel Proust dinner for this centenary.

It was on a terrace at Saint-Pierre de Tourtour, a paradise in the Haut-Var region, that I composed my menu as I reread Proust. To begin with, a cream of asparagus soup, to materialize that precious iridescence so well described in "Swann's Way"; then a sole *normande,* for which Swann had just asked Françoise the recipe in Combray. Following that, a dish of jellied beef, prepared just as the old cook had done for Monsieur de Norpois, which almost brought tears to the eyes of the old epicurean diplomat. Because, as we know, Françoise had poured all her talent into it:

> Since she attached the utmost importance to the intrinsic value of the materials that were to go into the creation of her works, she herself would go to the Halles to procure the finest cuts of rump steak, shins of beef, and calves' feet, just as Michelangelo spent eight months in the mountains of Carrara selecting the most perfect blocks of marble for the monument of Julius II.

Finally, a truffle and pineapple salad, prepared for the same Norpois dinner, as well as tea sherbet with the little *madeleines* of Combray. *Madeleines* and tea are the culinary strains of music throughout Proust's work, his very own "motif of Vinteuil."

Such a dinner, naturally, could be given only at the Ritz.

At the Ritz, where Proust gave his own receptions. At the Ritz, where he promoted the headwaiter Olivier to his confidant and even collaborator. At the Ritz, where, at dawn on November 18, 1922, he sent his servant Odilon out to find him some iced beer.

"The beer will be like everything else," he said; "it will arrive too late . . ."

That was true, and those were his last words.

Yes, I should have liked to organize that dinner. But Monsieur Charles Ritz, who had agreed to it, perhaps didn't do as much as he might have. And, in any case, I was unable to reach Madame Mante-Proust

Dîner pour le centenaire
de la naissance de Marcel Proust

₃·Ɛ

Crème Argenteuil
Sole normande
Boeuf en gelée
Salade de truffes et d'ananas
Sorbet au thé
Madeleines

₃·Ɛ

at the proper time. And, in any case, it required a great deal of time and preparation. And, well, I was perhaps a bit lazy . . . So the days went by, and the time was . . . past.

But no matter. That was, indeed, the dinner I should have liked to have.

Recipes for the
Marcel Proust Dinner

CREAM OF ASPARAGUS SOUP

To serve 6 persons

Prepare the base of the soup with 6½ cups milk, 1 small onion stuck with a clove, 1½ to 2 teaspoons salt, a few peppercorns, 1 *bouquet garni* (parsley, thyme and bay leaf), ⅓ cup rice flour.

Bring the milk to a boil with the aromatics and spices. Dilute the rice flour in a bit of cold milk and blend the mixture into the boiling milk, whisking to obtain a smooth cream.

Let the cream of rice cook slowly for 20 minutes. Remove the *bouquet garni* and the onion and strain through a fine sieve.

Cook ¾ pound of small green asparagus, or the same amount of large white asparagus tips, in salted boiling water. Drain them. Set one quarter of the asparagus aside and keep them warm. Sauté the remainder in butter for a few seconds and add them to the cream of rice. Strain through a sieve. Just before serving add ½ cup of heavy cream. Correct the seasoning. Add the reserved asparagus tips to the soup tureen.

SOLE NORMANDE

To serve 4 persons

Poach 4 flat oysters in their own liquid. Drain them and remove their beards.

Steam 12 well-scrubbed mussels open with some white wine; drain them. Filter their cooking juices.

Cook 4 crawfish (Louisiana crawfish) in a very spicy court-bouillon (p. 251). With the heads and bones of a few fish, prepare a fish *fumet* (p. 250) using half water and half wine as liquids, 1 onion and 1 carrot, both sliced, a *bouquet garni* and some pepper.

To the strained *fumet,* add the cooking juices of the mussels and oysters as well as the cooking juices of 24 small mushrooms cooked with a bit of white wine.

Cut the fins of a beautiful sole. Slit the sole down its center between the 2 fillets. Lift the skin and break the backbone in 3 places, just below the head, at the center, and at the tail.

Poach the sole in the *fumet* mixture. Drain the cooked sole; pat it dry. Remove the backbone and set the fish on a large heated platter. Surround the fish with the oysters, mussels and mushrooms.

With some butter and flour, make a golden *roux*. Moisten it with fish *fumet* and simmer slowly for 1 hour, skimming well. Strain through a muslin.

To 1 cup of this fish velouté, add the same amount of sole cooking juices. Mix 2 egg yolks with ¼ cup cream. Add this enrichment to the velouté mixture. Bring to a boil; stir over high heat with a spatula until the sauce has reduced by one third. Finish the sauce with an addition of 4 tablespoons butter and ⅓ cup heavy cream. Strain through a muslin again and add 24 peeled cooked small shrimps.

Pour this sauce over the fish and its garnishes. Cut a small truffle cooked in champagne into 6 slices, and decorate the sole with the slices.

Deep-fry 4 breaded small smelts tied head to tail and stretch the crawfish backward so they will sit proudly and elegantly on the dish. Alternate smelts and crawfish around the dish.

Decorate with 4 puff-paste croutons.

(Notes: For the initial velouté, use 4 tablespoons each of flour and butter for the roux *and 3 cups fish* fumet *to moisten the resulting* roux. *By the time you have simmered and skimmed the sauce for 1 hour, there will not be much more than a cup of velouté left in your pot. It will be very refined and purified. Since the velouté contains flour, the sauce can be reboiled even after the egg yolks have been added, and it is not by error that the author has you boil the sauce after adding the yolks. Remember though, that once the egg yolks have been added, the sauce must be brought to a boil extremely gradually. Once the sauce has boiled, continue stirring with a flat wooden spatula until it has reduced to the desired consistency. Ed.)*

JELLIED BEEF

To serve 4 to 6 persons

Lard 2¼ to 2½ pounds of face rump of beef. Marinate it for 24 hours in 6½ cups of dry white wine with 2 or 3 onions, 4 carrots and a *bouquet garni*.

Drain the meat, pat it dry, and brown it in butter in a *cocotte*. When the meat is well browned, flambé with Cognac and add the marinade. Add also 2 calf's feet split and blanched, salt and pepper. Cover the pot and bake in a 325°F. oven for 2½ hours.

Remove the meat from the *cocotte*. Strain the cooking juices through a fine strainer to discard the aromatics. Return the beef to the *cocotte* with 3 pounds of diced carrots. Bake again until the carrots are done. Cook separately in butter, and covered, 1 pound small early peas and ½ pound silverskin onions.

When the vegetables are done, decorate the bottom of a mold with them; add the beef and the cooking juices. Let cool completely. The juices will jell.

To serve, dip the mold into lukewarm water for a few minutes and unmold on a serving platter.

TRUFFLE AND PINEAPPLE SALAD

Mince some well-brushed raw truffles and dice the meat of a ripe pineapple. Mix both ingredients using by volume two thirds truffles and one third pineapple. Bind with a very light mayonnaise. Serve each portion in a large leaf of Boston lettuce.

TEA SHERBET

Prepare a very strong infusion of green tea flavored with essence of bergamot. To each quart of infusion add 1 generous pound of sugar and 1 quart of whipped heavy cream. Freeze in an ice-cream machine.

Conclusion

And that does it!

These are obviously not the only dazzling, extravagant, or ridiculous meals I ever ate.

Just think. Two meals a day for nearly forty years—two meals a day, never at home! I no longer recall who wrote the poem for Curnonsky that begins:

> The Prince of Gastronomes
> Has no dining room . . .

I don't either.

But, believe me, other people's dining rooms are full of surprises!

And while many of them may disappear, others open every day. They come in waves. We had the Greek wave after *Never on Sunday,* the Chinese and Vietnamese wave, which is still with us, and the Algerian wave. Now we are faced with the Japanese offensive.

There have been countless Japanese curios, written and oral, provoked among snobs by that cuisine—a cuisine of cutouts which little yellow men put together right before your eyes, and arrogantly, the way one imagines torturers used to act as they carved up their victims.

But there have also been countless disappointments provoked by French cuisine!

The cuisine of chefs who are like the frogs of the La Fontaine fable, each of whom dreams of being fat as a bull but ends up full of air, because a Parisian celebrity, a lady of culinary charity, or some hustling advertising executive has assured them they have genius.

Sometimes even a journalist who writes regular columns on food is guilty, whereas he should never lose sight of the following Ten Commandments:

1. His indispensable tool is not his style, or even a good jaw, but a scale. Weighing himself should be his first good deed every day, because although for some people getting fat means getting old, to him getting thin means losing face.

2. What comes to his lips most often should be not a fork but the word *No*. He should say no to temptations, no to outrageous sauces, no every time to "Do have a bit more."

3. He is told: "You are in a profession that feeds you." In moderation. The only professions that really feed you are those in which you can get the work done by others, and I have never found anyone who would eat for me for over a week.

4. Chefs are gentlemen who are convinced that the more complicated the cuisine, the greater it is. They will allow our columnist to prefer *andouillettes* to woodcock *flambé* only when he can accept them served with foie gras, sliced pineapple, and slivered almonds. They then call such a dish *andouillette du Prince* and will be disappointed when you make a face.

5. La Reynière said that one must beware of the music of amateurs and the cuisine of friends. Our columnist would do well to add *terrine maison* and any specialties of the chef.
When restaurant keepers suggest a dish, he should choose another, and if he is disappointed, he has only himself to blame.

6. A glass of mineral water every morning before breakfast, and before every meal, will protect him from superior wines and bad wines, which, in any case, are in the majority.

7. The secret of a good appetite is eating when relaxed.
And to be relaxed, our columnist should tell himself that nothing is ever as good as he would wish, but neither is it ever as bad as he fears.

8. When he is a guest of the restaurant keeper, he should always leave a very good tip for the waiter, who will then get the impression that he himself is the host.

9. Our columnist should always go and shake hands with the chef before leaving, just as a French general always goes and tastes the soup.

10. He should never forget Jules Renard's words: "The truly free man is he who refuses an invitation to dinner without giving any reason for it."

And Boileau had only one Ridiculous Meal!
How pleasant it is, Sacha Guitry used to say, when there are two of you and each one has his own partridge. How even pleasanter it is when you're alone. Or, rather, when there are two of you: the partridge and yourself!
Because so many meals that might be good or just decent are ruined by other people.

There are three afflictions with regard to eating:

1. The restaurant keeper—or chef—who persists in explaining his recipe to you, begs for praise, or assures you that his dish is superlative.

2. The professional gastronome, the fawning pot-licker, who takes the floor the minute you leave it, who doesn't let up until his hand is off the doorknob, and who messes up the entire evening with his slangy compliments and made-to-order enthusiasm.

3. Females at table. With a capital *F*. Yes, *F* for Futility!

Countless ordinary meals become intolerable, laughable, or odious because of the chef who tries to impress you, the pseudo connoisseur who tries to persuade you to accept his definitive opinions, and the lady whose only wish is that you admire her new dress, her so-called wit, the grace of her gestures, and the scent of her presence.

Owners of restaurants who respect your taste and know how to keep in the background are the exception. Hosts who have meditated upon Brillat-Savarin's aphorism: "Receiving a person at your table means attending to his happiness the entire time he is under your roof," are the exception.

Perfect dinners are the exception, which does not mean that exceptional dinners are perfect, alas! And therein lies the whole history of food.

APPENDIX

Concerning These Recipes

It is integral to the structure of French cuisine that many of its great dishes have component parts which are separately prepared and some of which—in a chef's kitchen—may even be assumed to be routinely on hand. The identity of these preparations is so specific that, in the writing of a recipe, a chef may well with a single word define an "ingredient" whose actual composition could take pages to describe. This is not laxity of language but rather economical exactness. A *brunoise*, a *fumet*, a *pâte feuilletée* are what they are. They may be made well or ill, but a classic basic procedure exists for each; there is no doubt as to what is meant.

The recipes in *Feasts of a Militant Gastronome* are naturally rife with such classic references and, also, with dishes American home chefs may relish in the reading more often than in the cooking. Nevertheless, the determined amateur bent on reproducing one of Robert Courtine's memorable meals can spend a glorious weekend in the kitchen, given the necessary information. And the armchair chefs cannot properly appreciate some of these dishes without the same information.

The publisher therefore asked Madeleine Kamman, translator and editor of the contributing chefs' recipes, to provide, from classic sources and her own trained knowledge, recipes for all preparations missing in the original text which are required for the completion of the many dishes in this book that are in fact possible to accomplish in this country and at home.

It should be made clear that this Appendix is a supplement to the original French text, provided especially for the American edition and its American audience. The recipes and information in it are not the responsibility of Robert Courtine or of the chefs whose work is the delectable burden of his book. They come, however, from precisely the same established tradition, with the added advantage that in a kitchen in Massachusetts, Madeleine Kamman has for some years labored long and hard to reproduce for Americans the culinary essence of her native France.

Stocks, Fonds, Fumets, Court-bouillons

FONDS DE VEAU BRUN (Brown Veal Stock)

To make 5 quarts (the recipe may be divided in half)

6 pounds veal shank (shoulder shank or osso buco*)*
5 pounds veal bones, finely chopped
2 tablespoons butter
4 medium-size onions, sliced thick
6 tablespoons chopped parsley stems
1 large Mediterranean bay leaf (½ only if using California bay leaf)
1 teaspoon dried thyme, or 5 sprigs of fresh thyme
1 cup dry white wine
6½ quarts lukewarm water
2 tablespoons salt

Place veal meat and bones in a large roasting pan and roast in a preheated 400°F. oven for 45 minutes, or until golden brown.

Sauté the vegetables and herbs lightly in the butter in a thick copper pot or in an enameled cast-iron braising pot. Place the meats and bones on the vegetables, cover the pot, and let cook over very low heat for 30 minutes.

Uncover the pot and raise the heat rather high to allow the meat juices at the bottom of the pot to concentrate and start to caramelize. This causes the stock to take on a deeper color. Add the white wine and let evaporate. Add 1 cup water and let evaporate again. Add a second cup of water and let evaporate again. Add now the remaining 6 quarts water and bring to a boil. Add the salt. Let simmer gently for 6 to 8 hours.

Strain first through a fine strainer and again through a muslin. Store in the refrigerator. When cold and jellied remove any trace of fat at the surface of the meat.

The stock keeps very well but should be reboiled every 5 to 6 days.

JUS OF LAMB

Use lamb bones and shanks to prepare a brown stock as described for brown veal stock above.

247

BROWN STOCK

To make 5 quarts

6 pounds beef shin, bone-in
5 pounds veal shank
6 carrots
3 large onions
6 cloves (2 stuck into each onion)
1 veal knuckle, sawed into 4 pieces
1 ham rind, scraped of all fat
6 quarts cold water
4 scallions
6 large leeks
2 celery ribs
1 tablespoon salt
large bouquet garni

Preheat the oven to 400°F. Roast the beef and veal meats and the carrots and onions for about 40 minutes. Blanch the veal knuckle. Put bones, meat and ham rind in a large pot. Cover the meats with the water and bring slowly to a boil. Skim very carefully. Add the vegetables and skim again. Add the salt and *bouquet garni*. Simmer for 6 to 8 hours.

Pour into large mixing bowls. Let cool at room temperature and refrigerate. The next day lift off the large layer of hardened fat and discard it completely. The stock is ready for use or storing.

GLACE DE VIANDE CLASSIQUE (Meat Glaze)

To obtain excellent meat glaze, pour some positively fat-free and well-strained beef or brown veal stock into a pot. Simmer until the mixture is reduced to a thick syrup which coats the back of a spoon with a shiny and rather thick layer. From 1 quart of beef stock one obtains ½ cup of meat glaze, from the same amount of brown veal stock about ⅔ cup.

Meat glaze is perfectly sterilized after boiling so long and can be preserved in a small covered jar in the refrigerator. Should it after 2 to 3 weeks develop a trace of mold, remove the mold with a clean spoon and reboil the meat glaze for at least 5 minutes. Pour meat glaze into a sterilized jar. A jar washed in an electric dishwasher can be considered sterilized enough for the storage of meat glaze.

BEEF CONSOMMÉ

To make 6 servings

2 cups ground, positively fat-free beef
2 carrots, minced
2 leeks, white part only, minced
1 egg white
1 eggshell
5½ cups cold brown stock

Mix together the raw beef and the vegetables cut into *mirepoix* in a large pot. Beat the egg white very lightly and add it to the pot. Crush the eggshell. Add it also to the pot. Pour the cold beef stock over the meat and bring to a boil, beating constantly to keep the egg white in suspension in the stock. As soon as the boiling point is reached, let simmer very slowly for 1 hour. Strain through a cheesecloth.

WHITE STOCK (Fonds Blanc)

To make 5 quarts

5 pounds veal shank or breast
4 pounds chicken carcasses
1 large veal knuckle, sawed into 4 pieces
a few chicken giblets (no livers, please)
6 quarts cold water
6 carrots
3 large onions, each stuck with 2 cloves
4 scallions
1 very small white turnip
6 large leeks
2 celery ribs
1 tablespoon salt
large bouquet garni
6 white peppercorns

Barely cover the meats and bones with lukewarm water. Quickly bring to a boil and discard the water. This cleanses the meats and reduces the amount of scum. Rinse bones and meats well.

Return the meats to the stockpot and cover with the 6 quarts of cold water. Bring very slowly to a boil and skim most carefully. Add the vegetables, salt and *bouquet garni*, and skim again very carefully. Simmer 6 to 8 hours. As evaporating brings down the level of the stock, add more boiling water. During the last hour of cooking, add the peppercorns. Line a strainer with cheesecloth and strain the stock into large bowls. Cool at room temperature and refrigerate. The next day, lift off and discard the layer of hardened fat on the surface of the stock. The stock should be as solid as a gelatin mold. If its flavor is not pronounced enough do not hesitate to reduce it as the flavor is liable to vary with the quality of the meat used.

FUMET OF DUCK OR GAME BIRDS

To make 2½ cups

Browned bones and giblets (without the liver)
      of ducks or game birds
1 tablespoon butter
1 onion, sliced
1 carrot, sliced
butter
bouquet garni
1½ quarts very gelatinous veal stock (see p. 247)

Brown the bones and giblets of the bird in a 400°F. oven. Sauté onion, carrot and *bouquet garni* in butter. Add the bones to the pot containing the vegetable aromatics. Add ½ cup veal stock. Let reduce completely. Add another ½ cup veal stock and let reduce again. Finally add the remainder of the veal stock and bring to a boil. Simmer until 2½ cups of very strong and very flavorful stock remain. Strain through a muslin and clarify, if desired, to use as aspic for ducks or game birds in *chaud-froid*. No additional gelatin will be necessary if the veal stock has been made according to the recipe given on page 247.

FISH FUMET

This is an all-purpose white-wine fish *fumet* that may be used as a base for all the fish dishes included in this book, with the exception of the "Dinner of the Century" sea bass recipe on page 105.

To make 1½ to 2 quarts

1 large onion, sliced thin
1 tablespoon butter
½ cup mushroom stems and pieces
4 pounds fish heads and bones without skin
2 cups excellent dry white wine
      (Graves, Pinot Chardonnay)

2 quarts water
1 teaspoon salt
bouquet garni
6 white peppercorns

Sauté the onion in the butter. Add the mushroom pieces and all the fish heads and bones. Remove very carefully the loose skins of the fish, which would give the finished *fumet* a doubtful gray tinge. Cover the pot and let steam until the fish falls apart. Add the wine and the water and bring to a boil. Add the salt and *bouquet garni*. Let simmer happily but not violently (to keep the finished *fumet* from being muddy) for 30 to 35 minutes. Longer cooking of the stock will give it a bony and chalky taste coming from an excess of calcium being extracted from the bones. Strain the stock through a sieve or strainer first, then strain it through a muslin. If the stock does not appear to be flavorful enough reduce it a little bit until it develops a pleasant powerful flavor.

ALL-PURPOSE FISH COURT-BOUILLON

4 quarts cold water
1 bottle dry white wine
1 cup mild wine or cider vinegar
3 carrots, peeled and sliced
5 onions, peeled and sliced
very large bouquet garni
3 tablespoons salt
1 teaspoon peppercorns

Mix cold water, white wine and vinegar. Put the vegetables and *bouquet garni* on the bottom of a large stockpot and add the liquid ingredients. Slowly bring to a boil. Simmer for 50 minutes, adding the salt after 20 minutes of boiling.

When the court-bouillon has simmered for 50 minutes, add the peppercorns and simmer for another 20 minutes. Strain and use.

This court-bouillon may be preserved frozen and reused. Add ⅔ cup water to each quart of court-bouillon to compensate for loss of moisture during the previous use.

NAGE POUR ÉCREVISSES
(Special Crawfish Court-Bouillon)

To make about 5 cups

1 quart water
1 cup fish fumet
1 cup dry white wine

2 carrots, sliced
2 onions, sliced
1 bay leaf, crushed
½ teaspoon dried thyme
large bouquet of parsley stems
1½ teaspoons salt
peppercorns

Bring the water to a boil; add the fish *fumet,* white wine, carrots, onions, bay leaf, thyme and parsley stems. Cook until the vegetables are completely tender.

If the crawfish is cooked for presentation in this court-bouillon, remove the bunch of parsley stems. Do so also if the vegetables are used to make a sauce as in the Troisgros recipe on page 97.

Note: A personal way to cook crawfish, which comes from the French chef who trained me. Add the crawfish to the wildly boiling court-bouillon. Bring back to a second boil and remove the pot immediately from the heat. Let the crawfish stand in the court-bouillon for 8 to 10 minutes before using them. The pot should remain covered.

RED-WINE FISH FUMET

To make about 2 quarts

2 small onions, sliced
½ small carrot, sliced
2 tablespoons butter
¼ cup mushroom stems and pieces
1 small garlic clove
4 pounds fish bones and heads
4 cups dry red wine
2 quarts water
large bunch of parsley
pinch of dried thyme
½ bay leaf
½ teaspoon salt

Sauté onions and carrot in butter, then add mushrooms and garlic and the fish bones. Cover the pot and let cook over very low heat for 15 minutes, or until the fish bones fall apart. Add wine and water and bring briskly to a boil. Add parsley, thyme and bay leaf plus 1 teaspoon salt. Cook over medium heat for 35 minutes. Strain.

GLACE DE POISSON (Fish Glaze)

Reduce some fish *fumet* by half. You will obtain a thick *fumet*. Recook this *fumet* with more fish bones and heads, using 2 pounds of fish for each quart of reduced *fumet*.

This preparation is called *essence de poisson*. It tastes better and is not as pungent as true fish glaze, which is obtained by reduction by three quarters of regular fish *fumet*.

FISH ASPIC (An all-purpose formula)

To make 2 quarts

1 scant pound of whiting heads and bones (no skins)
¾ pound sole heads and bones (no skins)
2½ quarts fish fumet
3 large onions, finely sliced
½ cup chopped mushroom stems and pieces
1 medium-size bouquet garni

Place all the fish heads and bones in a kettle. Cover with the cold fish *fumet*. Add the onions, mushrooms and *bouquet garni* and bring to a boil. Simmer for 45 minutes after the stock has returned to the boil. Strain through a muslin.

To clarify the aspic:
If the stock for the fish *fumet* and for the aspic has been made properly, no additional gelatin should be necessary; the natural gelatin should be strong enough to allow the aspic to coat very well once it has been clarified.

2 quarts fish aspic
2 egg whites
1 crushed eggshell
1 teaspoon dried chervil, or 1 tablespoon chopped fresh chervil
1 cup Champagne Brut, or Grand Cru Graves Blanc, or Alsatian Riesling
salt and pepper

Have the fish aspic barely lukewarm. Put the egg whites and the eggshell into a thick pot (stainless or enameled cast iron). Beat the egg whites until they appear grayish and full of large air bubbles. Bring slowly to a boil, beating constantly to maintain the egg whites in suspension in the liquid. As soon as the liquid boils, reduce the heat so it barely simmers and let simmer for about 30 minutes. Let cool and stand until the crust of egg whites falls to the bottom of the pot. Then lift the liquid aspic from the pot into a clean bowl. Add the champagne only when the liquid is almost cold; this keeps the aspic from being cloudy.

TRUFFLE ESSENCE

True truffle essence is made with fresh truffles steeped gently over very low heat with excellent *jus de veau* and a bit of excellent white port. Since fresh truffles are positively inaccessible for the average amateur chef in the United States, it would be a good idea to use this method.

Peel the truffle(s) used in the dish. Chop the peels extremely fine and add them to the amount of stock or *fumet* indicated in the recipe. Let simmer together until the stock or *fumet* is well permeated by the truffle taste. The stock and/or *fumet* strengthens as it simmers and acquires a strong truffle taste.

For example, in the recipe for cardinal sauce on page 257, the best procedure would be to use a total amount of 10 tablespoons of fish *fumet* and reduce it to 7 tablespoons, mixed with the peels of 1 or 2 truffles. The sauce will then need to be strained through a very fine strainer.to discard all the peels before serving.

Sauces, Butters, Coulis

SAUCE CLASSIQUE DEMI-GLACE

To make about 1 quart

2 carrots
2 onions
½ cup diced veal
2 tablespoons raw butter
¾ cup clarified butter
1¼ cups flour
4 quarts plus 1½ quarts plus 1 quart stock
2 tablespoons tomato paste
bouquet garni
1 cup dry white wine
⅓ cup Madeira

Stage 1:

Brown the *mirepoix* (carrots, onions, diced veal) in the raw butter until onions are golden brown. Meanwhile cook the *roux* (clarified butter and flour) until brown. Whisk 4 quarts very warm stock into the hot *roux;* bring to a boil. Add the browned *mirepoix,* the tomato paste, *bouquet garni* and white wine. Simmer for 2½ hours, skimming as much as possible. Strain the sauce into a large mixing bowl. Cool at room temperature and refrigerate overnight.

Stage 2:

Remove the layer of butter solidified on the surface of the sauce; it may be reused for vegetables. Return the sauce to a large pot, mix with an additional 1½ quarts cold stock, and bring to a boil again, stirring. The cold stock replaces the moisture lost the day before and facilitates further skimming. Let simmer until reduced to about 6 cups, skimming faithfully at regular intervals. The finished sauce should be fat-free and should coat the back of a spoon like a thick sticky syrup.

Stage 3:

Mix the finished sauce (there should be about 5 cups) with the last quart of brown veal stock. Bring back to a boil, and simmer together again until reduced to about 4 cups. Add the Madeira.

BÉCHAMEL

Sauce consistency—to make 1 quart:

1 small onion
1 small carrot
½ celery rib
½ cup butter
½ cup flour
4½ cups scalded milk
salt
pepper
nutmeg
small bouquet garni

Cut vegetables into *salpicon* (p. 267), and sauté in butter until onion is translucent. Add flour and cook for 4 to 5 minutes, stirring occasionally. Whisk in scalded milk. Bring back to a boil; add salt, pepper, nutmeg to taste, and the *bouquet garni*. Simmer for 45 minutes. Strain.

Soufflé base consistency—to make 1 cup:

1 small onion, chopped
3 tablespoons butter
3 tablespoons flour
1 cup scalded milk
large pinch of grated nutmeg
salt and pepper

Sauté the onion in butter. Add the flour and cook for 3 to 4 minutes. Add the scalded milk, whisking, and the nutmeg, salt and pepper. Bring to a boil and simmer for 10 minutes. Strain.

SAUCE MORNAY CLASSIQUE (Classic Mornay Sauce)

To make about 2 cups

2 cups Béchamel sauce (sauce consistency, above)
¼ cup finely grated Parmesan cheese
⅓ cup finely shredded Gruyère cheese
4 tablespoons unsalted butter

Have the Béchamel sauce very hot. Blend in the two cheeses and stir until the cheese has dissolved. Fluff in the butter divided in small pieces.

SAUCE MORNAY FOR FISH DISHES

When the Mornay is to be used with a fish dish, proceed as follows:

Add to 2 cups finished Béchamel sauce ⅓ cup of excellent fish *fumet*. Cook gently together until the mixture has reduced again to 2 cups. Then add the cheeses and butter as mentioned above.

SAUCE CARDINAL CLASSIQUE

To make about 1 quart

3¼ cups Béchamel sauce (sauce consistency, p. 256)
5 tablespoons fish fumet *(p. 250)*
5 tablespoons truffle essence (p. 254)
5 tablespoons heavy cream
½ cup lobster butter
pinch of cayenne

Have the Béchamel sauce ready.

Mix together the fish *fumet* and the truffle essence and reduce to 7 tablespoons.

Mix together the Béchamel sauce, the reduction of fish *fumet* and truffle essence and the heavy cream and simmer for about 10 minutes.

Finish the sauce by fluffing into it with a sauce whisk the ½ cup of lobster butter. Add the cayenne and correct the seasoning.

VELOUTÉ

To make 2 quarts of finished sauce

1 cup unsalted butter
1 cup sifted flour
3½ quarts white stock (chicken, veal, or fish fumet*)*
1 cup chopped mushroom stems or pieces
small bouquet garni
4 white peppercorns

Make a *roux* with the butter and flour and cook it for about 10 minutes. Add 3 quarts of hot stock of your choice (the recipe is valid for all types of velouté—chicken, veal or fish) and bring to a boil over medium heat, stirring constantly. Add the mushrooms and the *bouquet garni*. Let simmer for 30 minutes, skimming constantly the scum and melted butter coming to the surface of the sauce. Add the remaining ½ quart of *cold* stock and bring to a boil again, stirring. Let simmer and reduce to 2 quarts. Skim at regular intervals. The finished sauce should be absolutely fat-free. Strain through a fine strainer and, if desired, also through a muslin.

TOMATO SAUCE

To make 5 cups (for all classic French dishes)

10 pounds tomatoes, only fresh and sun-ripened
¼ cup olive oil
2 onions, finely chopped
2 teaspoons sugar
1 teaspoon salt
dash of pepper
potato starch

Wash and halve the tomatoes but do not peel them; squeeze out all seeds and water. Chop the tomatoes and measure them: they should measure up to about 12 cups well packed. Sauté the onions in the olive oil until they are translucent. Add the tomatoes, sugar, salt and pepper; mix well. Cook covered over medium heat for 1 hour. Uncover the pot and put the sauce to bake in a 300° F. oven for 3 more hours, stirring at regular intervals. Strain the sauce into a large saucepan. Thicken, if desired, with 1 teaspoon potato starch per cup of sauce.

This mixture is a tomato essence; to transform it into a tomato sauce, proceed as follows:

To each cup of essence add ½ cup of excellent chicken stock and the flavorings of your choice. Simmer until the sauce has reduced by one third.

HOLLANDAISE SAUCE

To make about 1½ cups

6 tablespoons water
3 tablespoons vinegar
pinch of fine salt
large pinch of mignonette
    (coarsely cracked white pepper)
5 egg yolks
1 generous pound unsalted butter
1 teaspoon lemon juice

Reduce the water, vinegar, salt and *mignonette* by two thirds. Add the egg yolks. Place the pot over very low heat and whisk the eggs until they foam up and look almost white and the bottom of the pot appears between the mass of egg yolks for a few seconds at a time.

Remove the pot from the heat and gradually beat in the melted and cooled butter. While the sauce cooks and is being fluffed up with butter, gradually add 1 teaspoon of water once in a while to lighten it. Add the lemon juice, and strain through a fine strainer or a silk strainer.

HOME HOLLANDAISE IN SMALL QUANTITY
TO BIND ANOTHER COMPOUND SAUCE

> *1 tablespoon each of water and lemon juice*
> *salt and pepper*
> *1 egg yolk*
> *6 to 8 tablespoons unsalted butter*

Proceed exactly as described in the basic recipe, using the smaller quantities. Use the sauce as a binder for a compound sauce.

CHAUD-FROID SAUCE FOR DUCKS
OR GAME BIRDS

To make about 1½ cups

> *1 veal bone, browned*
> *giblets and any available bones from duck*
>   *or game bird (no liver)*
> *1 large onion*
> *1 small carrot*
> *white part of 1 large leek*
> *⅓ celery rib*
> *4 tablespoons butter*
> *3 tablespoons flour*
> *4 cups hot brown veal stock (p. 247)*
> *½ cup dry white wine*
> bouquet garni
> *1 teaspoon tomato paste*

Brown the meats in a 400° F. oven if they are not already browned. Cut the vegetables into a *mirepoix* and brown the *mirepoix* well in the butter. Add the flour to the pot and cook until light brown. Whisk in the hot veal stock and bring to a boil. Add wine, *bouquet garni,* browned meats and tomato paste. Simmer until reduced to 1½ cups; skim the sauce of all flour scum and butter coming to its surface while it reduces. There should be no more traces of either of those in the sauce when it is finished. Strain the sauce through a fine strainer first, then through a muslin. The sauce should jell without the addition of any gelatin.

VINAIGRETTE CLASSIQUE

To make about 1 cup

¼ to ⅓ cup excellent wine vinegar, or a bit less (according to taste)
1 teaspoon salt
½ teaspoon ground black or white pepper (according to taste)
¾ cup oil—olive, peanut, corn, etc. (according to taste)

Mix the vinegar, salt and pepper. Gradually whisk in the oil. Keep any unused amount sealed in a jar. Shake the jar vigorously before using the sauce to restore the emulsion.

MAYONNAISE CLASSIQUE

To make about 2 cups

1 egg yolk
1 teaspoon vinegar
1 teaspoon Dijon mustard
¼ teaspoon salt
¼ teaspoon pepper
1½ cups oil of your choice (preferably olive
*   or part olive and part another oil)*
about 2 tablespoons cold water
1 tablespoon boiling water
lemon juice (to please your taste)

Place the egg yolk, vinegar, mustard, salt and pepper in a small bowl. Whisk the mixture until homogeneous. Dribble in about ½ cup oil. The sauce will thicken very regularly and turn quite thick. Lighten it with a scant tablespoon of cold water. Dribble in again another ½ cup oil and lighten again with another scant tablespoon of cold water. Add the last ½ cup oil, whisking well; then blend in the boiling water and as much lemon juice as you like. The mayonnaise will appear very fluid. Refrigerate it for several hours and it will set again. The consistency of a good mayonnaise should not be heavy and greasy with oil; the additions of water take care of lightening its consistency and color. The addition of boiling water slightly poaches the egg yolk and keeps the mayonnaise from "bleeding" droplets of oil on standing if it must be kept for several days. Mayonnaise keeps in the refrigerator for 1 week.

CRAWFISH BUTTER

Gather very carefully the heads, tails, shells and legs of cooked and shelled crawfish of which the tail meat has been used for a dish. Weigh the shells and weigh the same amount of unsalted butter.

Pound the shells to as fine débris as possible. Melt the butter; add the shellfish débris and let steep for 1 good hour; the butter will turn a pinkish or rose color, depending on the depth of the crawfish robe's color.

Use the butter as a finishing touch in fine fish sauces.

COULIS D'ÉCREVISSES

Please use exclusively Louisiana crawfish. Pound the shells of the crawfish. Add ½ cup scalded heavy cream for each 3½ ounces of pounded crawfish. Let steep for 10 minutes and strain through a muslin. Season with salt and pepper.

BEURRE DE HOMARD CLASSIQUE
(Classic Lobster Butter)

Pound to a smooth paste (this can be done in the blender) ½ cup of poached lobster coral and tomalley. Strain it through a fine strainer or sieve. Cream ½ cup of unsalted butter and add the tomalley and coral mixture. Add to sauces in the quantity mentioned in the recipes.

NOISETTE BUTTER

Heat some butter in a small pan and let it foam and turn light brown. Use only the browned butterfat, not the deposit of browned solids at the bottom of the pan.

BEURRE D'ESCARGOTS
(Snail Butter)

For 48 snails

3 large shallots, finely chopped
1 garlic clove, positively mashed
2 tablespoons finely chopped parsley
1½ cups very fine and fresh unsalted butter
2 teaspoons salt
½ teaspoon pepper

Chop the shallots and mash the garlic clove. Chop the parsley very fine until the chopping board starts turning green from the released parsley juices. Cream the butter; add all the aromatics, the salt and the pepper. Cream together and let stand in a cold place or in the refrigerator for several hours.

Strain the butter to discard the pieces of shallots and keep only their juices.

Notes: 1. Some authors also use a solid pinch of nutmeg. 2. Some authors do not strain the butter. 3. For the Troisgros recipe on page 97, strain the butter and after straining add another very generous tablespoon of very finely chopped fresh parsley.

Preparations for Particular Recipes

HOMARD À L'AMÉRICAINE (Lobster Américaine)

This is a classic version.

To serve 2 persons

1 live 1½-pound lobster
¼ cup olive oil
3 tablespoons butter for sautéing the lobster
2 shallots, chopped
1 pea-size piece of garlic, mashed
1 ounce Fine Champagne
¾ cup dry white wine (Pouilly-Fuissé, Pouilly-Fumé
*   or excellent white Graves)*
⅔ cup fish fumet
2 tablespoons melted meat glaze
3 sun-ripened tomatoes, peeled, seeded and finely chopped
1 tablespoon tomato paste
⅓ cup demi-glace sauce (see p. 255)
2 teaspoons chopped parsley
pinch of cayenne
½ cup unsalted first-quality grade AA butter
*   to finish the sauce*

Rub the head of the lobster with the thumb to put it to sleep and immobilize it. Plunge the tip of your large chopping knife into the little transversal line that separates the head from the tail; this will sever the spinal cord.

Cut off the claws and crack them open. Cut the tail into as many pieces as the tail has articulations. Cut the head into halves. Remove the gravel bag and gather the tomalley and coral, if there is any, into a small cup. Set it aside for later use.

Heat the olive oil and the 3 tablespoons butter in a large flat *sauteuse*. Add the lobster pieces and sauté them just until they turn bright red. Add the chopped shallots and the garlic. Cover the pot with the lid and, leaving the lid slightly ajar, pour out all the browning fats.

263

Heat the Cognac in a small pan, ignite it, and pour it flaming onto the lobster. Mix together the white wine, fish *fumet,* melted meat glaze, chopped tomatoes, tomato paste and demi-glace sauce; pour over the lobster. Sprinkle with the chopped parsley and the cayenne. Cover the *sauteuse* and cook in a 325°F. oven for 18 to 20 minutes.

Remove the cooked lobster pieces to a plate. Start reducing the sauce still in the *sauteuse.* It should reduce to about ¾ cup. While the sauce reduces, shell the lobster pieces and cut the meat into ½-inch cubes. You can, if you desire, leave the lobster in its shell and present it this way in a timbale.

To finish the sauce, mix some of it into the cup containing the tomalley and coral, then reverse the process and turn the whole amount of tomalley and coral into the bulk of the sauce. Reheat very well without boiling. Strain the sauce through a very fine strainer, so as to discard all traces of solids from the sauce. Reheat the sauce very well and fluff in the ½ cup unsalted butter, bit by bit. The finished sauce should not be red but a beautiful dark rose color. Pour the sauce over the lobster, sprinkle with a bit more chopped parsley, and serve promptly.

Note: Another recipe requires the use of *demi-glace maigre,* that is, a demi-glace sauce made with rich fish *fumet.* Considering the presence of meat glaze in the sauce, the use of demi-glace made with veal stock is not really a hindrance. In many of the more modern versions for this recipe, the demi-glace is completely omitted, which results in a thinner sauce lacking a bit in body.

CLASSIC PIKE FORCEMEAT (Godiveau Lyonnais)

To make about 4 cups

1 cup sifted flour
4 egg yolks
6½ tablespoons unsalted butter, melted and cooled
salt
ground white pepper
pinch of grated nutmeg
1 cup milk, scalded
8 ounces pike meat without skin or bones
2 egg whites
8 ounces extremely white and clean beef kidney suet
    with no nerves or sinews

Mix flour, egg yolks and butter in a small pot; add a good pinch of salt and pepper and a small pinch of nutmeg. Slowly blend with the scalded milk. Thicken over medium heat, stirring constantly, for about 5 minutes. When the resulting *panade* is smooth, pour it onto a buttered plate and let it cool completely.

Divide the pike meat into 2 equal portions. Cut each portion into 1-inch cubes and put it in the blender container with 1 egg white. Blend until very smooth. Repeat with the other half of the pike meat and the second egg white. Blend together the *panade* and the very finely crumbled beef kidney suet. Return the whole amount of pike forcemeat to the blender container and blend together until the mixture becomes slightly rubbery and leaves the sides of the blender container.

Attention must be given to the fact that not all blenders are able to accommodate such a large amount of forcemeat at once. If the blender shows signs of weakness, do not hesitate to do the last blending in two portions.

Place one quarter of the forcemeat in a mixing bowl. Add the salt and pepper. Gradually beat in the remainder of the forcemeat bit by bit so as to develop more elasticity in the *quenelle*. Keep the mixture well chilled before using it.

WHITE-WINE MARINADE FOR VENISON AND GRAND VENEUR SAUCE

To make about 1 quart

2 tablespoons olive oil
1 large carrot, sliced
2 large onions, sliced
3 shallots, sliced
2-inch piece of celery rib, sliced
2 peeled garlic cloves, crushed
1 tablespoon chopped parsley stems
¼ teaspoon dried thyme
½ Mediterranean bay leaf
3 white peppercorns
3 black peppercorns
2 cloves, crushed
1 bottle of excellent dry white wine
⅔ cup excellent white-wine vinegar

Heat the olive oil and sauté the carrot, onions and shallots in it. Add the celery, garlic cloves, parsley stems and all the other aromatics and spices; toss over medium heat until all the vegetables are light brown and well wilted. Add the wine mixed with the vinegar and bring to a boil. Simmer for 30 minutes. Let cool completely before pouring over the meat to be marinated.

This marinade can be used to make the Grand Veneur sauce mentioned in the Hôtel Meurice dinner on page 177.

QUATRE-ÉPICES

To make about 3 tablespoons

2 teaspoons ground cinnamon
4 teaspoons ground allspice
¼ teaspoon ground cloves
½ teaspoon ground cardamom
1 teaspoon grated nutmeg
2 teaspoons ground coriander

Mix all the spices in a bowl; stir well and pour into a small glass jar. Keep among your spices to use whenever a dish calls for *quatre-épices*.

Formulas for this basic preparation vary with the cooks; the spices are not necessarily limited to four. In France this is sold in jars already prepared.

RUSSIAN SALAD
(for garnish of Lobster en Bellevue, page 177)

To serve 6 persons

Cut into ⅓-inch dice enough carrots, white turnips, potatoes, fine green beans, chopped mushrooms and lean ham to make 1 cup of each ingredient. Add 1 cup of young green peas.

Cook the vegetables in boiling water until they are done but still firm. The mushrooms are better sautéed in a bit of oil until they have lost all their moisture.

Mix these vegetables with enough mayonnaise to bind them well but not overgenerously. Add as seasonings, at the last minute, 1 tablespoon small capers, 2 anchovy fillets, rinsed under running cold water and chopped, and 2 small sour pickles, chopped fine.

CLASSIC VEAL AND PORK FORCEMEAT
FOR COUNTRY PÂTÉ

To make about 4 cups

½ pound perfectly lean veal (shoulder or bottom round)
½ pound perfectly lean pork (tenderloin)
1 pound fresh unsalted pork fatback (no salt pork, please)
1 ounce quatre-épices-*flavored salt* (sel épicé)
1 teaspoon finely ground black pepper
⅓ cup Cognac or Armagnac
1 large or 2 small eggs

Grind the veal and pork separately, then the fatback, twice through the fine blade of a meat grinder. Put the meats in the large bowl of an electric mixer. Add all the spices, the Cognac and the egg, and beat on high speed until the mixture is perfectly homogeneous.

Note: If the mixture is to be used in a pastry, use only 1 egg.

QUATRE-ÉPICES-FLAVORED SALT (Sel Épicé)

To make about ½ cup

⅓ cup salt
4 teaspoons ground pepper
2 teaspoons ground coriander
1 teaspoon ground cinnamon
1 teaspoon grated nutmeg
½ teaspoon ground cardamom
⅛ teaspoon ground cloves

Mix the salt and all the spices together in a small jar and shake very well.

CHOPPED AND DICED VEGETABLES

In classic cuisine, the size of the vegetable dice determines the name of the composition; the vegetables are usually carrots, onions and sometimes celery.

A *brunoise* is a mixture of vegetables cut into ⅛- to ⅙-inch dice. A *brunoise* is often included in the sauce and the size is small to allow the vegetable to cook through.

A *mirepoix* is a mixture of vegetables cut into ¼-inch dice. The *mirepoix* is more often than not strained out of the sauce.

A *salpicon* is a mixture of vegetables cut into ⅓-inch dice. If the *salpicon* is made of vegetables to flavor a sauce they are usually strained. A *salpicon* of meat, shellfish or cooked vegetables is often used as a garnish in cold dishes.

Pastry and Preparations for Desserts

BASIC SHORT PASTRY

> *1½ cups sifted flour*
> *1 teaspoon salt*
> *9 tablespoons chilled butter*
> *3 to 4½ tablespoons chilled water*

Put the flour on the countertop; make a well in the center and add the salt and the butter cut into ½-inch cubes. Working with the tips of the fingers, rub flour and butter together until the mixture forms particles the size of a pea. Add the water, tablespoon by tablespoon. Mix it into the mixture with the tips of the fingers of both your hands extended downward toward the counter in such a way as to form a natural pastry cutter; the palms face each other. Push the dough from left to right, throwing it up from the bottom and fluffing it about 2 inches above the countertop. The more water is added the more difficult it becomes to break the lumps.

Gather the dough into a ball. With your right hand extended 45 degrees upwards, using only the heel of the hand, push the dough 6 to 8 inches forward, flattening nut-size pieces on the counter. When all the dough has been used, repeat the same operation. Wrap the finished dough in wax paper and keep it refrigerated. It will look and taste better if you prepare it 24 hours ahead of time.

BASIC PUFF PASTE (Pâte Feuilletée)

> *2 tablespoons cornstarch*
> *3⅞ cups sifted all-purpose flour*
> *1½ teaspoons salt*
> *1¼ to 1½ cups water*
> *2 cups (1 pound) unsalted butter*

Détrempe

Put the cornstarch in a 4-cup measuring cup, and sift enough flour on top to make a total volume of 4 cups. Pour the mixture onto the countertop and mix well. Make a large well in the center and put salt and ¼ cup water in it.

Dissolve the salt in the water. Slowly bring some of the flour into the water with the tip of the finger. When the liquid looks like a crêpe batter, start fluffing as for an ordinary piecrust (see p. 268). Continue fluffing, adding the water tablespoon by tablespoon, until the lumps of dough cannot be broken anymore by the fingertips. Try to use no more than 1¼ cups of water.

Gather all the lumps into one ball. Wipe all the particles off the counter, using the dough ball as a mop. Holding the dough in both hands, break it open twice as you would a piece of bread. *Do not knead or handle it anymore,* whether it is smooth or not. What is essential at this point is that the *détrempe* does not contain much of that tough material called gluten. Cut a cross ½ inch deep in the top of the dough and refrigerate it, *uncovered,* for 30 minutes.

Paton

After 30 minutes, remove the butter from the refrigerator. Let it stand at room temperature for 5 minutes; during those 5 minutes soak your hands in water as cold as you can stand it. Remove the wrapping from the butter and knead the butter with your bare hands until the water drips out of it and it has become soft enough for a finger to sink into it without resistance. Do not let the butter get oily.

Take the *détrempe* out of the refrigerator. With the heel of the hand gently pat the dough into a 9-inch square. Flatten the butter into a 7-inch square. Put the butter on the *détrempe* with each corner of the butter in one of the long sides of the *détrempe* square. Fold the four corners of the *détrempe* over the butter, edge to edge, without overlapping; the dough and butter package is now a *paton.* Let it stand for 5 minutes, with the rolling pin resting on it.

Turns 1 and 2

Roll the *paton* 9 inches away from you and 9 inches toward you, keeping it 7 inches wide and never less than ½ inch thick. Do not bear down on the dough; roll the dough parallel, not perpendicular, to the countertop. If the *paton* becomes wider than 7 inches, block it on each side by placing the rolling pin parallel to the edge of the dough and tapping it gently.

Fold the dough in three. Now, turn it by 90 degrees, so that it looks like a book ready to be opened. Roll out the dough again and fold it a second time exactly as described above. You will have given 2 turns. Punch 2 small depressions at the surface of the dough with a fingertip.

Put the dough on a lightly floured plate, covered loosely with a sheet of foil, and put it to cool *in the vegetable crisper* of the refrigerator.

Turns 3 to 6

Finish the dough by giving 2 more series of 2 turns each, exactly as described above.

Rolling out and cutting the dough

Roll out the dough when it is deep-chilled and still very stiff. Always cut the dough neatly perpendicularly to the countertop, so as not to produce stragglers that would prevent the paste from rising.

DORURE

This mixture is used to glaze pastries (short pastry, puff pastry and *choux* paste) before baking them.

Dark Brown Dorure
> 1 egg yolk
> 3 tablespoons milk

Beat both mixtures until liquid.

Golden Dorure
> 1 whole egg, beaten
> 1 tablespoon milk

GÉNOISE

Use a 10-inch round baking pan, or two 9-inch round baking pans if a 2-layer cake is desired.

> 6 eggs
> 1 cup flour
> 1 cup sugar
> ½ teaspoon salt
> 1½ tablespoons vanilla extract or liqueur of your choice
> ½ cup clarified butter

Warm the whole unbroken eggs in a bowl of warm water. Sift the flour. Prepare the baking pan or pans by buttering them evenly on the bottom and sides of the pans. Dust the bottom of pan or pans with just a veil of flour.

Place the eggs, the sugar and the salt in a fireproof mixing bowl (2 to 3 quarts capacity). Place the bowl over low heat, using an asbestos pad or any other device to control the heat. Beat the eggs until they become thick, foamy and almost white in color, and spin a very heavy ribbon when the beaters are lifted from the batter. Add the flavoring.

Fold in the sifted flour; then *fold in* the clarified butter. The folding in of the butter is essential or the cake will be flat and dry.

Turn the batter into the prepared cake pan and bake in a preheated 350°F. oven for 35 to 40 minutes.

PRALINE

2 cups sugar
¾ cup water
2 drops of lemon juice
2 cups chopped nuts (hazelnuts, almonds, pecans)

Mix sugar and water and bring to a boil. Add the lemon juice and cook to 310°F. Add the nuts and let cook to 325°F. Pour the mixture onto a buttered cookie sheet or a marble slab and let cool to a nut brittle. Break the brittle into pieces and crush with the rolling pin between 2 layers of wax paper. You can also pulverize the brittle to a fine powder in an electric blender. In all cases, keep either the brittle or the powder in a very well-sealed jar.

CRÈME ANGLAISE (English Cream)

To make about 2 cups

This recipe gives the sauce thickness. For Bavarian cream thickness use 1 more egg yolk per cup of milk.

3 egg yolks
¼ cup sugar
large pinch of salt
1 cup scalded milk
flavoring of your taste (1 teaspoon extract,
*   or 2 tablespoons liqueur or brandy)*

Mix egg yolks, sugar and salt and mix very well without producing too much foam. Gradually blend in the scalded milk.

Put the pot over medium heat and stir with a wooden spatula or spoon until the surface of the cream is positively free of foam and the foam does not rebuild again when the pot is taken off the heat. Remove the cream from the heat and whisk violently for a few minutes to prevent the sauce or cream curdling from the heat accumulated in the pot. Strain into a sauceboat; flavor with the flavoring of your choice.

Vanilla flavoring: When the sauce is flavored with vanilla, the very best way to flavor it is to scald the milk, add a 1½-inch piece of vanilla bean split open at the side, and let it steep in the milk for 2 hours. Reheat the milk before cooking the cream.

Where to Find Rare Ingredients

Crawfish

Since no shrimp, especially one delivered to a kitchen without a head, can ever replace crawfish, it is recommended to use only the beautiful American crawfish from Louisiana. Live crawfish can be obtained from

Battistela's Sea Foods Inc.
910 Touro Street
New Orleans, Louisiana 70116

The smallest airmailed shipment is 20 pounds; there are 6 to 8 crawfish in 1 pound. A 20-pound shipment is not difficult to dispose of. The air-freight costs as much as the crawfish.

Fresh Goose and Duck Foie Gras

There is no way to find fresh uncooked duck or goose livers, fattened and imported from France, for their entrance into the United States is forbidden by our health authorities. For this reason, the recipes using this type of liver have been left as descriptions. There is, alas, no replacement product.

Truffles

Fresh black truffles can be obtained from

Mr. Paul Urbani
130 Graf Avenue
Trenton, New Jersey 08607

Beautiful *première cuisson* truffles will be airmailed to you gladly by

Société Alimentaire Guillot
84 Grillon, France

Fresh truffles of course are by far the best, but a can of *première cuisson* truffles represents a good investment, for any unused truffle can be stored in melted goose fat or clarified butter and kept refrigerated for a long time. The best French restaurants in America use mostly *première cuisson* truffles.

Index of Chefs, Restaurants, and Restaurant Addresses

Recipe Index

ABOUT THE AUTHOR

ROBERT COURTINE is by all odds the most influential food writer in France and has made his gastronomic opinions known internationally as well as at home. A prolific journalist and cookbook author, his books have been translated into ten languages. His columns are syndicated throughout France, and under the pseudonym of La Reynière he has been writing the weekly feature "*Les Plaisirs de la Table*" for the newspaper *Le Monde* since 1949. His *The Hundred Glories of French Cooking* was published in this country in 1973. Both feared and revered by the best chefs of France, he possesses great breadth of knowledge of his subject and the most incisive sense of humor in the world of gastronomic reportage.

ABOUT THE TRANSLATORS

JUNE GUICHARNAUD is a professional translator whose credits range from the translation of the letters of André Gide and Paul Valéry to a recent biography of Edith Piaf.

MADELEINE KAMMAN was born in Paris. She acquired her culinary skills in the kitchen of a Michelin-starred restaurant and has diplomas from several well-known European cooking schools. She was also educated in languages at the Sorbonne and is one of the most effectively bilingual cookbook authors in this country, having written her first two books, *The Making of a Cook* (1971) and *Dinner Against the Clock* (1973), in English rather than her native French. She operates her own cooking school in Boston, Modern Gourmet, Inc., and teaches summer seminars at Lubernon College in Aix-en-Provence.